Speak with Confidence
A Practical Guide

Third Edition

Speak with Confidence
A Practical Guide

Albert J. Vasile
Harold K. Mintz
Bunker Hill Community College

Little, Brown and Company
Boston
Toronto

Library of Congress Cataloging in Publication Data

Vasile, Albert J.
    Speak with confidence.

    Includes bibliographical references and index.
    1. Oral communication.   I. Mintz, Harold K.
II. Title.
PN4121.V35   1983   808.5′1   82-21663
ISBN 0-316-89787-6

Library of Congress Catalog Card No. 82-21663

ISBN 0-316-89787-6

9 8 7 6 5 4 3 2 1

HAL

Published simultaneously in Canada by
Little, Brown & Company (Canada) Limited

Printed in the United States of America

To the three most important persons in my life —
my wife Evelyn and our two sons Albert J. Jr. and Walter B. —
who have taken particular interest in the chapter on listening,
and who never hesitate to lecture me, justifiably so,
on its contents.

And to the two persons who made it all possible —
my mother and father.

And to all my students, from whom I receive much inspiration
and knowledge.

    AJV

To my wife Edith, and to Andrea and Lloyd

    HKM

Acknowledgments

We owe special thanks to the following people and organizations:

Steve Miles for his cartoons, which express the spirit and humor of this book

Nazuna K. Comfort, assistant to the cultural attaché at the Japanese Embassy in Washington, D.C., for the Japanese words and their symbols

United Nations Photography Unit for insight in helping us select the most suitable photographs from their vast library

White House Liaison Office for the photograph of President Ronald Reagan

John F. Kennedy Library for the photographs of JFK

British Information Services for the photograph of Prime Minister Winston Churchill

Kathryn Daniel, our editor, for her many important contributions and constant communication that resulted in a very gratifying, professional relationship

Preface

We are delighted that the great success of *Speak with Confidence* has warranted this third edition. We thank all its users, both professors and students, who have communicated to us their enthusiasm and extremely helpful suggestions.

This third edition, we believe, has attained "flagship" status — a book that puts it all together for a one-semester course and that, if used properly, will enhance students' ability to speak with confidence, one to one, within a group, and to a group.

The major changes and improvements in this edition eclipse, by far, those that strengthened its predecessor. These current changes and improvements concern the following chapters and topics:

Chapter   *Changes and Additions*

2   A completely new chapter on nonverbal language
              that covers gestures, dress, facial expressions, body
              movement, artifacts, and so on. This chapter was
              written in response to countless requests from
              professors.

And, as usual, much of the material in this book is as *current* as the publishing deadline permits. Throughout the book, there are dozens of other changes, including relevant new anecdotes, cartoons, exercises, and topics for talks.

Speak with Confidence is *basic* in that it is designed for students who are taking a speech course for the first and perhaps the only time. It covers what we think should be included in one semester: from a detailed guide for planning and putting together your very first talk to informative, persuasive, and social speech-making. Our text is directed to all of you who want to sharpen your ability to converse and to listen and speak before a group — in short, to communicate with confidence now.

This text is *practical* because it focuses on the fact that you are now working or will soon be working, and thus you can use its contents immediately in your everyday lives. This pragmatic approach reflects our belief that the ability to communicate well is critical to you in achieving your career goals and in enjoying a full, rich life.

This text is designed to be a guide as the course progresses and after the course ends. We hope that it will benefit you as a student, a job seeker, or a job holder, or as a member of a political, social, labor, or consumer organization, and that you will refer to it as particular situations require. It guides you from your very first speech through your job interviews, to delivering researched reports, to special-occasion speeches (toasts and award ceremonies, for example), to panel discussions, and to informal conversations.

Because we want to increase your ability to communicate confidently, we have tried to make this book unique in several ways:

- It is written in a clear, vigorous, conversational style that "talks" to you.

- It is spiced with photographs, cartoons, practical hints, and real-life anecdotes relevant to the topics being discussed.

- It stresses the development of self-confident communicating, an ability that a surprisingly large number of people lack.

- It is loaded with ideas and guidelines gleaned not only from the world of work but also from the worlds of research and teaching.

And now one last thought. This third edition has been written, rewritten, researched, documented, checked, rechecked, revised, reorganized, edited, argued over, cursed, coddled, loved, sweated over. In other words, it has been forged in the fires of a creative friendship/partnership, all with one paramount objective: to help you students Speak with Confidence.

AJV
HKM

Contents

3

You Can Overhear,
but You Can't Overlisten   33

4

Your First Talk:
Getting to Know You   47

5

Make It Clear, Concise,
Correct . . . and Alive   67

6

Delivering Your Speech   89

7

Selecting a Topic
and Doing Research   103

8

Putting it
All Together   123

9

Know Your Listeners
and Speak Their Language   151

10
First Aid on
Audiovisual Aids   173

11
Inform Them   191

12
Persuade Them   207

13
Saying a
Few Words   227

14

Let's Meet
and Discuss It   249

15

"What Do You Say
After You Say Hello?"   267

16

Let's Go to Work   287

Speak with Confidence
A Practical Guide

1

Me Study Speech? You've Got to Be Kidding

More men have talked their way up the ladder of success than have climbed it in any other way.[1]

CHAPTER OBJECTIVES

After reading and understanding this chapter, you should know:

- The importance of this course to your personal life and to your career.
- The benefits you will get from working at this course.
- The importance of making business and social contacts.

CHAPTER DIGEST

Assuming that you do the assigned work, you will gain substantial benefits from this course: self-confidence; the ability to communicate one to one, within a group, and to a group; a keen sense of personal accomplishment; and a heightened ability to listen. These benefits can help you attain your full growth potential in the career and lifestyle you seek. In other words, as

---

[1] Bruce Barton, best-selling author, advertising pioneer, and lecturer.

1

many former students have said, this course may well turn out to be the most important one of your college years.

Let's face it, you're taking this basic course in speech, or oral communication, for one of two reasons:

1. You *want* to.

2. You *have* to.

If you *want* to take the course, you have nothing to worry about. Apparently, you appreciate the importance of oral communication and the boost that this course can contribute to the career and lifestyle you want. If you only exert the effort, you will develop into a self-confident communicator whom people will listen to and respect.

If you've been "drafted" into the speech course, this is now a different ballgame. To most Americans the idea of compulsion is self-defeating, destructive, and, in many instances, antilearning. Yet, while in college or after college, all of us sometimes have to do things that we don't want to do.

For example, if we decided to obey traffic lights and speed limits only at our own convenience, what would happen? If pilots decided not to abide by their pre-established flight patterns and procedures from takeoff to landing, what would happen?

If this course is required and you're not really ecstatic about taking it, try to control your enthusiasm by accepting this experience with an open mind. You may find yourself warming up to the challenge and even thriving on the zestful give-and-take of verbal jousting in class. Take the plunge on a positive note. Who knows, you may enjoy the course. Remember, you'll never know what you're capable of doing unless you try. Don't sell yourself short.

HOW IMPORTANT IS THIS COURSE TO YOU?

Every day you communicate orally without giving it a thought. You greet people. You express opinions and desires. You ask questions and you answer them. You agree with people and you disagree. Sometimes you try to influence them.

People will listen to and respect a self-confident talker.

Have you ever envied someone for his ability to express thoughts and opinions authoritatively? Have you ever experienced any situation when you wished you had had the confidence and ability to communicate ideas and opinions? Do you have problems meeting people and making new friends? Have you ever wished you were a better conversationalist?

If the answers to all, or some, of the above questions are in the affirmative, then get set for one of the most important courses of your life. You can accomplish all the above, if you want to, by plunging into this course with everything you've got. But you must have commitment.

Talking, listening, writing, and reading comprise areas of communication in which you participate throughout your life. Of the four areas, there is no question that talking and listening predominate in business, social, and political relationships. For every word you write, you may speak thousands of words to carry you through a typical day. Consider the following circumstances in which effective oral communication may be crucial to you:

- Being able to disagree with your boss or immediate supervisor without being disagreeable.

- Being able to "sound off" and file a grievance rather than suppressing your feelings and being miserable.

- Wanting some time off from your job without having to call in sick.

- Handling a delicate situation like being sexually harassed on the job (male or female).

- Evaluating and selecting courses with your faculty adviser. In order to receive maximum benefit from the adviser, you must be able to express your course selections in the light of your long- or short-range goals.

- Voicing your opinions at home, in classes, in politics, at the office, and at weekend orientations.

- Interviewing for a job or seeking a raise or promotion.

Like being sexually harassed on the job . . .

Unless you express yourself knowledgeably and confidently, what would your chances be?

- Participating in community, business, or political action groups. Consumer, taxpayer, environmental, and labor organizations, women's and men's liberation groups, and PTA's (to name just a handful) need people who have ideas and the ability to communicate as well as to execute them. How many of us shy away because we lack confidence in our ability to champion our beliefs?

- Trying to break the news gently to your parents that you've decided to move out of your home and into an apartment . . . with your boyfriend or girlfriend.

These represent only a few situations that require clear, confident talking. The point is that since these experiences will confront you throughout life, you should prepare yourself to cope with them to your advantage. No matter who you are, the keys to

"Mom and Dad, I'm going to live with Endicott."

achieving your lifetime goals are your competence on the job and your ability to communicate effectively with your fellow humans.

Having certain abilities and occupational goals is advantageous, but not having the opportunity to put them to use is, at first, discouraging and then depressing.

MAKING BUSINESS AND SOCIAL CONTACTS

Almost all adults would agree that making contacts and knowing the "right people" are invaluable aids in moving ahead.

Making contacts can help you move ahead in your career and in many other ways. Perhaps your son, daughter, or other relative is looking for summer or part-time work, perhaps you want a favor from a politician — a letter of recommendation or introduction, perhaps you are seeking college admission or membership in a prestigious organization. Your chances of obtaining these favors will be immensely improved if you know the right people.

You should realize that it's no shame to ask for a favor. What is a shame is to need something and not get it because you don't know anyone who can help. (This topic is discussed further in Chapters 15 and 16.)

Since knowing the right people may make a significant impact on your life, you should strive to meet and interact with as many people as possible. You never know when they may be able to "come through" for you. By the same token, you should be helpful to others if you can, because helping is a two-way street.

Your sincere desire and ability to meet people should become an integral part of your daily life. The way to do this is to communicate orally — speaking, listening, questioning, answering, getting involved. Every time you speak, you make an impression, good or bad.

WHAT WILL YOU GET FROM THIS COURSE?

Provided that you expend the effort — and it is vital that you do — this course will enable you to:

- Develop self-confidence when interacting with people, one to one, within a group, and to a group.

- Be more assertive.
- Improve your ability to listen.
- Learn how to present your ideas clearly, logically, and forcefully.
- Acquire a sense of accomplishment.
- Learn the secrets of meeting and being liked by people.
- Be more convincing.
- Develop a more positive self-image.
- Sell yourself to employer, group or friends.

These benefits and advantages are so closely related that they seem to overlap or blend into each other. You'll develop them by exerting yourself in the following ways:

1. By giving many talks on various topics. In this way you'll communicate your views, experiences, and feelings with your colleagues.

2. By responding to questions from the audience after your talk. The key to performing well in the question-and-answer period is to know your subject thoroughly. If you've done your homework, you will, like most people, be charged up and exhilarated by your effort. The adrenalin racing through your veins could produce a new "high" for you. As a result, you will speak more forcefully and fluently than ever before.

3. By asking questions after others have spoken. Listening intently and having some knowledge of the subject under discussion will enable you to ask interesting and penetrating questions. Perhaps you will disagree with the speaker or perhaps you can shed light on some questionable point; in that case, think first and then speak your mind. Your self-confidence will grow once you notice that others listen to you. Remember, the more often you speak, the more self-confident you'll become.

4. By talking or debating with fellow students. After a talk is given, the question-and-answer session often triggers discussion among class members, sometimes without involving the original speaker. Someone may ask a question

or present an opinion that incites others to reply. This may result in a sizzling, crackling demonstration of the power of the spoken word to move people.

After each talk, you'll feel a sense of accomplishment, and rightfully so. Even after your maiden effort, you'll admit not only to great relief (which you've earned) but far more important, to a feeling of tremendous satisfaction. With each new talk given, you can only become more confident, and that glow of achievement will intensify.

Keep in mind that this course will not only teach you how to research, prepare, and deliver an effective speech in public or private, but will help you develop your self-confidence when interacting one to one or in a small group, or when speaking before a large gathering. Remember, once you achieve self-confidence, you will be able to do almost anything you want, provided, of course, that you prepare for it.

"And then I shoulda said . . ."

Nothing is more frustrating than having something to contribute to a discussion at school, at home, at work, at a social affair — but not contributing for lack of self-confidence. "To sin by silence," said Abraham Lincoln, "when they should protest makes cowards of men." This course will help you make your contribution.

THINGS TO THINK ABOUT AND DO

1. List a few topics that you can talk about for at least three minutes.

2. How would speech training help you in your current occupation or the one that you plan to enter?

3. Name a few benefits that you hope to gain from this course.

4. What public figure do you consider an excellent speaker and why?

5. What public figure do you consider a poor speaker and why?

2

You Don't Have to Say It to Convey It

When the eyes say one thing, and the tongue another, a practised man relies on the language of the first. [1]

CHAPTER OBJECTIVES

After reading and understanding this chapter, you should be able to:

- Define what nonverbal communication is.

- Explain the vital role that nonverbal communication performs in the daily verbal messages we transmit and receive.

- Observe and explain the various modes that communicate nonverbal messages.

- Explain the roles of objects, time, space, and environment in nonverbal communication.

CHAPTER DIGEST

This chapter deals with nonverbal language — the language without words that you use throughout life, consciously or

---

[1] Ralph Waldo Emerson, "Behavior," *The Conduct of Life* (1860).

subconsciously, to convey and receive messages. This language is often termed body language, face language, silent language, and silent messages. You may, in fact, lean more on this wordless language than you do on words.

Some personal elements of nonverbal language include posture, eye contact, facial expressions, tone of voice, body movement and gestures, clothes, smell, taste, and touch. Some impersonal elements are environment, weather, lighting, objects (artifacts), space, and time.

Your appearance, for example, creates powerful first impressions, even before you utter a word. How often have you misjudged someone initially because he wore a beard or she exuded a perfume that you couldn't stomach? On the job and in your social life, your appearance can help you or hurt you — tremendously.

Impersonal aspects of nonverbal communication also create impressions about you. Time and how you use it in relation to others tells something about you. If you're a high-ranking manager, for instance, you can keep your employees waiting. Space, or turf as it is sometimes called, is another impersonal element that denotes your status and authority. As a manager, you probably have an office with a large desk, windows, a rug, extra furniture, air conditioning, recessed lighting, plants, and paintings on the walls. All these objects, or artifacts, represent power, prestige, prosperity.

Our personal lives are influenced through the use of nonverbal language. Depending on how we control it, career decisions may be positively or negatively affected.

WHAT IS NONVERBAL COMMUNICATION?

Nonverbal communication is the conscious or subconscious transmission and reception of unspoken messages. An authority on nonverbal communication concludes from his research that 93 percent of the meaning we receive from another's message derives from the nonverbal part of the communication — facial expression and tone of voice — and only 7 percent from the words.[2]

[2]Albert Mehrabian, "Communication Without Words," *Psychology Today*, September 1968, p. 53.

One immediate observation comes to mind: what we *do* say may not be as important as what we *don't* say or as important as *how* we say it. Since so much of our message's impact depends on nonverbal aspects, how much more effectively would we communicate if we could become more proficient in this vital form of communication?

Nonverbal communication is a vast and ever-growing field for further study and research. Some elements of this type of communication include: environment, weather, lighting, objects, space, time, sight, taste, smell, touch, clothes and colors, and the hearing of sounds. Other elements include: facial expressions, eye contact, gestures, and other body movements; and *paralanguage* — laughing, coughing, throat clearing, vocal pitch, and pauses. This is just a partial list of nonverbal elements, and we will discuss only those over which you may have some control and which you may find important in your daily lives.

VERBAL REMARKS WITH NONVERBAL MEANINGS

We have all heard any number of sayings and phrases which clearly demonstrate the importance of nonverbal communication, such as:

> "Actions speak louder than words." Perhaps you can recall, as a child, the number of times you were told (verbal) not to do something, but you persisted to the point that the only "language" you really understood was a slap (nonverbal) on the hand or rear.

> "It wasn't so much *what* he said, but *how* he said it." Try to recall the number of situations that this statement applies to.

> "She had a look that could kill." If your mate "discovers" you where you shouldn't be, with someone you shouldn't be with, you'll appreciate this remark.

The nonverbal elements of communication are extremely important and in some instances more so than the spoken words. In fact, when a person's actions and words appear contradictory, the actions often communicate the true feelings.[3]

---

[3]Albert Mehrabian, *Silent Messages*, (Belmont, California: Wadsworth Publishing Co., Inc., 1971), p. 56.

Nonverbal communication is often referred to by other terms such as: the silent language, body language, face language, silent messages, and beyond words. No matter what it is called, it means the conscious or subconscious transmission and reception of messages, other than spoken words.

HOW WE COMMUNICATE WITHOUT WORDS

We cannot NOT communicate. Our very presence or absence "says something." If, for example, you had registered for a certain course and then failed to attend class, what messages could your absence transmit to the professor? He might think you were ill, or that you were still vacationing, or that you had changed your mind and signed up for another course. In actual fact, maybe you had changed jobs and your new hours prevented you from going to that first class, or you had to stay home with an ill child. The professor, though, might interpret your absence as apathy.

If you sign up for a course and attend from day one, your presence alone may transmit some of the following messages to your professor. He would know your sex, approximate height and weight, probably your taste in clothes or make-up. He may even know your socio-economic background and your general health, or from the way you dress, whether you're a conservative or a moderate. Your facial expressions may announce that you're happy, sad, nervous, friendly, shy, frightened, or restless. Where you sit in class (front row, back row, near the door) and how you sit (straight up, slouched, feet resting on chair in front of you) are other nonverbal signs of communication transmitting messages to your professor. These messages and others are transmitted by your presence — and even before you speak a word.

Nonverbally we communicate by: who we are, our appearance, the way we walk and stand, our facial expressions and eye contact, the way we move, gesture, and touch — and our vocalics or paralanguage.

Other nonverbal modes which strongly affect communication are time, space, environment, and objects. Let's discuss each of these modes.

WHO WE ARE

Just *being* we communicate. Messages are received and transmitted by such bodily qualities as: our sex; bodily frame; scars, birthmarks, and other visible features; color and hair style; skin and eye color as well as the quality of our complexion. How many of us have made initial judgments of people from a superficial first glance — and been wrong?

Our *self-image* is very critical not only to us personally, but to how others perceive us. More and more people, regardless of age, are spending thousands of dollars for plastic surgery simply to look and feel more appealing or to change their image. Vive la sex appeal!

OUR APPEARANCE

Before we even open our mouths, we make an impression, favorable or unfavorable. The clothes we wear often communicate our status in life and our degree of self-confidence. Just from observing a person's apparel, you may have heard or said that the person "has class."

A survey of one hundred top executives of major corporations showed:

- 96 percent said that their employees had a better chance of getting ahead if they knew how to dress.

- 72 percent said they would stall the promotion of a person who didn't dress properly.

- 84 percent turned down people who dressed improperly for job interviews.[4]

An authority on apparel writes, "When you step into a room, even though no one in that room knows you or has seen you before, they will make ten decisions about you based solely on your appearance." He further states: "To be successful in almost any endeavor, you must be sure that these decisions about you are favorable, because in that first impression you make — *you are what you wear.*"[5]

For example, what impression would you make if you appeared before a group impeccably dressed, but with messy hair

[4]John T. Molloy, *Dress for Success* (New York: Warner Books, 1975), p. 36.
[5]William Thourlby, *You Are What You Wear* (New York: New American Library, 1978), p. 1.

and dirty fingernails? Your perfume, your cosmetics, your after-shave lotion, and deodorant (or lack of it) convey messages. Is your breath always fresh and your body clean? If not, it will be no secret.

Posture often reflects our attitude, pride, confidence, and general health. If your professor observes — and he's adept at this — that you're sitting erect and looking at him, he'll probably conclude that you're alert and interested in his lecture. If, on the other hand, you're drooping in your chair, he'll conclude that you're tired, bored, or daydreaming.

At the next chance, notice the way people walk. You can almost tell a person's mission by his posture and stride: Is he fast-paced, slow-paced, skipping, ambling, hunched over or walking tall? Is he in a hurry? Perhaps he's late for a date. Is he slouching along? Maybe he's dreading a dentist's appointment. Good posture projects a positive image.

OUR FACIAL EXPRESSIONS

There is, perhaps, no other nonverbal code which can be so easily misread as facial expressions because so many people control them so well. Controlling these expressions can camouflage true feelings. We are better prepared to lie with our face than with any other nonverbal cue. Perhaps you can recall a situation when you were eating something you really didn't like but, so as not to offend the cook, you said it was "delicious" and your remark was reinforced by your feigned facial expression. You've heard the expression, "He lied through his teeth." This is understandable when you consider that our facial muscles can create thousands of different expressions.

To insure credibility, we should strive to have our facial expression and verbal message coincide. Imagine the reaction if you smiled at a funeral or flashed an expression of indifference while congratulating someone on a happy occasion. Conversely, crying at a wedding is acceptable because, presumably, these would be tears of joy.

Research tells us that facial expressions can communicate the following meanings: surprise, fear, happiness, sadness, contempt, disgust, anger, interest, determination, and bewilderment.[6] The

---

[6]Ekman, W. V. Friesen, and P. Ellsworth, *Emotion in the Human Face* (New York: Pergamon Press, 1972), pp. 57–65.

following quote is appropriate: "A man finds room in the few square inches of his face for the traits of all his ancestors; for the expression of all his history, and his wants."[7]

| Surprise | Fear | Happiness | Contempt |

| Disgust | Anger | Determination | Bewilderment |

OUR EYES

Eye contact is necessary to establish and maintain a beam of communication. If you're listening to a lecture and suddenly the speaker starts reading a long passage verbatim, the chances are he has disrupted his strong line of communication and may lose your attention.

Eyes can convey approval or disapproval; they can include and exclude a person during a conversation; they transmit happiness, sadness, confusion, and even terror. Eyes tell us if someone is interested or bored. Eyes can communicate at a glance. If you've ever visited a singles bar, you've probably experienced the dynamics of communication which takes place via glances, winks, and stares.

Our culture teaches us it's impolite to stare. The next time

[7]Ralph Waldo Emerson, "Behavior," *The Conduct of Life* (1860).

you're on a bus or train, single out a person and stare at him. See how long it takes before the situation becomes awkward. When children are being scolded, they try to avoid eye contact but are ordered to, "Look at me when I talk to you."

The next time you're in an elevator, notice how little eye contact takes place because of the occupants' proximity to each other. They will stare at the flashing floor numbers, the floor, or ceiling, but seldom at each other unless, of course, they're seeking contact. Most people tend to increase eye contact with those from whom they seek approval or recognition.[8]

OUR BODY MOVEMENT

To appreciate the almost total power of nonverbal communication, watch a professional pantomimist perform — it is sheer artistry. Some of the classic characterizations in show business belong to such superstars as Jackie Gleason, Red Skelton, Marcel Marceau, the late Charlie Chaplin, and Jerry Lewis. Their artful use of apparel, movement, eye contact, gestures, and facial expressions brings laughter and tears to millions of all ages. The ways in which they move their arms, hands and fingers, their heads and eyes, the ways they sway, stoop, and bend are sheer genius. They never utter a word, but their messages are always understood.

When you speak, you can significantly reinforce your verbal message by your body movement. Such movement adds variety to your overall delivery, as opposed to standing rigidly in one spot. To get more personal with your listeners, move closer to them. To make emphatic points, take a step for each point. Movement can also help you relax by releasing some of your excess energy.

OUR GESTURES

Gestures play a large role in our daily communication and are usually most effective when performed naturally. You've probably heard the statement, "If his hands were tied, he couldn't speak." Gesturing can enhance verbal communication. If you wish to make

---

[8]Efram Broughton, "Effects of Expectancies for Social Approval on Visual Behavior," *Journal of Personality and Social Psychology*, 86 (1972), pp. 29–33.

several points, when making point number one, show one finger; for point number two, show two; etc.

A hitchhiker pointing his thumb, an umpire calling a player out at home plate, and a policeman directing traffic at a busy intersection are examples of communicating explicitly without words, as is sign language of the deaf.

When giving directions, many people find it easier to accompany spoken words with hands — straight, to the right or left, up or down. We've probably all been shown, by the extension of the arms, "the size of the fish that got away."

A scholar of nonverbal communication has aptly stated, ". . . we respond to gestures with an extreme alertness and, one might also say, in accordance with an elaborate and secret code that is written nowhere, known by none, and understood by all."[9]

"Really, you should have seen it!"

[9]Edward Sapir, *Human Message Systems* (New York: Harper & Row, 1976), p. 82.

OUR TOUCHING

Perhaps the most personal mode of communicating without words is touching. It can signal both positive (a handshake) and negative (a slap in the face) attitudes, depending upon the individual being touched and his culture patterns. Touching is a crucial aspect of most human relationships. It can communicate approval and encouragement, tenderness and passion, disapproval and punishment.

Touching starts at birth when babies get slapped in the rear, and continues when mother takes charge with breast feeding, holding, cuddling, rocking, stroking, burping, bathing, and changing. Studies show the staggering importance of touch: orphaned babies placed in institutions have died because they were never cuddled or held.

Touching can symbolize different things to different people, depending on a specific situation, environment, time of day, anticipated intent, etc. Some individuals enjoy, and even crave, touching and being touched. Touching can be an expression of being friendly and liking someone, and could signal sexual desires. Other individuals may regard being touched as disrespectful and even offensive.

Our culture teaches us it's improper for an individual of lower status to touch one of a higher status unless encouraged to do so. For example, it may be acceptable for a professor to put his arm around a student, but not for a student to embrace a professor; or a manager may touch someone from the mailroom but not vice versa.

Our culture frowns upon a male hugging, embracing, or kissing another male. If you saw two women dancing or holding hands, you probably wouldn't think much about it; but if you saw two men dancing or holding hands, you might think it strange. This would generally be interpreted as an act of femininity or homosexuality. However, the exception to this code is often displayed in sports, when a player hits a game-winning home run, scores a winning touchdown, goal, or basket, and is spontaneously hugged by his fellow players showing their joy.

Although our culture has established certain taboos regarding male-to-male touching, there are times, for example at a funeral, when no action could equal a warm embrace for manifesting affection, love, or sympathy.

How we touch, what part of the body we touch, and the duration of the touch are all important factors in interpreting the message. Notice people shaking hands, hugging, kissing, or pinching. Can you "read" them and their intentions? Touching, according to the messages communicated, can range from the very impersonal to the very personal.[10]

OUR VOCALICS

Another word for vocalics is paralanguage. For example, let's assume that your professor had a female colleague from New England tape-record the following message: "All of you are lucky to be in this speech course." After listening to this tape, the class would probably agree that the speaker had a message; it was conveyed in English and everyone in the class understood it. But *beyond* this, the class would probably be able to say other things about the voice on the tape machine. They would be able to identify the voice as a white American female, probably from the Northeast, because of her regional accent. They probably would agree that her voice sounded professional. Her diction was articulate and pleasant, she pronounced her words correctly, and she had no problem breathing. The class could probably tell if she were young, middle-aged, or older.

They might have received other messages as well, such as her voice was soothing and sexy. She sounded alive and happy, and would probably be fun to be with. Whatever it was that enabled the class to infer these messages — other than the actual spoken words — is paralanguage, or vocalics.

Paralanguage is the "how we say it" as opposed to "what we say." The quality of our voice — its pitch, rate of delivery, inflection, emphasis, and even pauses play an important role in transmitting nonverbal messages. Take the sentence, "Yes, I love you." Say it aloud but each time put emphasis first on the word "yes," then on the word "I," then on the word "love," and finally on the word "you."

Yes, I love you.
Yes, I love you.
Yes, *I* love you.
Yes, I *love* you.
Yes, I love *you*.

---

[10]R. Heslin, "Steps Toward a Taxonomy of Touching," paper presented to the Midwestern Psychological Association, Chicago, May 1974.

"Yes, I *love* you, dammit!"

You should have no difficulty interpreting the various messages received from the same sentence. *How* we say things is often more important than *what* we say.

OTHER CODES

There are other codes equally significant in nonverbal communication, such as time, space, artifacts (objects), and environment.

TIME

Most of us are very time-conscious, and time plays a vital role in the messages we convey. Many people consider time more valuable than money, and indeed, most of our lives are influenced by a time schedule.

How important is time? To many people, time represents status and power. For example: a boss can keep a worker waiting, and can also be late for a meeting, without consequence. A doctor can keep a patient waiting. A college president can keep a dean waiting, who in turn can keep a division chairperson waiting, who can keep a department chairperson waiting, who can keep a professor waiting, and who in turn can keep a student waiting. The more influential your position, the more command you have over your time and other people's time.

Being late or even last to arrive may be interpreted as a symbol of status, depending on a person's importance or popularity. It's common knowledge that, on occasion, airline flights have been delayed for the arrival of a V.I.P. At a candidate's fundraiser the candidate is usually the last to arrive. At a nightclub or concert the star is usually the last to perform. When Nancy Reagan represented the president at the royal wedding in London in July 1981, she outraged her hosts by arriving late at various functions.

You've heard the expression that "people don't usually appreciate what they have until they no longer have it." It's true. Persons in hospitals and prisons appreciate time because they are forced to do things when other people want them to. This can, and often does, lead to frustration, anger, and hostility.

Remember . . . You can "use time." You can "waste time." Or, you can "kill time."

"I wonder if she forgot me . . ."

SPACE

Anthropologist Edward T. Hall coined the word *proxemics* to describe the study of space as a communicative mode. "Every living thing has a physical boundary that separates it from its external environment."[11]

We take our space very seriously. Daily you can see signs declaring, "No Trespassing," "Keep Out," or "Private Property." These signs indicate private ownership and an intruder enters at his own risk. You should never invade another's space or territory. In a home it's not unusual for members of the family to sit in the same chairs at every meal.

Throughout history, millions of people have been killed in wars due to the infringement on someone else's space. Territorial waters and air space are usually respected by all governments mutually.

Territorial behavior is often evidenced in our daily lives. While walking down the street at night, it may bother us to "sense" a stranger approaching us from behind. While eating in the crowded "cafeteria," some people would resent a stranger asking permission to sit at the same table. How would you feel if you were waiting in line at a restaurant or theatre and someone stepped in front of you?

Most people carry an invisible "bubble" of personal space around with them, and any attempt to enter that area constitutes an intrusion. Notice how uneasy people become in crowded situations like an elevator, bus, or at the theatre when a stranger sits uncomfortably close. If you would like to experiment, the next time you're talking with a friend, slowly inch a little closer and a little closer — then observe your friend's physical reaction.

Space may also indicate a person's status and authority. Many wealthy people live in very large homes and estates where the servants' quarters are removed from the rest of the house. At one time a two-car garage symbolized status — now it's a three-car garage.

A person's position and influence in his company can usually be determined by the size of his office and its view and by his private parking space.

When a company plans to build a new facility or move to new quarters, a great deal of time, money, and thought is devoted to

---

[11]Edward T. Hall, *The Silent Language* (New York: Anchor Books, 1973), p. 163.

the new office layout to maximize the productivity of employees. Should all the desks sit in an open area or should they be clustered? Who should have private offices and who should share them? Should walls or separators be used to offer a degree of privacy? What type of furniture and wall hangings should be purchased? In what areas or offices should the furniture be placed and how should it be arranged? These are some of the considerations that daily influence the working world.

OUR ARTIFACTS

The artifacts or objects in our possession transmit clear messages about us. Our clothes, furniture, paintings, cars, home, and jewelry can be explicit indicators of our behavior and status. A wedding band says we're married. A ring on the right hand may say we're available. A policeman's badge shouts authority, and a uniform may announce a person's occupation.

Some people, upon entering one room, feel comfortable and warm, whereas in another room they may feel nervous. Is there any question that furnishings, including rugs, lamps, mirrors, and wall covering, contribute to the room's personality? People communicate more easily in comfortable surroundings than in uncomfortable ones.

A person driving a Mercedes 450 SL and one driving a dune buggy will communicate vastly different messages. And so will the individual who skippers a 45-foot yacht as opposed to one who owns a 12-foot Boston Whaler.

Many people derive a sense of pride and self-worth from their collections. The wealthy may collect paintings, jewelry, diamonds, and gold worth a fortune. Other popular collector's items are cars, stamps, coins, dolls, trains, Waterford crystal, guns, butterflies, and fine wines. Many people not only enjoy their collections, but some look upon them as symbols of power, status, challenge, and accomplishment.

OUR ENVIRONMENT

Environment affects all communication messages. Natural factors include weather elements such as rain, snow, fog, sunshine, day and night, temperature, and humidity. They also include such things as mountains, lakes, valleys, oceans, and outer space.

Business and industry have learned that a happy employee is a more productive employee and that the working environment influences an employee's performance. As a result, thousands of companies have improved lighting, temperatures, and air for their workers. Sometimes employees are even encouraged to bring in plants and flowers to brighten their own personal areas. More attention is now paid to color coordination and furnishings to make the working environment more appealing and pleasant. Such companies, by their actions, say they care about their employees.

"Are you there, Miss Froehmer?"

WE CANNOT *NOT* COMMUNICATE

Sigmund Freud once summed up nonverbal communication in this way: No mortal can keep a secret. If his lips are silent, he chatters with his fingertips.

As mentioned earlier, certain nonverbal cues can be faked and may contain a message different from what's actually being transmitted. It is easy to misinterpret parts of nonverbal language. Remember, nonverbal cues are not absolute. We must consider them in the total context of a given situation in which they are produced.

Because of the importance of this subject, certain elements of nonverbal communication are briefly repeated in Chapter 4.

THINGS TO THINK ABOUT AND DO

1. Listen to a voice on the radio and jot down as much information as possible based on the voice's paralanguage. Discuss them in class.

2. Traveling to or from work, make a list of as many nonverbal messages you have perceived. Discuss them in class.

3. The next time you're talking with a friend, slowly move closer and closer. Tell the class of your friend's reaction.

4. Select someone in your neighborhood with whom you've never spoken. Tell the class as much as you can about that individual based on that person's nonverbal codes.

5. Explain to the class what nonverbal messages you think you transmit to others. The class may wish to respond as to its interpretations of your messages.

6. Discuss the verbal and nonverbal cues that your professor employs in teaching this class.

If your class has access to a videotape recorder (VTR), you may wish to record some of the following exercises as a learning experience in nonverbal communication. Play back the videotape to see how many members of the class received the nonverbal messages that you feel you actually transmitted. The exercises should not run more than a few minutes.

1. Through facial expressions and your eyes, try to convey different moods. For example, anger, fear, happiness, sadness, and surprise.

2. Pretend that you're at a market place in a foreign country. The vendor, who doesn't speak or understand English, shows you something. You admire it, try it on, but feel it's too expensive. You want it. Nonverbally, communicate this to the vendor and bargain for a lower price.

3. Again, you're in a foreign country where a language barrier exists. You're at a restaurant and when the waiter arrives you attempt to order a full-course breakfast nonverbally.

4. You're in a pet shop. Without words, convey to the class where you are and what you see. You look at various pets and then pick up the one you intend to purchase.

5. In silent language, demonstrate a line of work performed by a member of your family. First, you must identify the individual and then that person's occupation.

6. Using body language only, describe a vacation spot you would like to visit and the mode of transportation to get there.

7. Visually describe your favorite hobby or avocation.

8. If you have a full- or part-time job, describe it.

9. Communicate your major and your short- and long-term educational goals.

WHAT DO YOU REMEMBER FROM THIS CHAPTER?

1. Approximately what percent of the meaning we derive from another's message is nonverbal?

2. Define nonverbal communication, and give several examples.

3. List five phrases or sayings which demonstrate the importance of nonverbal communication.

4. Explain the statement "We cannot NOT communicate."

5. What can posture tell us about a person?

6. What nonverbal code can be easily misread? Explain.

7. List five types of messages that a person's eyes may transmit.

8. List five gestures which convey explicit meanings.

9. Explain paralanguage and give five examples.

10. Give an example of time being interpreted as a symbol of status.

11. What is proxemics?

12. How important a role does the environment play in nonverbal communication? Explain.

VITALIZE YOUR VOCABULARY

You can have a clear, musical voice, an attractive appearance, good eye contact, and a solid knowledge of your subject; but if your vocabulary is weak and vague, your presentation will also be weak and vague. Whether you're communicating with one or two people or a group of thirty, a strong and varied vocabulary is a major asset. That is why, starting now and continuing with each succeeding chapter, we include a list of words (and their most basic meanings) that educated people should not only understand but also be able to use.

The lists of words vary considerably. Some lists contain families of words that relate to the same subject; for example: government and politics, court and law, business and finance, computers and data processing. Other lists comprise synonyms, words based on Latin and Greek roots, words from American Indians, and words from Japan that have entered our language.

We hope that these brief glimpses into the intriguing world of words will galvanize you into exploring deeper into that world.

A solid knowledge of synonyms (words that have the same basic meanings but may differ in tone and appropriateness) will impart vigor and variety to your speech. An excellent and proven source of synonyms and antonyms (words that mean the opposite) is *Roget's Thesaurus of Words and Phrases*. It doesn't, however, explain differences in meanings; for those different shades of meaning you should consult a modern authoritative dictionary.

Consider the basic meanings of the adjectives *slim* and *slender*; synonyms are *trim* and *svelte*. These four adjectives are complimentary. On the other hand, synonyms like *bony*, *gaunt*, and *skinny* are anything but complimentary and may even be insulting. The word *thin* falls somewhere between the first four adjectives and the last three. These examples prove the vital importance of understanding different shades of meanings.

Synonyms

big, huge, large (adj.)   immense, vast, massive, kingsize, enormous, tremendous, colossal, mammoth, jumbo, gigantic, gargantuan.

brave, courageous, fearless (adj.)   bold, valiant, heroic, game, valorous, gallant, lionhearted, spunky, plucky, dauntless, audacious, adventurous, nervy, intrepid, gutsy.

cash, money, bread (n.)   legal tender, currency, greenbacks, dough, dinero, lucre, bucks, wherewithal, scratch, wampum, moolah, loot, smackers, cabbage.

complain, gripe, bitch (v.)   grouse, whine, beef, "weep," bellyache, wail, crab, squawk, lament, mutter, fuss, moan and groan, grumble.

fake, phony, artificial (adj.)   counterfeit, spurious, adulterated, ungenuine, make-believe, mock, substitute, ersatz, bogus, pseudo, simulated, synthetic.

famous, great, outstanding (adj.)   distinguished, noted, renowned, celebrated, prominent, illustrious, foremost, eminent, notable, honored.

friend, acquaintance (n.)   companion, pal, buddy, chum, sidekick, partner, associate, colleague, amigo, comrade, crony, alter ego, confidant.

grouchy, cranky, disagreeable (adj.)   cross, crusty, irritable, cantankerous, irascible, snappish, churlish, mean, waspish, ornery, touchy, peevish, petulant, grumpy, sour, surly, morose.

holler, shout, yell (v.)   shriek, bellow, hoot, howl, bawl, roar, whoop, scream, bark, screech, shrill.

stubborn, obstinate (adj.)   inflexible, rigid, immovable, bullheaded, adamant, unyielding, unbending, uncompromising, intransigent.

swindle, double-cross, deceive (v.)   dupe, bamboozle, victimize, hoodwink, bilk, flimflam, cheat, defraud, con, fleece, gouge, shortchange, hoax, hornswoggle, rip off, hustle, take, hose, frame, screw, shaft.

3

You Can Overhear, but You Can't Overlisten

Nobody has ever listened himself out of a job.[1]

CHAPTER OBJECTIVES

After reading and understanding this chapter, you should know:

- The importance of listening well.
- Some major reasons why we listen.
- Some ways to become a better listener.
- The different types of listening.

CHAPTER DIGEST

The act of listening comprises a significant portion of our daily activities. It is the other half of the communication process since, without listeners, we cannot communicate orally. Yet, few of us pay attention to improving our ability to listen.

Hearing is a biological function, but listening is, or should be, an intellectual function that involves your mind, eyes, ears,

---

[1]Calvin Coolidge, thirtieth president of the United States, 1923–1929.

and memory. As a listener, you influence speakers by your reactions. If you show interest through your facial expression or body language, you will see speakers perk up. If you show boredom or confusion through inattention or lack of eye contact, you will see that they tend to change their approach to avoid risking failure.

There are several reasons why we should listen: to become informed, to understand, to evaluate, and to enjoy. Any intellectual activity that can affect your life to such an extent deserves to be done well. Suggestions for sharpening your listening skill are offered, but they will benefit you only after you make the commitment to help yourself.

When you were a child, how often did your parents criticize you for not *listening*? As a parent, how frequently do you direct your children to *listen*?

At one time or another all of us are guilty of not really listening to what's being said. It could lead to embarrassment, argument, and, at times, even more serious consequences.

All too often in interpersonal communication, we absorb only what we want to, at home, school, work, or play. Many a time we choose not to pay attention to certain people because they are boring. We have that arbitrary ability to "tune out" certain people, and let's face it, sometimes it can be beneficial.

A study conducted by one of the leading universities found that adults spend about 70 percent of their waking hours engaging in communication activities. It concluded that the average adult devotes 9 percent of this time to writing, 16 percent to reading, 30 percent to speaking, and 45 percent to listening.

We wake up in the morning to the sounds of an alarm clock, radio, or someone's voice. There may be conversation at breakfast, at work, at school, on public conveyances, in a car pool. We might attend a business meeting, a lecture, or a luncheon. We might hear someone speak in person or on the radio, TV, or telephone. We might attend a concert, a movie, or a social or civic function. Think of all the times in one day, for example, that we listen. How much of that listening experience will we be able to recall? Are we actually *listening* and *understanding*, or are we just *hearing* things? There's a world of difference.

Despite the above statistics, listening, the communication activity we engage in most of our waking hours (a third of our lives) is the one that our educational system ignores the most. In most colleges today, courses in basic writing are mandatory for all freshmen. With increasing alarm over our low national reading scores, reading courses are offered and at some colleges they're required. Courses in public speaking and oral communication are offered on most college campuses and, in some instances, taking at least one is a requirement for a degree. But how many institutions require a student to take a course in listening?

That arbitrary ability to "tune out" certain people.

Perhaps because we spend so much time listening we feel that we can do it efficiently. What a false conclusion this is!

The fact is that from the business and educational communities comes the disturbing complaint that workers and students "just don't know how to listen." To address the seriousness of this problem in the business world, a Fortune 500 international corporation took two steps.[2]

1. It set up special listening programs worldwide for all their employees who may wish to attend.

2. It invested hundreds of thousands of dollars in a 2-page color advertising campaign in several national magazines which ran for months. The theme was "We understand how important it is to listen."

LISTENING AS AN INTELLECTUAL ACTIVITY

You can listen more effectively and improve your comprehension markedly if you work at it. Listening is just as important to interpersonal communication as speaking; in fact, "listening is the other half of talking. If people stop listening, it is useless to talk — a point not always appreciated by talkers. . . ."[3]

While hearing is a biological activity, listening is an intellectual one because it requires more than just ears. Effective listening is an holistic activity that should include the active efforts of your mind, eyes, ears, and memory.

- **Your mind.** You should summon your logical reasoning capacity to grasp the real intended meaning of the speaker's message. Learn the differences between fact, opinion, and inference.

- **Your eyes.** You should observe the speaker, her posture, gestures, facial expressions and mannerisms, and her movements. All these combine to communicate vital messages.

- **Your ears.** Listen carefully to her voice. Is it pleasant, harsh, reassuring, authoritative, or weak? How about her inflection, rate of speaking, pauses, loudness, and animation? Are they "in synch" with her message? In other words, is her nonverbal message enhanced or contradicted by her oral one?

---

[2]Sperry Corporation, *Newsweek*, 20 October 1980, p. 89.

[3]Stuart Chase, "Are You Listening?" *Reader's Digest* (December 1962), 1980.

■ **Your memory.** Try to recall as much as you can, if possible, about the topic at hand. Are you hearing new or different information? Did the speaker omit anything? If so, what and why? By recalling as much as possible about the speaker's message, you should have a solid basis on which to compare or contrast the message.

As a listener you not only have a responsibility to the speaker, but you can also aid her during her talk. Your facial and body reactions are quickly communicated to her. If you're looking at her, show interest: lean forward occasionally and appear to catch her every word, even jot down a few notes or a question you may wish to bring up later. These positive indications tell the speaker that the message is getting across to you.

If you slouch in your chair, whisper to your neighbor, read a book, or look just plain bored, the speaker will be well aware that she has problems.

REASONS FOR LISTENING

Following are some of the major reasons why we listen:

1. To enjoy.

2. To become informed.

3. To understand.

4. To evaluate.

To enjoy. This is light listening, for example: a pleasant conversation, listening to music, watching a movie or TV show for relaxation. Listening to enjoy should not involve any strain but should be casual and relaxed. The change of pace should be enjoyable and pleasant.

To become informed. Here you seek new information. You listen to the radio for the weather report or no-school announcement, you attend a class lecture or a business, social, or civic meeting. You should establish in your mind the motive for listening, and therefore you should direct complete interest, attention, and concentration to the speaker. If your professor announces that there'll be a quiz following her short lecture, you're motivated to listen.

Listening is an intellectual activity.

"Know how to listen and you can learn even from those who speak badly," said Plutarch, Greek essayist and biographer, about two thousand years ago.

To understand. How often have you formed an opinion of a speaker and her subject before she has even opened her mouth or before she has concluded her talk because of preconceived opinions or prejudice?

Many people find listening to understand most difficult because it requires restraint, fair mindedness, and objective thinking. As a consequence, many of the world's problems have resulted from selfishness, disregard of other people's opinions, and a failure to attempt honestly to understand another's viewpoint. Listening to understand doesn't mean that you must agree or disagree, but that you must approach the subject with an unbiased, open mind. You must also listen totally to the message, striving to understand why and what is being expressed. Allow yourself to grasp the entire message before you react.

To evaluate. Of all the types of listening, evaluative listening is the most difficult and the most critical because it requires the most effort. There are a number of questions to bear in mind when listening to evaluate:

> What is the main purpose of the talk?
>
> Is the talk informative, entertaining, persuasive, inspirational, or is it a talk to actuate?
>
> Is the speaker making logical and valid points?
>
> Are the arguments convincing? Are they based upon fact or opinion?
>
> Is the speaker an authority on the subject or does she just have an axe to grind?
>
> To what needs of the audience is the speaker appealing?
>
> Can you clearly understand the speaker's message?
>
> Do the nonverbal elements of her talk coincide or conflict with her verbal message?

These are only some of the countless questions you should consider when preparing to listen to evaluate. You now have some idea of the complexity and depth of evaluative listening.

Do you usually take statements uttered by a well-known figure as the last word, or do you make an effort to seek out the other side before formulating an opinion? If you're in a position to disagree or question people, do you? Remember that you may disagree without being disagreeable. Evaluative listening, whether the issues are international, national or local, business or educational, political or social, is especially critical.

HOW TO BE A BETTER LISTENER

Diogenes, a Greek philosopher 2300 years ago, put it very wisely when he said, "We have two ears and only one tongue in order that we may hear more and speak less."

To be a better listener you must first *want* to be one. You must realize the many benefits of improved listening, and you must be prepared to exert the required effort. When you come to class you know that you'll hear people talk, so prepare yourself to listen. Develop a positive attitude toward the speakers. Tell yourself that you'll hear some exhilarating topics and that in all probability you'll learn something new. Motivation can spell the difference between just hearing something and listening and understanding it.

If you're planning to attend a lecture or listen to a speech outside class, you can get ready for it by learning what you can about the speaker. Who is she? What's her background? Is she an authority on the subject? What's her motive for speaking? By increasing your interest in the speaker and her subject before the event, you can't help but listen more effectively.

Below are some suggestions for honing your ability to listen:

1. Concentrate.

2. Keep an open mind.

3. "Read" the speaker.

4. Get ready for the wrap-up.

5. Put yourself in the speaker's shoes.

Concentrate. Interpersonal communication should be on a constant beam from the speaker to the listener and back to the speaker. Don't interrupt this beam by daydreaming or succumbing to distractions. Try not to think about last night, this morning, or tonight. If your thoughts begin to wander, take charge and direct them back to the speaker and her message. If the speaker is boring, you're really faced with a challenge.

Another obstacle to total concentration is the fact that we think much faster than we speak. As mentioned in Chapter 5, a comfortable speaking rate lies between 130 and 160 words per minute. The brain, however, can deal with approximately 500 words per minute. So you can see that while we're listening, we have quite a bit of spare time. It is during this spare time that we must try not to become distracted.

From the moment the speaker approaches the stand, rivet your eyes onto her. Remember that eye contact is as important to the speaker as it is to the listener. Look interested and you will be interested. Watch her facial expressions and gestures while she's speaking. You can receive many clues to her meanings by observing her mannerisms. As discussed in Chapter 4, gestures can be eloquent, indeed.

Beware of distractions. Little things can throw you off . . . books dropping, people talking and coughing, fire engines roaring. The speaker herself can be distracting. Her dress may be as loud as the fire engine, her gestures may be uncontrollable, or she may be constantly swaying. If these or any other distractions occur, then you must intensify your concentration on the message.

Nothing inspires a speaker more than an interested audience.

Keep an open mind. Don't have the attitude, "I know what she's going to say and she's all wet." Preconceived opinions narrowly limit your ability to benefit from a true communicative experience. Be objective. Hear the speaker out to the end. Then, if you disagree, ask her to clarify certain points. Give the speaker every courtesy that you would want if you were speaking.

"Read" the speaker. If the speaker opens with a title, grasp it. Closely follow her introduction and the main points she's making. In her introduction she should state what will be covered. Take note and anticipate the main points. How do they relate to the other points mentioned? Is she accomplishing what she set out to do? What about the soundness of her ideas? Are they valid? Is she logical? Does she have supporting material and how does she use it? These are just some thoughts to consider while you're listening.

Being able to "read" a speaker will give you the added advantage of listening with greater insight.

Get ready for the wrap-up. Be ready for the conclusion of the talk. It will be the speaker's final chance to imprint her message in the minds of the listeners. At this time she may repeat some important points that you may have missed during the talk. Listen for them and ask yourself the following crucial questions: Did I get her message? Do I agree, or do certain points need clarification? What were her strongest and weakest arguments?

Never be too embarrassed to ask questions. There is no more important process in education than asking questions. (Refer to the section on the question-and-answer period in Chapter 4.)

Put yourself in the speaker's shoes. You may be able to better understand and absorb a talk if you try to put yourself in the speaker's place. This means you must strive to feel, think, act, and react like the speaker. What motivated her to select this topic? What is her educational and professional background? Is she married or single? Does she have any children? What action or reaction is she seeking from the audience and why?

If you can successfully place yourself within the speaker, not only will you understand her message better, but you will have taken a giant step toward becoming a more effective and responsive listener.

THINGS TO THINK ABOUT AND DO

1. Describe a job environment or school environment or social environment that you consider ideal for listening.

2. Do you agree that attentive listeners help a speaker communicate better? Explain.

3. What distractions hamper your listening in this class? What can you do about them?

4. What have you observed to be people's most common listening deficiencies? Prepare to discuss them.

5. Honestly evaluate your own listening habits. Can you improve your listening habits? How?

6. Plan to attend or view a speaking situation involving an audience. Evaluate the listening habits of some members of the audience, especially those who fail to become involved in a genuine listening experience. Plan to discuss.

7. After each student has given a short talk, could you briefly summarize the main ideas of the talk? You may do this by yourself, or your instructor may call upon members of the class at random for a response. Be prepared.

WHAT DO YOU REMEMBER FROM THIS CHAPTER?

1. Approximately what percentage of your waking hours is involved in listening?

2. Can a listener aid a speaker? If so, how?

3. Name some types of listening.

4. Explain some hints for better listening.

5. Is it permissible to take notes while a person is speaking?

6. Is there a difference between hearing and listening? Explain.

7. Explain listening as an holistic activity.

VITALIZE YOUR VOCABULARY

Words from Japan

At the end of World War II, Japan, land of the rising sun, was a vanquished and demoralized nation. Since then, Japan, with guidance and financial aid from the United States, has emerged as the number one nation in technological expertise and industrial productivity.[4] Today, Japan is a world-class power, and a linguistic spin-off from that status is that some of its words have entered our language; a few of these words were part of American English even before World War II.

Here is a sprinkling of Japanese words that you should know, together with their symbols:

Banzai 万歳

Literally "10 thousand years," "banzai" is a carryover from the Chinese language where it means something like "long live the king." Now, it means "three cheers" or "hip-hip hooray." It is said when celebrating something (usually three times in succession), and is accompanied by raising both arms.

Bonsai 盛栽

Japanese dwarf tree cultivation.

Geisha 芸者

A female entertainer who serves at a private party.

Hancho (frequently misspelled "Honcho") 班長
Boss, literally squad leader

Harakiri 腹切

Suicide by disembowelment.

Hibachi 火鉢

A charcoal grill.

Ikebana 生花

Japanese flower arrangement. In its earlier stage of evolution, ikebana was closely related to the tea ceremony as a special way of decorating the tea room. Later, many schools and styles of arranging flowers developed.

---

[4]*Newsweek*, 9 August 1982, page 48, column 2.

Judo 柔道

Japanese art of self-defense. The fundamental principle of Judo is to utilize the opponent's strength to one's own advantage.

Kamikaze 神風

A suicide pilot. A divine wind, specifically the typhoon that wrecked the Mongol invasion of Japan in the thirteenth century.

Karate 唐手

The Loochoo (Ryukyu) art of self-defense, of hitting or jabbing an opponent with one's fist or kicking him. It was introduced from China and gradually became a unique art of combat that uses no weapons.

Kimono 着物

A traditional Japanese robe.

Nisei 二世

Americans of Japanese descent.

Rickshaw 力車

Man-pulled cart.

Samurai 侍

This is the noun form of the verb saburau, which means "to serve." The samurai were the warrior class in Tokugawa (sixteenth through eighteenth century) Japan who served clan chieftains. They were ranked above the common man and were permitted to have surnames while commoners were not.

Sayonara さよなら

Good-bye

Shogun 将軍

A feudal generalissimo.

Tsunami 津波

A tidal wave.

Zori (es) 草履

Thonged sandals.

4

Your First Talk: Getting to Know You

The first time I attempted to make a public talk . . . I was in a state of misery . . . my tongue clove to the roof of my mouth, and, at first, I could hardly get out a word.[1]

CHAPTER OBJECTIVES

After reading and understanding this chapter, you should be able to:

- Appreciate the importance of knowing your subject well.
- Prepare a short, interesting talk about yourself.
- Deliver the talk about yourself.
- Grasp the importance of eye contact and gestures.
- Realize the importance of good posture, some movement, and the limited use of notes.
- Broaden your circle of friends.
- Understand that nervousness strikes almost everybody, rich and poor, young and old, black and white, educated and uneducated.

---

[1]Lloyd George, Prime Minister of England and one of the most eloquent speakers in this century.

47

CHAPTER DIGEST

This chapter will guide you into some of the ways of giving a good, stimulating talk.

Since it's easier to talk with people you know, the sooner you get to know each other, the better. That's why your first talk will probably be an autobiographical sketch from three to five minutes long.

Thorough knowledge of the subject gives more self-confidence to speakers than anything else. And since you know yourself inside out, if called upon to do so, you should be able to talk for at least a few minutes.

All of us like attention and respect. When you're "front and center," you're the focus of attention. If you follow the suggestions in this chapter and those in later chapters, you will earn the respect of your peers and other listeners.

Everybody, including professional speakers and actors, gets nervous before a performance. It's a normal reaction that usually diminishes soon after you get involved in your message. Since it's almost impossible to eliminate all nervousness, you should strive to control it.

Eye contact with your listeners is vital, so look them right in the eye. This arouses them initially and gives you the momentum to keep them interested. Eye contact also provides you with feedback on how you're doing.

Gestures support and dramatize your ideas. As long as your gestures are spontaneous and vigorous, use them. In addition, they're an excellent outlet for your nervous energy.

If using note cards will give you confidence, use them; professional speakers often do. Just don't read so much from the cards that you disrupt eye contact with your listeners.

This first talk will probably be the toughest one of all. From then on, your other efforts should be easier. Remember that giving good talks requires that you do your homework beforehand. Homework includes rehearsing, preferably with at least one listener.

If you've never addressed a group before, this will be an exciting and memorable experience. Although your talk will probably be short, it could provide you with the challenge and motivation that could have a positive impact on your life.

Your professor may either ask you to talk about yourself or ask you to interview a classmate and then give a talk about him. No matter which talk you give, this chapter will guide you in how to plan and give it.

"What am I doing here?"

Since almost all of you are more relaxed when communicating with people you know, your instructor may feel that it's a good idea for everyone to give a brief autobiographical sketch. In this way you'll learn to know each other sooner and also get the "feel" of giving a prepared talk before a group.

This short autobiographical talk will afford you an opportunity to listen to everyone in the class introduce himself. What an excellent chance to find out which classmates have the same interests as yours. Perhaps, while listening to someone interesting, you'll look forward to the class break or a chance to meet at the cafeteria to develop, on a one-to-one basis, a more personal relationship. So "psych" yourself to absorb what your classmates have to say and listen carefully for possible clues of mutual interest or concern. This talk is an important first step in developing new friends.

The speaker's stand may be only fifteen feet away from your seat, but it may seem like a mile to you. This is understandable because of your anxiety about what's to come. Many things will zip through your mind, like "I wonder if I'll be able to move when I'm called. I'll just play dead — on second thought, who'll be playing?" or "What the hell am I doing here?" Believe it or not, you're here to give your first talk.

KNOW YOUR SUBJECT

Most professors of speech agree that *knowing your subject* is 90 percent of delivering an effective talk. No one knows you better than you do yourself, and no other topic should interest you more or provide you with more material, so your autobiographical talk is an excellent first topic.

Knowing your subject is one of the crucial secrets of self-confident interpersonal communication, on a one-to-one basis, and within or before a group. As long as you know your subject thoroughly and practice its delivery, you'll communicate competently.

You shouldn't let this talk upset you because, in all probability, you won't be graded or critiqued. Your professor may only wish to introduce you to how it feels to stand up and speak before a group — and to convince you that there's nothing mysterious or impossible in doing so.

Preparing your first talk should be a simple exercise. With paper and pencil at hand, conduct a self-inventory and make notes. Think about your childhood, parents, and relatives. Where were you born and raised? How about the schools you attended? What made you decide to attend college? Why this one? Has any one person had a strong influence on you? How about your major study and why did you select it?

Were you in the service? If so, what branch and what rank did you hold? How was basic training and where did you take it? What type of work did you do in the military and where were you stationed? Did you have any spine-tingling encounters?

Maybe you're working. Do you like your job — why or why not? How long have you worked there?

Did you ever travel? Where have you been and with whom? How long were you there? Would you like to return — why or why not?

Don't overlook your hobbies or other interests. Do you play a musical instrument? Perhaps you play for a group — if so, where and how often? Maybe you're into karate, automobile repair, ceramics, exercising, or gourmet cooking. Beautiful, share your experiences with us.

Are you married or single? Do you have children — if so, how old are they? Maybe you're a grandparent. What made you decide to return to school? How much of a challenge is it? Are you a full-time or part-time student? What are your plans when you graduate?

Have you ever met any interesting people or celebrities? Tell us about them. When and where did you meet them and under what circumstances? What were your impressions of them? If you've never met a celebrity but if you could, who would it be and why?

You should now have some ideas on how to prepare for your first talk. Go over the preceding questions again and use them as a guide. We're sure you can expand upon them.

Remember, you can be an interesting person. You have something to say: you do things, you have likes and dislikes, you have opinions and dreams and ambitions. Here now is your chance to express them. Good luck.

Perhaps for your first talk, you may wish to choose the following format as a guide or outline:

My name is _____

My friends call me _____

I live at _____ and my family consists of _____
_____

I attended the following schools _____
_____

My favorite subject(s) were _____

My extracurricular activities consisted of _____
_____

I am presently employed at _____ and my
responsibilities are _____
_____

The days and hours I work are _____

What I like best about my job is ＿＿＿＿＿＿＿＿＿＿
What I don't like about my job is ＿＿＿＿＿＿＿＿＿＿

I've decided to come to this college because ＿＿＿＿＿＿
and my major is ＿＿＿＿＿＿＿＿＿＿＿＿＿＿
My plans after I graduate are ＿＿＿＿＿＿＿＿＿＿＿
I participate in the following college activities ＿＿＿＿＿＿

I am married/single and my family consists of ＿＿＿＿＿＿
＿＿＿＿＿＿＿＿＿＿＿＿＿＿＿＿＿＿＿＿＿＿＿＿
I am a full-time/part-time student and I'm taking courses in
＿＿＿＿＿＿＿＿＿＿＿＿＿＿＿＿＿＿＿＿＿＿＿＿
My biggest obstacle in coming to college is ＿＿＿＿＿＿
As far as what my family thinks about my coming to
college ＿＿＿＿＿＿＿＿＿＿＿＿＿＿＿＿＿＿＿＿＿
The reason I decided to return to college is ＿＿＿＿＿＿

I enjoy traveling and have visited ＿＿＿＿＿＿＿＿＿＿
Of all the places I visited I enjoyed ＿＿＿＿＿＿＿＿ the
most because ＿＿＿＿＿＿＿＿＿＿＿＿＿＿＿＿＿＿
I was a member of the Armed Forces (mention branch,
length of service, duty stations, and occupational specialty)
＿＿＿＿＿＿＿＿＿＿＿＿＿＿＿＿＿＿＿＿＿＿＿＿
My short-term goal is ＿＿＿＿＿＿＿＿＿＿＿＿＿＿＿
My long-term goal is ＿＿＿＿＿＿＿＿＿＿＿＿＿＿＿
Some of the things I enjoy doing are ＿＿＿＿＿＿＿＿
Some of the things I don't enjoy are ＿＿＿＿＿＿＿＿
My biggest gripe is ＿＿＿＿＿＿＿＿＿＿＿＿＿＿＿＿
The one thing that gives me great pleasure is ＿＿＿＿＿
I think the biggest problem facing our society is ＿＿＿＿

Answers to most of these statements should give your class-mates a handle on who you are, where you come from, and could lead to some stimulating relationships.

After you've finished your talk, you may answer questions from the class. This question-and-answer session (further discussed at the end of this chapter), more than any other exercise, will help you develop self-confidence because you'll have completed your formal talk, and all you do now is to relax and answer questions on a subject that you thoroughly know — you.

Questions-and-answer sessions have uncovered the following unusual experiences:

- A young woman appeared on TV programs several times a week, and communicated to deaf viewers in sign language.

- A mother and her son and daughter attended this school at the same time. Each was enrolled in a separate section of my speech classes (AJV, one of the authors).

- A young man enrolled in the course because he wanted to enter politics. He did and he won his campaign.

- A student told the class she signed up for this course to meet a prospective husband. You guessed it; a year later she was married.

- During semester breaks and summer vacations a student works at Disneyworld in Florida.

- A female student told the class of her two hobbies — sky diving and hang gliding.

- A mother of two children worked one summer driving a cab. She was robbed twice and shot at once. She no longer drives a cab.

ICE CUBES IN THE STOMACH

Suddenly the professor calls your name — it's your turn to address the class. Your heart pounds with such force that you think it can be heard across the room, your forehead breaks out with beads of perspiration, your mouth goes dry, and your stomach quivers.

You're experiencing an attack of nerves that is not unique to you. Most people get it, whether they admit it or not. This sensation, in varying degrees, occurs thousands of times daily: on an individual's first day on a new job, on a first date, on a student's first day at a new school, to actors and actresses just before the curtain goes up or the camera starts to roll, to students in other speech classes throughout the country ready to give their first talks, and to your own classmates who have spoken before you and to those who will follow you. Even professors aren't immune.

For example, the week before each semester begins, I'm (AJV) a bear to live with. The thought of facing four classes, each of approximately thirty strangers, rattles me. The thought of walking alone into each classroom, with students staring and trying to assess their "prof," and knowing that this first encounter is critical in establishing respect and rapport for the entire semester, leads to many anxious moments. But once I start two-way communication and break the ice, the problems melt away. Then, when the first class ends, I enjoy a tremendous feeling of relief and accomplishment.

Nervousness, we assure you, can be a form of positive energy that will keep you on your toes. If you accept it as normal, which it is, it will help you do your best. In a new environment there is no stigma to feeling nervous or even frightened before speaking. It is a normal reaction, and its intensity will lessen the more you speak.

Even the great and the powerful suffer from attacks of nerves. In a talk before London journalists years ago the famous British cartoonist David Low said that every time he had to make a speech he felt as if he had a block of ice, nine inches by nine inches, in the pit of his stomach.

Later he was approached by a member of the audience, Winston Churchill, the greatest speaker of this century. "Mr. Low," asked Churchill, "How large did you say that block of ice is?"

"Nine inches by nine inches," replied Low.

"What an amazing coincidence," said Churchill, "exactly the same size as mine."

There's no cure for nervousness, but to help control it, you should:

- Admit it.

- Talk about it.

It's no shame to admit that you're nervous, a bit uptight, queasy, even petrified; some text books call it "stagefright." You should be greatly relieved to learn how many of your peers share your feelings. And really, things don't always seem quite that bad if you're able to talk about them freely. Discuss them at home, school, or work, with other members of your class, and certainly with your professor.

Remember, there's nothing wrong with admitting, at the beginning of your talk, that you're nervous. You should gain sympathy and understanding from your classmates.

Even royalty suffers from pangs of nervousness. At the royal wedding in July 1981, the bride, Lady Diana Spencer, called the groom "Philip Charles Arthur George" instead of Charles Philip

Arthur George. He, in turn, omitted (or forgot?) the word "worldly" in pledging to share all his worldly goods with her.[2]

FRONT AND CENTER

After the initial shock of hearing your name has subsided, slowly draw a few deep breaths. This should help ease that uptight feeling. Walk to the front of the classroom with purpose and confidence. Don't shuffle your feet, don't look at the floor, and don't make any remarks to class members. Once you begin your talk, all attention is riveted on you.

Before starting to speak, you may find it reassuring to look around the classroom. You may sense encouragement from familiar faces. You may also observe a look of genuine understanding from those who appreciate your feelings because it will soon be their turn. You now realize that you're not alone. The preceding speakers sweated through the same experience, and the following speakers will do the same. The quicker you appreciate this, the more relaxed you'll become.

Just as soon as you get wrapped up in what you're saying, after perhaps twenty to thirty seconds into your talk, your nervousness should diminish. This is why we emphasize knowing your subject thoroughly. (In this regard, it may be helpful to memorize the first few sentences.)

SAYING IT WITHOUT WORDS

First impressions are critical to communicators, and all of you are communicators. Every day you see people, you greet people, you meet people — at work, at school, and at social or business functions. Before you even say a word, you transmit impressions, favorable or not, in various ways:

- **Your walk.** Is it slow, fast, or listless; jerky, confident, or hesitant? Do you march, saunter, strut, shuffle, or stalk?
- **Your posture.** Are you straight as a drill sergeant? Do you

---

[2]*New York Times*, 30 July 1981, page 1, column 3.

slump, shift from one leg to the other, droop, lean on the lectern?

Keep your cool.

- **Your facial expressions.** Do you smile, frown, smirk, look condescending, absorbed, disappointed, troubled?

- **Your eyes.** Are they expressive, twinkling, shifty, piercing, friendly, cold, penetrating?

- **Your dress.** Are you neat or sloppy? Is your hair combed? Are your colors coordinated or clashing?

- **Your cosmetics.** Odors from aftershave lotion, cologne, perfume, hairspray, antiperspirant (or lack of it) as well as the amount and application of other cosmetic aids also transmit messages.

- **Your gestures.** What you do with your hands, head, and shoulders also conveys impressions. The firm handshake versus the listless one. The nod of your head or the shrug of your shoulders carries messages, and you must be aware of them.

First impressions are usually long-lasting. How many times have you prejudged a person by any of the above criteria, only to change your assessment after he has spoken or you've become better acquainted? How many times have you reached a negative opinion of a person before he has had the opportunity to communicate orally? When was the last time you admitted that you couldn't stomach someone before he even said a word?

It's OK to relax, but . . .

Indeed, nonverbal communication can often influence your opinions more forcefully than the spoken word. The old aphorism that actions speak louder than words is more than mere rhetoric.

In interpersonal communication you don't always have to say it to convey it, and in nonverbal communication you may often transmit messages entirely different from what you think you're transmitting. Call it what you like — body language, the silent language, soundless speech, or nonverbal communication — it is an eloquent form of message transmission and reception.

(For more on nonverbal communication, you can refer to Chapter 2.)

IMPORTANCE OF EYE CONTACT

Perhaps you know the feeling of approaching several of your friends who are involved in a discussion. When you join the group, you notice that the speaker doesn't look at you but continues looking at the others. He doesn't even acknowledge your presence, and you experience a left-out feeling.

Eye contact with your audience is extremely important. Without it you will have immense difficulty conveying interest and sincerity. What is your reaction when you listen to someone who doesn't look you in the eye, at least occasionally? Believability is seriously impaired. When you appear before a group, you should remember that they are not only listening to you, they are also looking at you.

As tempting as it is, don't gaze out windows, at notes, or at the floor or walls. Some speakers, by looking at people in the last row of a large audience, can give the impression that they're looking at everyone in front of them. In a smaller group look at the students to your left, then to your right, then in between. Don't make the mistake of some beginning speakers who focus their eyes solely on the professor. Just remember that people like to be talked to and looked at simultaneously.

Eye contact means that you, the sender, are making contact with your audience, the receiver. You're transmitting a message and without eye contact the transmission is broken and communication is disrupted.

By maintaining eye contact with your audience you can receive visual feedback. Your listeners' eyes can tell you if they're getting your message. Do they look confused, bored, doubting, satisfied, or interested? Do they seem to enjoy and understand what you're saying? Do they look drowsy? As long as you're aware of telltale signals from your audience, the communication cycle can be complete. You have a message to communicate with your mind, your voice, your body, and your eyes — you maintain eye contact with your audience and you receive messages in response to your spo-

Eye contact with your audience is extremely important.

ken thoughts. If you fail to look at them, you can't receive any reaction from them.

WHAT ABOUT GESTURES?

Many people gesture as naturally as they breathe. Perhaps you know people who would be speechless if their hands were tied behind their backs. If you find it natural to move your hands and arms while communicating, fine, continue to do so. If, however, you tend to be carried away by gestures, don't be too concerned about them now because you'll learn to control them as the course progresses.

Your professor will make suggestions as to the degree and effectiveness of your gestures. A practical exercise is to speak before a mirror and watch your body movements. Without question, being videotaped is the best way to see yourself exactly as you appear to others.

Try to become more aware of how people gesture (nonverbal communication is also discussed in Chapters 2, 5, and 16) when they talk; for example, groups of students, your teacher, friends, family, boss, speakers, and performers on TV. Are their gestures meaningful and expressive? Or do they look awkward and meaningless?

Gestures can be natural.

Hands always seem to be a problem for inexperienced speakers, but they don't have to be. Putting one hand in a pocket is permissible, and many experienced speakers do it. In his early days of public speaking, the late President John F. Kennedy used to jingle coins in his pocket. He was "cured" by the constant criticism of his mother. His favorite position, when addressing either a press conference or large gathering, was to keep one hand in his jacket pocket; it contained no coins.

On occasion you may clasp your hands behind your back and, if there's no lectern, you may hold notes in them. Be sure to keep your hands away from your face, hair, neck, ears, and nose. Also, if you wear necklaces, pendants, earrings, or bracelets, leave them alone. Fiddling with them distracts people.

MOVING AROUND

As far as movement is concerned, many speakers feel that they must stay in one place and remain completely motionless. Not so. You should feel free to move around. Taking a few steps in either direction from the stand is desirable as long as you move smoothly, not jerkily like a puppet.

However, avoid perpetual motion; for example, swaying back and forth or from side to side, crossing and uncrossing your feet, or fidgeting with your hands and fingers. Movement can be effective when done in moderation, with purpose and naturalness. It helps you develop poise and confidence, and it constructively channels your nervous energy.

STANDING TALL

Good posture — standing straight, but not like a ramrod, and squarely on both feet — conveys an impression of confidence and alertness. Your posture communicates attitude, just as your face and voice do. Don't slouch, or lean against a table, or drape yourself over the speaker's stand. These actions detract from your overall appearance and create a negative effect on your audience.

Perhaps the best way to improve your posture is to observe yourself on a videotape recorder or in a full-length mirror. Then you can see if you're standing tall or hunched over, if your head is held high or drooping, and if your weight is equally distributed on both feet.

There's no question about it — erect posture helps you look sharper and feel more alert.

TAKE NOTE

Without a doubt, using notes is recommended because it can give you a feeling of confidence and security. In fact, many professional speakers use them. Just be careful not to rely on them to the point that you read the entire talk and do not look at your audience.

If there is no speaker's stand or lectern, 3 by 5 cards can fit comfortably in the palm of your hand without annoying the audience. If your classroom is equipped with a lectern, 4 by 6 cards (or even standard-sized 8½ by 11-inch paper) may rest on it without being noticed. Try to keep your cards lying flat so they won't distract your audience. Write or print on only one side of note cards.

If you have more than two cards, number them just in case they are dropped or misplaced.

QUESTION-AND-ANSWER SESSION

As you conclude your talk, don't lower your voice so that it becomes almost inaudible. Keep it strong and confident until you finally ask, "Are there any questions?" Some of your classmates and even your professor may have a few. If they do, you should feel complimented and, by this time, relaxed enough to answer them easily and naturally.

While you're answering questions, try not to focus your attention solely on the questioner. If the answer is long, you may glance around the class but when you're concluding your reply, look again at the questioner. Pause a second or two as if to ask, "Did I answer you satisfactorily?" Then field the next inquiry.

When you've handled all the questions, breathe deeply and return to your seat confidently. Don't rush. Don't crumple your notes and stuff them into your pocket. And don't collapse into your chair; just sit down quietly.

Congratulations! You've given your first talk. Now, was it as difficult as you thought it would be? Was it as traumatic an experience as you envisioned? You're damn right it was. But you did it, and this was the most difficult talk you'll ever make — your toughest obstacle course. Your other talks will become easier and more enjoyable. We're even willing to bet that your nervousness wasn't detected as much by the audience as you may think it was.

THINGS TO THINK ABOUT AND DO

1. Be aware of eye contact among your friends, colleagues, speakers, and TV performers. When you are personally involved, observe the importance and effect of eye contact among your associates.

2. Using the biographical outline in this chapter as an aid, prepare and rehearse a two- to four-minute introductory talk.

3. Select two or three individuals who make their living primarily by speaking. Ask them about nervousness and what they do to control it. Be prepared to discuss their replies in class.

4. If you gesture a lot when you speak, by all means don't stop, but become more aware of your gestures. Do other people comment on them? Be ready to discuss this.

5. Notice how people gesture when they speak. Do the gestures of anyone in particular impress you? Why or why not?

WHAT DO YOU REMEMBER FROM THIS CHAPTER?

1. What two elements in speaking do more than anything else to help you acquire self-confidence?

2. Is getting nervous before speaking uncommon? Explain.

3. Why is eye contact so vitally important?

4. When you speak before a group, why is it important to constantly look around at individuals in the audience rather than focus on a limited area?

5. Do gestures enhance one's ability to communicate? Why?

6. Is it permissible to move around when you speak?

7. Is the use of notes recommended when you speak? Explain.

8. What must you be aware of when you use notes?

9. What two things can you do to help control nervousness?

VITALIZE YOUR VOCABULARY

English words derive from countless languages, although principally from Latin and Greek, and from other sources such as literature, art, and science. Among the most fascinating words are *eponyms* — words based on the names of real or mythical people who have accomplished something unusual. The following words are derived from the names of people who really lived:

Eponyms

casanova (n.)   a man who has a reputation for being a promiscuous lover, with many female conquests. After Giovanni Casanova, an Italian adventurer and writer of the eighteenth century.

chauvinist (n.)   an extremist in any cause, often militaristic or patriotic. Derived from Nicolas Chauvin, one of Napoleon's most fanatic followers.

diesel (n.)   an engine named after its inventor, Rudolf Diesel (1858–1913), a German engineer.

guillotine (n.)   a device for beheading people, named after J. I. Guillotin, a doctor who invented it during the French Revolution.

hooker (n.)   a prostitute. During the Civil War, General Joseph Hooker's troops were encamped for a time in Washington. Prostitutes who "serviced" them became known as "Hooker's Division" first. After the troops moved out, the women were then called "hookers."

levis (n.)   blue jeans, named after Levi Strauss, a Texas merchant who popularized them in the 1800s.

machiavellian (adj.)   deceitful, unscrupulous, crafty, in accordance with the political ideas explained in *The Prince*, a book written by Niccolo Machiavelli (1469–1527), Italian statesman, political philosopher, and author.

maverick (n.)   a dissenter, usually in politics, art, or literature, one who takes an unorthodox stand and refuses to conform. After Samuel Maverick (1803–1870), the Texas rancher who refused to brand his cattle.

nicotine (n.)   from Jean Nicot, a seventeenth-century French diplomat who introduced Turkish tobacco into France.

sadist (n.)   a person who enjoys inflicting pain on another. Named after Marquis de Sade (1740–1814), French soldier and novelist who conducted experiments on pain and wrote about them.

watt (n.)   a unit of electrical power, named in honor of James Watt, the Scottish inventor of the steam engine.

5

Make It Clear, Concise, Correct ...and Alive

All the great speakers were bad speakers at first.[1]

CHAPTER OBJECTIVES

After reading and understanding this chapter, you should know:

- The several skills that contribute greatly to effective delivery.
- How to sharpen these skills.
- Why a voice is pleasant or unpleasant.
- The importance of good diction.
- How to be more expressive in your speech.

CHAPTER DIGEST

This chapter zeroes in on various aspects of delivering a talk: voice, pronunciation, rate of speaking, pauses, and expression. Emphasis is placed on voice and pronunciation.

---

[1]Ralph Waldo Emerson, "Power," *The Conflict of Life* (1860).

Your voice influences your speech and also your daily interpersonal communication. A pleasant, expressive voice is an asset in school, on the job, in your social life. Such a voice is capable of inflection, the ability to go up and down comfortably in order to express different feelings, emotions, and ideas.

Almost all voices can be improved. Listening to your own voice on a tape recorder may spur you to act to improve yours. Some practical suggestions on pitch, volume, and proper breathing are offered.

Your pronounciation immediately marks you as either an educated or an uneducated person. Sloppy speech and rigid lips result in sounds being omitted, syllables being slurred, and incorrect sounds being tacked on. Again, ideas are presented to bring pronounciation up to the standards recommended by authoritative dictionaries.

Other topics discussed in the chapter are rate of speaking, use of pauses, and the importance of expressing our inner feelings and emotions.

Every spring, college campuses throughout the nation are visited by representatives from industry and government to recruit potential employees. Several large state universities asked the various recruiters to explain why they had rejected students. In almost 70 percent of the cases, the primary reason given was that the rejected student did not "talk effectively during the interview."

My speech consulting practice (AJV) affords me a rewarding opportunity to train men and women in groups and individually, at all levels (from entry to top executive) in both the public and private sectors.

Over the years I have asked many executives who were in a position to approve an employee's promotion to a supervisory level, what qualities they considered paramount in making their final decision. The overwhelming response was the ability to communicate orally in clear and understanding language.

CLEAR AND UNDERSTANDING LANGUAGE

How many times have you called a company, spoken to a salesperson, heard a lecture at school, or talked to someone on the telephone only to recoil in shock over the gibberish which left you exclaiming, "I don't believe this!" You've found it almost impossible to understand the individual. Perhaps she mumbled, ran words together, didn't articulate, had a monotone, took a breath mid-word or phrase, or spoke too fast or too slow. It's amazing the number of people who daily communicate with the public and don't realize their speech shortcomings or who fail to improve their oral communication skills.

Through months and years of study, discipline, practice, trial and error, perseverance, and even failures, people can develop their speaking abilities. You should understand that Luciano Pavarotti was not *born* a great singer, Chris Evert Lloyd was not *born* a great tennis player, Albert Einstein was not *born* a great physicist, and Sir Lawrence Olivier was not *born* a great actor.

The art of speaking to communicate knowledge, ideas, and feelings is no exception. All the theoretical knowledge of public speaking will not make you outstanding in the art, and it will not improve your ability unless you're willing to commit yourself totally. It will take work, perhaps even a bit of needling from your family and friends, but if you have the will and motivation to sharpen your speaking effectiveness, nothing can deter you.

For as long as I (AJV) can remember, I have wanted to be a radio announcer. I practiced reading, pronunciation, enunciation, interpretation, projection, and the most difficult challenge of all, eliminating my Boston accent. I practiced in the bathroom, in the cellar, even in my brother's car. I took my share of ribbing, but even today I enjoy these reminiscences every time I appear before a microphone or TV camera. *If you want to do something, make up your mind to do it; then go at it with gusto.*

Certain elements contribute to effective and lively delivery: your voice, pronunciation, rate of speaking, duration, pacing, breathing, expression, pauses, and oral visualization.

YOUR VOICE

There is no more versatile instrument in the world than your voice. Yet, as with any instrument, its effectiveness depends solely on the way you practice with it and use it.

The immediate reaction of almost all people when they hear themselves played back on a tape recorder is usually shocked disbelief. You may recall such statements as, "That sounds horrible," "Good God, that's not *me*!" or "You mean I sound like *that*?" In almost all instances the sad fact is that you *do* sound like that. If you're serious about speech development, you should use a good tape recorder to hear yourself as others hear you. It is an invaluable aid.

"*I* sound like *that?*"

Speech skill doesn't remain on a plateau; either it improves or it regresses. You must always work to improve it because that's the only way to banish poor speaking habits. Your tape recorder will "tell." The sound of your voice may play as great a role in getting your message across as the words themselves.

Stop a moment and think about the voices of some of your friends and acquaintances. Try to describe each one's voice quality. Is it beautiful, soothing, too high, too low, unpleasant, friendly, unfriendly? Let's briefly discuss some important factors of voice quality.

HERE COMES THE PITCH

Every voice has a pitch. Pitch refers to the highness or lowness of your tone or sound. A person whose pitch is too high, too low, or monotonous (on the same level) may not only transmit a negative impression when communicating, but risk losing listeners completely.

The pitch is too high. Under normal circumstances, this frequently occurs because of nervousness (remember your first talk?), fright (if you're able to sound off at all), or from being overanxious to respond. If you suffer no physical problems that may affect your voice, the more often you speak, the more relaxed your throat muscles will become, resulting in more pleasant vocal sounds. A good exercise to lower a high pitch is to read aloud solemn passages very slowly.

Every voice has a pitch.

The pitch is too low. You may know some people who speak with a very low, bass-like sound. Usually they speak slowly. Reading aloud happy, lively material — children's stories, for example — at a fast pace is a good exercise that may help slightly to raise a low pitch.

The voice is monotonous.   The person who speaks in a monotone is like the kid who constantly strikes one note on a piano. After a short while the sound is boring, dull, and lifeless. The voice lacks inflection, that is, the raising and lowering of pitch.

To avoid or eliminate a monotone, you must find your normal range. This is the vocal area that is most comfortable for you to carry on a normal conversation and from which you may easily raise or lower your pitch.

One way to find your normal range is to match your vocal tones with the tones of a piano. Most women can usually start around middle C on the keyboard, and men an octave lower (if you're not familiar with the keyboard, ask someone who is). Your normal pitch range should be the notes in the scale that feel comfortable for you as you sound them, and from which you may comfortably go up and down. An acceptable range for a normal, healthy voice is about one octave (for example C to C, or 13 half-notes inclusive).

Once you establish your normal pitch range, it is crucial to maintain it. Listen to how it sounds and feels when you use it so that whenever you speak, it becomes as natural as breathing. The up-and-down inflection of your pitch adds color to your delivery.

WARNING

Your voice box is such a delicate, complex mechanism that abuse of it can lead to irreparable damage. Never force yourself to lower or raise your pitch. Be sure to consult with your professor before attempting to change your pitch drastically.

VOCAL VOLUME

Some people have naturally loud or soft voices. If you speak too loudly or too softly, your audience will communicate this message to you nonverbally. For example, when you start to speak, do they all move back in their chairs as if blown there by a gust of wind? Or do they move up to the edge of their seats turning their ears in your direction?

The size of the room and audience should determine the volume of your voice. If you have a soft voice, start by asking the audience, "Can you hear me in back?" Speaking too loudly or too softly is not only annoying, but it also leads to a breakdown in speaker-listener communication.

BREATHING

Proper breathing is vital to speech communication. Perhaps you know someone who takes several breaths in mid-phrase or sentence. You feel that any minute she will require a tank of oxygen.

Practice and learn to breathe deeply, filling your lungs with as much air as possible and as quickly as possible. This healthful exercise will enable you to communicate a message-idea without interruption. Take deep breaths, mainly through your mouth, read something aloud, and stop when you have to breathe. Time yourself to see how long you can read.

Lung capacity varies widely among people. Some professional singers can hold a note comfortably from twenty to thirty seconds, and some seasoned speakers can complete a marathon sentence in one breath. The ability to speak from fifteen to twenty seconds on a single breath is attainable through deep breathing, and should allow you to surmount any difficulty in finishing a sentence without gasping for air.

Lung capacity varies.

NOTE
Public speakers should learn to breathe from the diaphragm. It is a special kind of breathing that is covered in advanced speaking classes.

PRONUNCIATION

Nothing stands out more negatively in a speaker than the way she mispronounces words. Pronunciation, rate of speaking, volume of voice, and proper breathing all contribute to the effectiveness of your communication. Defects in any of these areas can, unfortunately, impair your communication style.

It's very easy to develop and retain poor speech habits. Your environment — your family, friends, city or section of the country where you live — has a tremendous influence on your pronunciation and speech habits. Regional accents or "dialects" abound throughout our country. The three major accents are:

- General American — spoken by the largest segment of our population — includes the Midwest, the West, and parts of the Southwest. This dialect is most often heard on radio, TV, and in movies.

- Northeast — includes the New England and Middle Atlantic states.

- Southern — includes those areas south of the Mason-Dixon Line.

We should point out that even within these geographical areas, local and regional dialects exist. Bostonians can easily be identified because they do not pronounce the letter r in the middle or at the end of words. For example, they say, "Pahk yah cah in the Hahvahd yahd." They also tend to sound an *r* when one doesn't appear, as in *Cuber* for *Cuba*, *Americer* for *America*, *delter* for *delta*, *tuner* for *tuna*.

A great aid for improving your pronunciation is an accepted standard dictionary. Even though recognized dictionaries are accepted throughout the country, some of their recommended pronunciations are ignored in certain locales. Generally, it is wiser to use the pronunciation typical of the region you're in, even though it may not be correct, rather than allow yourself to sound like an eccentric. Be flexible enough to bend a little to avoid embarrassment.

Another way to improve your pronunciation is to pay close attention to professional speakers, actors, and actresses and then try to emulate them. A tape recorder will verify your progress.

Learning to pronounce words correctly and clearly will require time and effort but once you achieve this goal, it will pay you life-long dividends at work and socially. Remember Eliza Doolittle, the flower girl in *My Fair Lady*? She learned to speak like an educated person in six months. However, she did enjoy a supreme advantage — daily instruction from Professor Henry Higgins, played by Rex Harrison.

It's important to produce sounds clearly in a word. Voice each syllable carefully so that the entire word sounds crisp and understandable. Sloppy speech results from not taking the time to pronounce all the sounds in a word and from running words together. For example:

Whatimes zit?	for	What time is it?
What'sitdoin outside?	for	What's it doing outside?
How'ya doin?	for	How are you doing?
Ahdunno.	for	I don't know.
Whaja say ya name is?	for	What did you say your name is?
Howzitgowen?	for	How is it going?
Whatchadowen?	for	What are you doing?
Whujasay?	for	What did you say?
Whutsamatta?	for	What's the matter?

Not opening your mouth enough is a major cause of poor diction, especially among beginning speakers. Because the mouth is not opened sufficiently to allow all the sounds to evolve into clearly spoken words, the sounds seem to be struggling somewhere down in the throat. A beneficial exercise is to repeat vowel sounds slowly and aloud, holding the sound of each vowel a full breath (AAAAAAAAAA — EEEEEEEEEE — IIIIIIIII — and so on). Practice until you produce a full, forceful sound and can feel the muscles in your lips and mouth working. Don't hesitate to overexaggerate your lip and mouth movements. Do this every time you speak until the feeling becomes second nature.

Nothing in our spoken language is more beautiful than the fully stressed sound of vowels and vowel sounds. When you sound them within a word, voice them a little longer. This is called *duration* and it refers to the length of the sound. You will notice the different length, or duration, of the *aw* sound in the words "draw" and "fog." Duration of vowel sounds adds color to your speech delivery. Notice how professional singers, actors, and speakers treat these sounds within words of a song, or speech — it's sheer artistry. If you can listen closely to the delivery of such public figures as Mary Tyler Moore, Ed Asner, Richard Burton, the Reverend Billy Graham, or Angie Dickenson. The next time President Reagan holds a press conference or makes a speech on TV, listen to what he does with the vowel sounds within words.

We would like to emphasize that there are more than five vowel sounds. For example, note the different sounds produced by the symbol *a* in the following words: aggravate, fat, hall and bah; or the letter *e* in: be, been, sex, feet or term; or the letter *o* in: hot, go, out, order, and oil. We're sure you get the idea. Duration of these sounds adds color to speech.

You too can learn to produce more colorful sounds in your speech which can lead you to a more captivating delivery. However, it will take commitment, time, and effort. Practice the following vowel sounds aloud and listen to them carefully:

A (ay)	betrayed	be-traayed
	delayed	de-laayed
	conveyed	con-vaayed
E (ee)	received	re-ceeved
	believe	be-leeve
	reprieve	re-preeve
I (eye)	divide	di-viide
	revise	re-viise
	coincide	coin-ciide
O (oh)	behold	be-hoold
	resold	re-soold
	foretold	fore-toold
U (you)	preview	pre-vyuu
	review	re-vyuu
	through	thruu

As we emphasized earlier, there are many other vowel sounds that you may practice.

Another cogent reason to stress vowel sounds is that they impart carrying power to your voice. Relax your neck, throat, mouth, and lips, breathe deeply, open your mouth wide, and let these sounds roll out full and strong. As a result, your listeners will hear you better, understand you better, and appreciate you more.

Below are common pronunciation problems to be aware of:

Not pronouncing all vowels and consonants

Bar*br*a	for	Barbara
Bat*try*	for	battery
Boun*dry*	for	boundary
Ca*ni*date	for	candidate
Cho*clit*	for	chocolate
Di*m*ond	for	diamond
Feb*u*ary	for	February
Go*v*ament	for	government
Gran*it*	for	granted
Jew*l*ery	for	jewelry
Li*bry*, Li*bary*	for	library
La*bra*tory	for	laboratory
P*lee*ce	for	police
R*a*member	for	remember

Producing incorrect sounds of letters

Dem	for	them
Dis	for	this
Exscape	for	escape
Jist	for	just
Pitchah	for	picture
Wid	for	with
Winduh	for	window
Yestiday	for	yesterday
Tuday	for	today
Tunight	for	tonight
Tumorrah	for	tomorrow

Eliminating word endings (especially *-ing* in verbs)

Walkin	for	walking
Talkin	for	talking
Coughin	for	coughing

Slep	for	slept
Crep	for	crept
Fine	for	find
Fie	for	five
Ben	for	bent
Sen	for	send
Reveren	for	reverend
Fence	for	fenced

Adding or reversing vowels and consonants

Athaletic	for	athletic
Athalete	for	athlete
Alumnium	for	aluminum
Acrost	for	across
Calvery	for	cavalry
Evuning	for	evening
Interduction	for	introduction
Laundary	for	laundry
Mischievious	for	mischievous
Often	for	offen
Perduce	for	produce
Pervent	for	prevent
Wunst	for	once
Skoowull	for	school
Skejoowull	for	schedule

It's important not to go completely overboard and o-v-e-r — e-n-u-n-c-i-a-t-e. Doing that will result in stilted and phony-sounding speech.

RATE OF SPEAKING

For almost everyone a comfortable speaking rate lies between 130 and 160 words per minute. Speaking too fast can cause poor diction — running words together, slurring words, and dropping word endings — which could result in listeners complaining "What did she say?" A machine-gun delivery can easily lose your listeners.

On the other hand, talking too slowly is just as bad. Actually, it can irritate your listeners even more than talking too fast. When a speaker takes, like what seems, five minutes to draaaaag out a phrase or sentence, she is setting up her listeners to yawn or mind-wander. A sluggish speaker can easily convey an impression of shyness, lack of confidence or intelligence, or illness.

From this moment you should be conscious of your delivery rate. Listen to yourself on a tape recorder.

PAUSES

We pause for one of four reasons:

- To provide emphasis
- To breathe
- To provide variety in delivery
- To pull your thoughts together

Pausing is an art which every professional performer strives to master in order to achieve maximum effectiveness. At your next opportunity, listen closely to how performers like Rex Harrison, Frank Sinatra, and Sarah Vaughn orchestrate pauses in their songs. Notice how comic pros Johnny Carson and Phyllis Diller use pauses to get laughs.

However, you must be careful not to pause excessively since it could lead to a stacatto delivery which can be abrasive to the ear and can short-circuit communication. With practice and determination, the right number of pauses sprinkled at the right times can give your delivery more variety, excitement, and interest.

PACING

If you were on a long drive and kept your speed at exactly 55 miles per hour, chances are you would soon be bored, and later, perhaps, drowsy. A wise driver thus slows down, then speeds up for awhile, then returns to average speed. This tactic is repeated until the driver reaches her destination.

The professional runner practices the same basic procedure. She may start out with a burst of speed, slow down a bit, pick up speed, continue at a comfortable clip, then, when approaching the final stretch, a surge of energy and speed carries her to victory.

Both the driver and the runner performed a very important function of delivery — they paced themselves. It would be wrong to say that you should never talk quickly or slowly. It's only when you do either of these constantly that you sabotage communication.

Pacing means an interesting rate of delivery, with enough variety to hold your listeners' interest. To describe excitement you would speed up your delivery. When quoting statistics or emphasizing several points, you would slow your pace. Speaking at a constant rate, either fast or slow, can only lead to monotony and loss of your audience.

EXPRESSION

When you speak, you express yourself through facial and body actions as well as by the words you choose and how you say them. Do these words convey exactly what you intend them to? Are you saying them with conviction and feeling or are you just mouthing them? There is a difference between a person who bids you "good morning" with a warm smile and one who mutters it like a robot.

After you've prepared your speech, go over it carefully, noting the important points you wish to make. Review the title, opening remarks, main body, and transitional phrases. What points do you want to drive home in the conclusion? What is your appeal and to whom?

Understand what you want to say and practice saying it. Pause to attract attention, show your fingers to enumerate steps, raise an eyebrow to ask a question, frown to show disbelief, or lean toward the audience to make a personal point or to let them in on a secret. Don't hesitate to repeat a point several times if necessary.

What you are doing is making your talk come alive, and this will entice your audience to be more interested and motivated by your message. *Strive to convey emotions and feelings in your words.*

ORAL VISUALIZATION

A highly effective way to express yourself with animation is to recall as many experiences as possible. Select what you need for your talk and visualize it when you're communicating.

When was the last time you were frightened, thrilled, or pleased? Can you recall the incident vividly? Have you ever been hungry, cold, hot, very thirsty, in extreme pain, grief-stricken? Think about it until you're practically reliving it. If you're trying to convey some of these emotions and experiences, recall them again and again and visualize them as you communicate with your audience. Feel and live your words.

By mastering this technique in expression, you'll not only be able to communicate deeper meaning to your audiences, but you'll also be able to generate "electricity" from your message to the audience who will generate it back to you through their expressions. You will have successfully completed the full cycle of successful interpersonal communication. "Eloquence lies as much in the tone of voice, in the eyes, and in the speaker's manner, as in his choice of words."[2]

THINGS TO THINK ABOUT AND DO

As previously mentioned, no instrument is more useful in speech development than the tape recorder. Most speech classes have access to one — so use it, whenever possible, as you record some of the following exercises. There's no better learning experience for personal and instructor evaluation than listening to your own voice.

1. Record about a minute of your voice onto a tape machine. The material may be pre-selected or it may be impromptu. The purpose of this exercise is for you to hear your voice and delivery as others do. As you listen to the playback, be alert to your pitch, inflection, pronunciation, rate of speaking, breathing, and expression.

2. Remember, when you breathe, you should inhale as much air as possible to avoid taking a breath in the middle of a word, phrase, or sentence. You should be able to read each sentence on a single breath.

   a. The future belongs to those who are willing to prepare for it.

   b. They say money isn't everything, but you must admit it sure beats poverty.

   c. Breathing is a basic biological process that continues as long as life is maintained.

   d. More people could enjoy much happier lives, if they could only learn to be more assertive.

---

[2]La Rochefoucauld, *Maxims* (1665).

e. "Nature has herself appointed that nothing great is to be accomplished quickly, and has ordained that difficulty should precede every work of excellence."
— *Quintilian*

3. Here are some words which are often mispronounced; usually one sound is substituted for another. Use a dictionary, if necessary, to write the correct pronunciation beside each word before you record.

anesthetist   _____

chasm   _____

chiropodist   _____

diary   _____

et cetera   _____

handkerchief   _____

hearth   _____

indict   _____

masochist   _____

pantomime   _____

pitcher   _____

pronunciation   _____

radiator   _____

robot   _____

4. Here are some words which are often mispronounced; usually one or more sounds are omitted. Follow the same instructions as in exercise 3.

accessory   _____

arctic   _____

asphyxiate   _____

casualty   _____

correct   _____

environment   _____

February   _____

figure   _____

length   _____

picture   _____

probably   _____

recognize   _____

regular   _____

twenty   _____

5. Here are some words which are often mispronounced; usually one
   or more sounds are added to the word. Follow the same
   instructions as in exercise 3.

accompanist _____

across   _____

athlete   _____

athletics   _____

chimney   _____

disastrous   _____

escape   _____

film   _____

laundry   _____

monstrous   _____

often   _____

positively   _____

statistics   _____

6. Here are some words which are often mispronounced; usually the
   accent is placed on the wrong syllable. Follow the same instructions
   as in exercise 3.

admirable   _____

amicable   _____

autopsy   _____

barbarous   _____

comparable   _____

guitar   _____

impotence   _____

incomparable _____

irreparable   _____

magnanimous   _____

mischievous   _____

police   _____

preferable   _____

theater   _____

7. Here are some words which are often mispronounced; usually two or more sounds are reversed. Follow the same instructions as in exercise 3.

asterisk   _____

cavalry   _____

hundred   _____

introduction _____

irrelevant   _____

perspiration _____

prescription _____

prevent   _____

professor   _____

solemnity   _____

voluminous   _____

8. As you read the following sentences, prolong the vowel sounds within words to produce full, rich tones.
   a. The most beautiful sounds in our language are produced when we open our mouths and prolong the vowel sounds within words.
   b. Be nice to people on your way up the ladder, because you'll meet the same people on the way down.
   c. The friendly, round-faced native traded corn and coffee for a large amount of cinnamon-flavored honey.

d. Noreene maintained that Gregory Wayne should not be blamed for the injury which became inflamed.

e. Running into debt isn't so bad; it's running into your creditors that could produce problems.

f. Round and round went the wheel and when it came to a stop, it landed on my lucky number — thirteen.

g. The orange was large, perfectly round, seedless, firm, deliciously juicy, and sweet.

9. Read the following sentences with feeling and expression. Try to visualize the words and thought-ideas as you read.

a. The battalion of tall, determined waves, slowly, but steadily, approached the unsuspecting, jagged shore like military columns. When they arrived, their fury was unleashed as they exploded against the rocks and ledges.

b. The raindrops happily tip-toed across the barn's metal roof almost in unison. Then, as if playing a game, they decided to slide off onto the soft, soggy ground.

c. "We shall fight on the beaches. We shall fight on the landing grounds. We shall fight in the fields and in the streets. We shall fight in the hills. We shall never surrender."
— *Winston Churchill*

d. "If a free society cannot help the many who are poor, it cannot save the few who are rich."
— *John F. Kennedy*

e. He rose, shivering, chilled, infected, bending beneath this dying man, whom he was dragging on, all dripping with slime. He walked with desperation, without raising his head, almost without breathing.

10. You may find this reading interesting since it contains all the sounds of the English language.

It is usually rather easy to reach the Virginia Theatre. Board car number 56 somewhere along Churchill Street and ride to the highway. Transfer there to the Mississippi bus. When you arrive at Judge Avenue, begin walking toward the business zone. You will pass a gift shop displaying little children's playthings that often look so clever you will wish yourself young again; such things as books and toys and, behind the counter, a playroom with an elegant red rug and smooth, shining mirrors. Beyond this shop are the National Bank and the Globe Garage. Turn south at the next corner; the theater is to your left.

WHAT DO YOU REMEMBER FROM THIS CHAPTER?

1. Name several elements that contribute to effective delivery.

2. How can you find your normal pitch range?

3. What is a good exercise that will help eliminate a monotonous delivery?

4. Why is proper breathing important to oral communication?

5. What are some poor speech habits that are common?

6. What is the average comfortable speaking rate?

7. Explain oral visualization.

8. Comment on the statement, "She was a born singer."

9. Explain pacing.

10. Explain duration.

VITALIZE YOUR VOCABULARY

Court and Law

accessory (n.)   one who knowingly aids a criminal.

acquittal (n.)   the freeing of a person from an accusation of wrongdoing.

affidavit (n.)   a written statement made under oath before an authorized officer.

appellant (n.)   one who appeals to a higher court for a retrial of his case.

arraign (v.)   to summon before a court to answer a charge.

circumstantial evidence (n.)   evidence not directly relevant to the facts in a lawsuit.

defendant (n.)   the person against whom a legal action is brought.

deposition (n.)   written testimony given under oath.

exonerate (v.)   to free from an accusation.

extradition (n.)   the surrender of an alleged criminal by one state for trial by another.

felony (n.)   a serious crime, such as burglary, rape, or murder.

habeas corpus (n.)   a legal order to produce a prisoner and to determine if there is just cause to detain him.

indictment (n.)   a formal written statement listing charges against an accused person.

injunction (n.)   a court order prohibiting or requiring a specific course of action.

intestate (adj.)   having no legal will.

litigant (n.)   a person engaged in a lawsuit.

malfeasance (n.)   misconduct, especially by a public official.

misdemeanor (n.)   an offense less serious than a felony (*see above*).

perjury (n.)   the willful utterance of false testimony while under oath.

plaintiff (n.)   a person who brings a lawsuit against another (defendant).

reprieve (n.)   a temporary postponement of punishment.

subpoena (n.)   a legal order requiring a person to appear in court and to give testimony.

6

Delivering Your Speech

You have all it takes to become the next President of the United States, but you must do something to improve your public speaking.[1]

CHAPTER OBJECTIVES

After reading and understanding this chapter, you should know:

- The various methods of delivering a talk.
- The advantages and disadvantages of each type of delivery.
- The differences between an extemporaneous and impromptu talk.
- How to deliver a talk that you have prepared.

CHAPTER DIGEST

There are three methods of delivery: speaking extemporaneously, reading from a manuscript, and speaking from memory. For almost everyone, an extemporaneous talk is the most effective. It requires you to know your subject in depth and allows you to

[1]President Herbert Hoover to Thomas Dewey, Governor of New York and Republican presidential nominee in 1944.

use note cards. You can also look at your listeners and speak in the language most appropriate to them and to you.

Those who have significant statements to make to the public or to a special audience often read from a manuscript. Beginning speakers who need 110 percent security also tend to read.

The disadvantages of reading are that, usually, the talk sounds "read," eye contact is lost, and the speaker may become addicted to reading all the time. If, however, you must read your talk, try to follow the suggestions given in this chapter.

Speaking from memory invites trouble. What do you do if you forget a word? In addition, this method of delivery can sound cold and mechanical to almost everyone. Memorizing, however, can help you in your introduction and conclusion. Memorizing is also recommended for very short talks, such as introducing a speaker or presenting or accepting an award. (See Chapter 13.)

However, there is another type of speaking. If you are called upon to say a few words, without prior notice — you are doing impromptu speaking. An impromptu talk means that you've had no previous notice and therefore have not prepared for the sudden invitation to speak. The best advice on speaking impromptu is to have some remarks prepared just in case you're called upon without warning.

SPEAKING EXTEMPORANEOUSLY

In our opinion, the most successful speakers in business, politics, religion, and education prepare their talks ahead of time: they've researched their topic, thought about it, outlined it, and rehearsed their performance with or without notes — preferably to a few critical listeners. By taking these steps they smooth their delivery and bolster their self-confidence.

This is what we mean by an extemporaneous talk. If you follow this method, explained in Chapter 7, you should be so immersed in your topic that you need refer only occasionally to your note cards or outline (see Chapters 7 and 8).

An extemporaneous talk enables you to speak in your own style, even to the extent of choosing some words on the spur of the moment. Thus your presentation will not sound memorized or mechanical. You'll be able to maintain that all-important eye contact and, at the same time, enhance your ability to convey sincerity and spontaneity. In addition, this method of delivery will permit you more mobility and the opportunity to use gestures that develop naturally.

As you can see, this type of delivery offers you a great deal of latitude. If you wish to quote someone, you can read the quotation verbatim or recite it from memory. If you give the same talk more than once, chances are that you will not use the exact same wording each time. The talk will be conversational and spontaneous, and this is the reason for advance preparation.

There is no question in our minds that this kind of speaking is the most effective method of delivery and the one that you should try to master.

The talk will be conversational and spontaneous.

READING FROM A MANUSCRIPT

We strongly urge beginning speakers to refrain from reading their entire talks. There are, however, circumstances in which very limited reading may be helpful, such as when you're using statistics or a quotation.

Inexperienced speakers who require a feeling of total security often read from a manuscript. A good example is the person who holds a high position in public or private enterprise but lacks public speaking experience. When he must make policy statements, he doesn't want to risk omitting points or being misunderstood or misquoted. Sometimes he provides advance copies of the speech to the press, for example:

- The President of the United States addressing the Congress and the nation on his proposed massive budget cuts as part of his economic program.

- An industry spokesman explaining to stockholders the reasons he is recommending a merger.

- A school committee spokeswoman announcing the reasons for the massive layoffs of teachers and administrative personnel.

- A university spokesman explaining why the institution is involved in a controversial scientific program.

- A chief justice announcing a landmark decision.

All these speakers are fully justified in reading their statements; they can't afford a wrong word. As a non-professional, reading your entire speech word for word could create one or more of the following problems:

- Your speech will sound read and will therefore lack spontaneity.

- You may communicate only isolated words instead of idea patterns.

- You may become so engrossed in your manuscript that you forfeit rapport with your audience by not looking at them.

- You may be so "glued" to the manuscript that you can't move about and gesture.

- You may become so addicted to reading your talks that you will not develop skill in the other two methods of delivery.

If, however, you feel compelled to read your speech verbatim, then consider the following tips:

1. Don't use words you don't normally use because you'll run the risk of mispronouncing them or hesitating when you approach them. Nothing could blow your credibility more. Don't try to impress your listeners with polysyllabic profundity!

2. Be sure that your sentences are short and understandable. In a newspaper or magazine one sentence can be a lengthy paragraph, but that's understandable because the reader can review the material as often as he wishes. A listener has only one chance to hear what you're saying (unless, of course, you repeat very important points). Keep this in mind when you write your speech. Remember that you're writing for the ear — which likes short conversational sentences — and not for the eye. (See Chapter 9 for a comparison of oral and written styles.)

3. Type your speech all caps, either double-spaced or triple-spaced. Number each page and type only on one side of the page. For ease of reading and quickly finding the right place of your talk after looking at the audience, use the large ORATOR style type which is available for electric typewriters with interchangeable elements. When you finish a page, turn it or slide it aside quietly.

4. Read your speech aloud over and over until you know it so well that you can look at your audience more than at your manuscript and so that your speech will sound conversational. This will take a great deal of practice, but it'll be worth the effort.

Rehearsing is imperative. Once I (AJV) listened to a speaker who read his entire speech and had not practiced sufficiently. The last line at the bottom of one page was repeated as the first line of the next, and he read both! Can you imagine the audience's reaction?

Without question, one of the most polished public speakers of this decade when reading his speeches verbatim is President

Ronald Reagan. His delivery — voice, diction, inflection, pronunciation, rate of speaking, duration of vowel sounds, pauses, pacing, breathing, expression, and eye contact — is flawless. The President's impeccable performance evolved from many years of training and experience in front of radio microphones as well as motion picture and TV cameras. Even his critics agree that he is a virtuoso at reading a speech.

Treat your manuscript with care.

SPEAKING FROM MEMORY

The riskiest method of delivering a talk is to memorize it completely. This method of delivery often lacks warmth, feeling, and emphasis since the memorized words usually pour forth mechanically. The chilling risk is that forgetting a word or key phrase could throw you into a state of confusion.

Very few people can deliver memorized speeches effectively. Those who can are very likely professionals who have been speaking this way for years because they have trained their memory.

Many years ago one of my college speech classes was assigned a short memorized talk. I (AJV) chose to speak on memory development since I was always interested in improving this ability. I started by explaining how important memory can be in everyday living, how it is a God-given talent but one that can be developed with perseverance and application.

I stated "basically there are three important factors involved in the development of memory. One is association." On the blackboard I wrote the words, "One — Association." "Two," I continued, "is repetition." Again, approaching the blackboard, I wrote, "Two — Repetition." Then, facing the class I announced, "And three!" . . . dead air, silence. I drew a blank. The silent seconds seemed like horrendous hours and for the life of me I couldn't remember the third point.

The class thought my performance was humorous, as I stood motionless with a look of desperation. After getting myself together, I embarked on an impromptu talk on the fallacy of attempting memorized speeches.

Despite the danger of memorizing an entire speech, this method can help you with introductions and conclusions, which are the most crucial parts of a talk. Memorizing your opening and concluding remarks allows you to begin and end confidently, and enables you to look around at your audience directly instead of glancing at notes. By the same token, it's wise to memorize a short talk (a minute or so), for example, introducing a speaker or presenting or accepting an award (discussed in Chapter 13). But attempting to recite an entire talk from memory could lead to trouble.

SPEAKING IMPROMPTU

Impromptu speaking is more often a predicament you may find yourself in than a method of delivery. Since an impromptu talk is one for which you've had no previous notice, you're denied the advantage of preparation. Yet, if you analyze your daily conversation, you'll find that most of it, by far, is impromptu: in class, over coffee, at home, on the phone, with a date, or somebody else's date, and during interviews. In all these cases, except interviews, you may be conversing with one or a half-dozen people. You talk, they listen; they talk, you listen.

Because of your experience or degree of involvement in a group or organization, you should have a pretty good idea whether or not you may be called upon "to say a few words" at a formal meeting. Before going to a meeting, banquet, social, political, or fraternal gathering, ask yourself, "If I were called upon to speak, what would I say?"

Suppose you forget a word?

An impromptu situation doesn't require a fifteen-minute talk. Driving home one sharp point in a few minutes of a carefully prepared "off-the-cuff" talk can make you look like a pro. If there's any possibility, no matter how remote, that you may be asked to say a few words, prepare some comments. It's better to be prepared and not called upon than to be called upon and not be prepared.

An "off-the-cuff" talk can make you look like a pro.

Although you may be ready to say a few words, once called upon, you must focus your thoughts on the specific subject and occasion. Following are some ideas that may help:

- Refer to what previous speakers have said.

- Comment on some of the topical views expressed by people at your table. They could be a fertile source of ideas.

- Compare the past and present, with possibly a word on the future.

- Compare certain advantages and disadvantages.

- State the problem and a possible solution. (Perhaps you may wish to recommend that a special committee be named to investigate the matter further and then file a report at the next meeting.)

- State the importance of the problem and its effect on our families and our daily lives.

- Consider the topic from the viewpoints of childhood, adulthood, old age.

- Consider the topic from political, economic, or social aspects.

- Consider a topic geographically — by city, state, country, the world.

One or more of these approaches should work for you, because your obligation is to speak only two or three minutes. But you do have to think fast; make no mistake about that. And under no circumstances should you start by apologizing.

If you're completely unprepared and don't wish to address the group, bow out as gracefully as possible (again, prepare a short statement ahead of time).

There's no question that the best preparation for an impromptu performance is to have had practice in giving prepared talks and to have a mind well stocked with information and opinions. The most important suggestion, however, is to prepare ahead of time. Before you go to any gathering, plan a few pertinent remarks so that the audience will not only listen to you but will also envy your ability to speak "off-the-cuff."

You'd be wise to learn from Mark Twain's experience. After many years of successful platform speaking, he said, "It usually takes more than three weeks to prepare a good impromptu speech."

In this chapter we covered the three methods of delivery — making an extemporaneous talk, reading a manuscript, and speaking from memory. We also discussed impromptu speaking. Since the most effective speech delivery may contain a combination of all these, experiment with them to establish the most comfortable style for you.

THINGS TO THINK ABOUT AND DO

1. Which methods of delivery do you think are used by political campaigners? Discuss this.

2. Which method of delivery annoys you the most and why?

3. As a listener, which method of delivery do you prefer? Why?

4. Become more aware of speakers, for example, politicians, clergymen, professors, and their methods of delivery. Ask a few of them which methods of delivery they prefer and why. Discuss in class.

5. Cite two or three examples of speakers you've recently heard and discuss their methods of delivery. In your opinion, which delivery was the most effective? Why?

WHAT DO YOU REMEMBER FROM THIS CHAPTER?

1. List three methods of delivering a talk.

2. Explain the advantages and disadvantages of each method.

3. Is it permissible to use more than one method of delivery in the same talk?

4. Give a few examples in which a speech might be read verbatim.

5. Explain the differences between extemporaneous and impromptu talks.

6. How would you prepare an impromptu talk?

7. Why is practicing a talk important?

8. What method of talking do you engage in most of your waking hours, and why is it easy for you?

VITALIZE YOUR VOCABULARY

Government and Politics

bipartisan (adj.)   representing members of two parties.

bureaucracy (n.)   the whole body of nonelected government officials, often accused of red tape and insensitivity to human needs.

caucus (n.)   a closed meeting of a political party to decide policies.

center (n.)   a moderate approach to political, economic, and social problems, somewhere between liberal and conservative positions.

conservative (adj.)   tending to oppose change and to favor traditional ideas and values.

constituent (n.)   a voter in a politician's district.

electorate (n.)   the people qualified to vote in an election.

envoy (n.)   a person sent to represent his government to another government for a specific mission.

filibuster (n.)   use of delaying tactics, such as nonstop speeches, to prevent voting on pending issues.

grass roots (n.)   the local level, as opposed to the centers of political power.

gubernatorial (adj.)   pertaining to the governor.

impeach (v.)   to legally charge a public official with misconduct in office.

inaugurate (v.)   to install into office with a formal ceremony.

incumbent (n.)   the current holder of an office.

left wing (n. and adj.)   see *liberal*.

legislate (v.)   to enact laws.

liberal (adj.)   favoring civil liberties and the use of governmental power to promote social reforms.

lobby (n.)   usually a group of people trying to influence lawmakers in favor of the group's special interest.

pacifism (n.)   a philosophy that promotes peace and opposes war as a national policy.

platform (n.)   a formal statement of a political party's goals and principles.

protocol (n.)   ceremonies and etiquette observed by diplomats and heads of state.

radical (n. and adj.)   an extreme approach to social, economic, and political problems, can be either left wing or right wing.

republic (n.)   a country governed by representatives elected by the people.

quorum (n.)   the minimum number of members of an organization who must be present to conduct business officially.

referendum (n.)   the practice of submitting a measure to the voters rather than to the legislature.

registration (n.)   the official enrollment of citizens eligible to vote; if not registered, they cannot vote.

right wing (n. and adj.)   see *conservative*.

7

Selecting a Topic and Doing Research

Nature has herself appointed that nothing great is to be accomplished quickly, and has ordained that difficulty should precede every work of excellence.[1]

CHAPTER OBJECTIVES

After reading and understanding this chapter, you should know:

- How to go about selecting a topic.
- Several ways to conduct research.
- How to use library facilities.
- How to take research notes.
- How to summarize, paraphrase, and select apt quotations.
- How to prepare notes.

CHAPTER DIGEST

If you're able to select your own topic, choose one that interests you, one that you can handle, and one that suits your audience. Your next step usually involves paring down the topic to a

[1]Quintilian, eminent Roman teacher of speech (A.D. 30?–96?).

manageable size that you can cover in a short talk. When the topic is focused clearly in your mind, it's time to seek solid information — very often the only basis of effective interpersonal communication in business and professional careers.

There are several ways to find information, and you should feel free to use the ways that will suit your needs best: dredge up your own experiences, opinions, and observations; contact various organizations and agencies, both public and private; consult nonprint media (television, radio, documentary films, and recordings); interview specialists from all walks of life; and utilize libraries.

You'll probably find the bulk of your information in print — newspapers, journals, magazines, books. It's vital that you read and take notes with a critical eye. Question constantly and don't swallow anything whole. The fact that a statement is published does not guarantee its accuracy or truth.

CRITERIA FOR SELECTING A TOPIC

Before you can give a brief, stimulating talk, you need a topic and information on it. Sometimes your professor may assign a topic and ask you to research it. At other times she may specify a general area, for example, inflation, unemployment, or white-collar crime, and request you to select a particular facet of it. Some students prefer to have a specific topic selected for them, because it's easier than having to choose one themselves.

Or the professor may tell you to choose your own topic. If this is the case, your first reaction will probably be, "What will I talk about?" Without question this is the most common response by students of speech. With a little thought and with the suggestions in this chapter, you may find that selecting a topic is not as difficult as you first imagined. In any event, you should weigh the following guidelines in searching for a topic:

- Your interest in it.
- Your capability of handling it.
- Its appropriateness to the audience.

The topic should be interesting to you. If you're not interested in the topic, chances are that nobody else will be, and your talk will probably fizzle. Interest, enthusiasm, zeal — call it what you will — are reflected in your voice and by your nonverbal communication (facial expressions, emotions, gestures). (Nonverbal communication is discussed further in Chapters 2, 4, 5, 8, 15, and 16.) Audiences sense enthusiasm, or the lack of it, in a speaker, and they respond accordingly.

Audiences sense enthusiasm, or the lack of it.

What you are going to talk about depends on what interests you. Perhaps you're engaged in one of the following hobbies:

- Repairing and reconditioning antique cars.
- Stamp or coin collecting.
- Candle making and design.
- Rug braiding or needlepoint.
- Shooting pictures and developing them.

- Music.
- Ham radio.
- Comic book collecting.
- Playing an instrument.
- Reading.
- Painting.
- International doll collecting.

If you're interested in politics and government, you may consider one of the following:

- Don't say, "What's the use of voting?"
- Judges should be elected instead of appointed.
- What we need is a woman president.
- The vice-president should be elected by the people and not selected by the presidential candidate.
- The president should be elected by popular vote.
- Forced busing as a means of integration.
- How does a bill get through the legislature?

How about choosing one of the following topics if you enjoy sports?

- The adventure of scuba diving.
- Getting high by sky diving.
- The case against expansion teams.
- Is jogging healthful or harmful?
- Pro athletes are overpaid.
- Pro athletes should have the right to strike.
- Our Olympic sports teams should be federally subsidized.

If you have strong feelings on education, how about one of these?

- Politics in education.

- Speech should be a mandatory subject.

- Students should be permitted to evaluate their teachers.

- Attendance in class should be required.

- Earning a college degree should take three years instead of four.

- Students should be able to attend their state colleges free of charge.

Do you still want more topics for talks? Then you and your classmates might venture into a brainstorming session, a technique used occasionally in the business world to dredge up solutions to problems (see Chapter 14). In brainstorming, the cardinal rule is complete freedom to think of, and then say, anything, without being criticized: No matter how wild or cockeyed an idea seems, *nobody can ridicule it.* Following these wide-open, nonthreatening rules, a cooperative group can often create answers to a problem — in this case, producing more topics for your talks.

All the suggestions should be recorded on the chalkboard and in your notepad, and evaluated at the next class when everybody has simmered down. The worthwhile ideas can be used and the poor ones discarded.

If you're deeply interested in a particular topic, chances are your audience will be too. Your enthusiasm can't help but be transmitted to your listeners, because it's contagious. If you can get totally wrapped up in your subject, the end result could be electrifying.

John Wesley, founder of the Methodist Church in the eighteenth century, was once asked how he attracted such large audiences and held them spellbound. "I set myself on fire," he replied, "and they come to watch me burn."

The topic should be within your capability.   In other words, can you handle the topic based on your personal experiences, book learning, first-hand knowledge, family background, personal convictions, and acquaintances in specific fields? If some or all of these factors are in your favor, then the odds are that you'll be able to prepare and speak intelligently on your selected subject.

For example, if you're planning to select as a subject the operation and safety of a nuclear power plant — a vital concern since the Three Mile Island accident in Pennsylvania in 1979 — you need a strong technical background, several visits to a nuclear plant, and interviews with engineers and administrators. Then, you face the challenge of compiling all this scientific information and translating it into a level of English that your audience can understand.

Suppose, however, that you want to address the question, "Should use of marijuana be legalized?" You could easily find yourself knee-deep in facts, opinions, half-truths, and myths. Consider the sources of information available to you, for example, acquaintances who smoke pot and swear by it, law enforcement officials who think otherwise, doctors involved in drug treatment, and legislators determined to control the problem. Remember to check out as many sources of information as possible, because almost all controversial issues are complicated and many-sided and seldom lend themselves to simplistic solutions.

The topic should be suitable to the audience. Knowing the makeup of your listeners will help you shape a more effective person-to-person communication. To know your listeners, you should think about and try to answer several questions about them: What are their age levels, ethnic backgrounds, occupations, financial status, sex, educational levels, and any other elements that may affect your performance?

Consider a speaker at a meeting of the Women's Liberation Movement. If she explains innovative tactics that would help qualified women break into public school administration, higher echelons of civil service, or corporate executive suites — the three areas in which women have traditionally been shut out — she might receive a standing ovation.

In other words, try to assess the problem from the standpoint of the audience. Put yourself in the role of an active listener and ask yourself: What do I expect from this speaker? Will her message be interesting, informative, understandable? Will I want to hear more? (Audience analysis is discussed in depth in Chapter 9 and Chapter 12.)

SELECTING MATERIAL AND
NARROWING DOWN THE TOPIC

A common tendency among beginning speakers is to select a subject that is so general in scope that it cannot be realistically covered in a short presentation. You should bear two questions in mind: Is the subject too broad? Should you zero in on a specific phase of it?

Suppose that you find a subject that really piques your curiosity, for example, coping with violence in our society. Should you use this subject for a talk? Definitely not, because it's so vast and complex that you couldn't even dent its surface in a half-hour. Your subject must be limited to a topic that you can discuss in the allotted time — usually five to ten minutes. Select a phase of that subject, for instance, stiffer court sentences or more stress on rehabilitation in prison or greater use of capital punishment.

"I'd like to talk for a minute on nuclear power . . ."

Now you have a vital, current topic that you can sink your teeth into in a short speech. And you'll find more material in newspapers, magazines, books, radio and TV programs than you can possibly utilize.

Let's say that you've now found an idea that complies with the suggested guidelines. If the subject is new to you, you'll probably need to engage in some research. True, some people can talk on anything, but do they communicate any substance if they have not thoroughly researched their topic?

DOING RESEARCH

The difference between a speech stocked with the latest, accurate information and a speech lacking it can be the difference between acceptance or rejection by the audience. We say "acceptance" because most audiences listen to and respect a knowledgeable speaker. This hard-won knowledge will give you an injection of self-confidence and, together with your listeners' respect, you're off and running. Let's assume that you're contemplating buying a house — an old American dream that is vanishing now that banks are charging around 15% or more interest on mortgages — and you want to find out if banks are exploiting potential home buyers. If you're lucky, consumer advocate Ralph Nader may be booked to delve into this very question on a national TV talk show. You might tape-record the interview and wind up with confidential information that might be presented publicly for the first time. Can you imagine the impact on your audience when, somewhere in your presentation, you could play back excerpts of that tape? Dynamite!

Below are some ideas on how to ferret out information on any topic:

Probe your own knowledge, experience, and observations. If you stop to think, you'll probably discover opinions, ideas, and knowledge that you didn't know you had. Jot them down. And don't forget to question friends and acquaintances because some of them may know a good deal about your topic.

Write to organizations. Government agencies, corporations, labor unions, research consultants, colleges, and publications are often helpful in providing information. If you do write to them, be very specific in your requests. The only drawback to this approach is that you may wait weeks for answers.

Check out TV and radio documentaries and talk shows, tapes, films, film clips, and cassettes. In recent years these nonprint media have assumed more and more importance as carriers and recorders of vital information.

Suppose that you're curious about the solemn occasion and exact wording of President Franklin D. Roosevelt's Declaration of War against Japan on December 8, 1941. You could, of course, turn to the Congressional Record, biographies of FDR, or history books to find the answer. But another approach will allow you to capture the real-life gravity of that momentous day. Ask your audiovisual department to get the recording of the Declaration so that you can listen to it in President Roosevelt's own unique voice and speaking style.

Talk to people. Authorities on various subjects are everywhere, and many of them are willing to share their expertise. Be sure to have a list of questions ready so that you won't waste the expert's time. After she has answered your questions, thank her and leave immediately.

A tape recorder can be used in a face-to-face information quest because it is a time saver, but first request permission to use the recorder. Some people are "allergic" to being taped and tend to clam up.

Don't feel that you must always seek out authorities sitting on top of the organizational pyramid. Some of them tend to be "long" on administrative plans, policies, and procedures but "short" on nitty-gritty savvy. On the other hand, many people in everyday positions essential to the functioning of society can brief you on problems in specialized areas, and they may do so if you ask. You'll be astonished at what you can get by simply asking.

Do you want to know about muggings, rapes, and armed robberies? Talk to police officers, judges, prison officials, and victims. Do you want to learn about financial hardships plaguing welfare families? By all means, talk with sociology professors, but don't forget to talk with welfare mothers, social workers, and members of legislative committees on human services. This many-sided approach to gathering information allows you to "see" an issue as it is in the real world.

Talk to the man (or woman) under the street.

Read.   Reading, the most dependable of all sources, opens endless horizons to you. Just about "everything you ever wanted to know about anything but were afraid to ask" can be found in books, magazines, journals, newspapers, government reports, almanacs, encyclopedias, dictionaries, diaries, and so on.

To extract the maximum benefit from the printed word, you must know how to use a library. So, let's touch upon the highlights of exploiting your library's resources. Every library has a card catalog that lists all its books. This catalog is broken down by author name, title, and subject, which means at least three cards pinpoint each book. In addition, each card contains a call number that indicates the book's location in the library. Figure 7-1 shows a typical card from a library catalog.

For periodicals (magazines, journals, and newspapers), visit the periodical section where you'll find the latest authoritative information on countless specialized fields. This is the tremendous advantage that periodicals offer — information that may be only weeks or days old, in contrast to books that require several months or a year to publish.

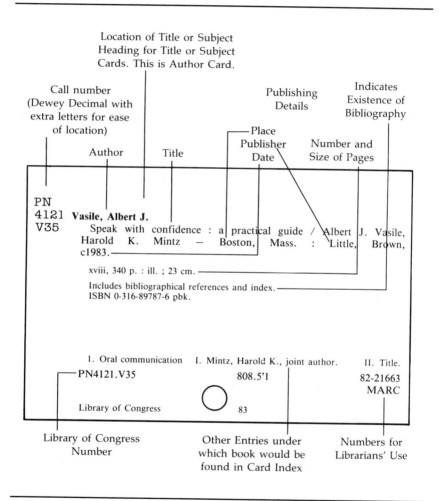

Figure 7-1
A card from a library card catalog.

To find articles in periodicals relevant to your topic, turn to the indexes, especially *The Reader's Guide to Periodical Literature*. The

Guide lists, by subject, the contents of more than 125 American publications and is an excellent aid in getting your research started. Other sources of information are listed below.

If you're searching for material on business, industry, education, or public affairs, consult some of the following indexes:

Bibliography Index
Business Periodicals Index
Christian Science Monitor Index
Education Index
The New York Times Index
Public Affairs Information Service
Ulrich's Periodical Directory
United Nations Documents Index
The Wall Street Journal Index

For statistical data, you might dig into the following:

Government Publications
Information Please Almanac
United Nations Statistical Yearbook
U.S. Statistical Abstracts
World Almanac

To learn about people, consult the following:

Current Biography
Dictionary of American Biography
International Who's Who
Leaders in Education
Who's Who in America
Who's Who in Finance and Industry
Who's Who in Law

As speech students and, in fact, all through life, you should make a habit of mining these wordbooks:

Funk & Wagnall's New Standard Dictionary
Random House Dictionary of the English Language
Roget's International Thesaurus
Webster's Dictionary of Synonyms
Webster's Third New International Dictionary

When you're searching for appropriate quotations, use the following excellent sources:

Bartlett's Familiar Quotations
Oxford Dictionary of Quotations
Stevenson's Home Book of Quotations

For general information and for an overall view of thousands of subjects, check the following standard encyclopedias:

Collier's Encyclopedia
Encyclopedia Americana
Encyclopaedia Britannica

Here are two hints for using libraries wisely:

First, browse around your college or public library. Explore the card catalog, periodical section, reference section, and open stacks. After you do that a few times, you'll be amazed at how much faster you'll find the facts, figures, and authoritative opinions that will help you master your topic, communicate your message, and earn your listeners' respect.

Second, get acquainted with your reference librarians. Almost all librarians like to have their libraries used. No matter how sharp you are, research is a time-consuming process that librarians can speed up by guiding you to the right reference aids. However, don't expect them to do your research; that's your task.

At this point you're primed to dip into reference works in order to locate sources of information. Magazines, journals, newspapers, books — they're all fair game in this hunt. Whether you plan to refer to a few sources or a dozen, you should number and list them on note paper or cards (5 by 7 is a good size). This list is your bibliography. Figure 7-2 shows a sample bibliography for a talk on the soaring cost of higher education.

Before studying your sources, you might save time by evaluating them and weeding out the poorer ones. Some yardsticks for judging the worth of a magazine or newspaper article or a book chapter are:

- Recency of publication (not always a reliable measure).

- Reputation of author (is he a recognized authority in his field?).

- Reputation of publisher (what's his "track record"?).

1. From *Readers' Guide to Periodical Literature, March 1979–February 1980*

   Cost
   College tuition: soaring out of reach? How college costs strap 3 affluent families. il U.S. News 86:48-50 Ap 30 '79
   Does daddy owe her a college degree? Zimmerman vs. Zimmerman takes a parent to court; tuition payment dispute. M. Vespa. il por People 12:57 Ag 20 '79
   Higher education; address. June 10, 1979. C. R. Wharton, Jr. Vital Speeches 45:744-6 O 1 '79
   How to have the money you need when your children are ready for college. P. Gross. House & Gard 151:38 + Mr. '79
   Save for college: a tax-free plan; Uniform Gifts to Minors Act. T. Tilling. il Parents Mag 54: 94-6 F '79
   Should tax credits for tuition payments to colleges and nonpublic schools be enacted? symposium. Cong Digest 58:10-32 Ja '79
   Tuition tax credits in 1979. America 140:465 Je 9 '79
   > *See also*
   Medical education—Cost
   Student aid
   Student loans

2. From *New York Times Quarterly Index, 1979*

   Finances. Note: Includes all fees and costs, and student loans
   > *Carter Adm to propose $11.1 billion educ budget for fiscal '80, up $1 billion from '79 figure;* major changes are keyed to higher requests for appropriations for

Figure 7-2
Sample bibliography on costs of higher education. Note that abstracts of articles, not titles, are given from the *New York Times Quarterly Index;* also (L) indicates a news story longer than two columns, (M) a story of up to two columns, and (S) a story of a half-column or less.

For example, an article in the *New York Times* or *Chicago Tribune* carries far more clout than an article in a small-town newspaper. Admittedly, one or both of the last two yardsticks may be difficult to apply, but they do help in comparing one work against another and in deciding which would make a better source.

TAKING NOTES

There are various ways to take notes: Write a summary, write a paraphrase, or copy a direct quotation. If you can capture the essence of an important paragraph in a few sentences, you are sum-

scholarship and loan programs for coll students; HEW and educ orgns say $2.4 billion proposed for such programs will be wholly inadequate; law raising income ceiling for families receiving aid to $25,000 a yr from $15,000 increased number of eligible students by 1.7 million (M), Ja 6,1:1

Article on improvements in Fed loan program for coll students, which have led to considerable reduction in bad debt; new strategy is to keep billing the defaulter until he pays; more businesslike execution of loan and better methods of tracking down defaulters also cited (Winter Survey of Educ), Ja 7,XIII,6:5

3. From *Business Periodicals Index, 1980*

College costs

Coping with college costs. tab Bus W p96-8 S 4 '78

Corporate executives taxable on EBT payments to children. J. Taxation 48:325-6 Je '78

Educating your kids: decisions and dollars. J. S. McClenahen. il tabs Ind W 198:52-3+ S 4 '78

Further look at the Hansen-Weisbrod-Pechman debate [higher education subsidies] J. Conlisk. bibl J Hum Resources 12:147-63 Spr '77; Discussion. 13:566 Fall '78

How to finance your children's college education. R. Nurock. Super Mgt 24:39-41 Ja '79

Universities: no love story. il Economist 268: 49 S 16 '78

When — and how — to start saving for college. B. Hitchings. Bus W p 121-2 O 9 '78

marizing. You may summarize often. Figure 7-3 shows an original paragraph and a summary of it.[2]

When you rewrite a sentence or paragraph in your own style and in about the same number of words as the original, you're paraphrasing. Figure 7-4 shows a paraphrase of the same original paragraph.[3]

Occasionally you'll run across a key idea phrased so strikingly that you can't summarize it or improve the wording. In that case, copy it exactly, word for word, and enclose it in quotation marks (see Figure 7-4). Be sure to jot down the author's name and other information needed to document the quotation (detailed above).

---

[2]Harvey S. Wiener, *Total Swimming*. (New York: Simon and Schuster, 1980), p. 33.

[3]Ibid.

Original paragraph

Sometimes the commitment to swimming borders on private psychotherapy, so deep and abiding are the mental rewards of the sport. Don Mantell, an art teacher at Deer Park High School, turned to swimming for peace of mind. Tension, restlessness, anxiety manifested in sky-high blood pressure, all pushed him into recreational activity just to ease his worries. He admits to shock at the results. Within weeks of starting a regular swim program recently he dropped his blood pressure thirty points. His friend, Mario Vecchioni, dropped not only his blood pressure by an equally astonishing degree, but also more than fifty pounds as well. The two men relate their physical change to the way they feel about their exercise and to an altered mental state. First, they really enjoy swimming. They don't have to convince themselves to do it only because it's good for them. Next, they're more relaxed, less apt to fly off the handle in spite of histories marked by short-tempered outbursts and inner tension.

Summary of original paragraph

Swimming offers tremendous mental and physical rewards. A high school art teacher, suffering from tension and high blood pressure, tried swimming regularly. Within weeks his pressure dropped 30 points. An overweight friend reduced his pressure similarly and lost more than 50 pounds. Since they enjoy swimming, their mental states improved; they've become more relaxed, less tense.

Figure 7-3
An original paragraph and its summary.

When you take notes, you may sometimes think of a question to ask, a doubt to ponder, a lead to follow up. Record these thoughts immediately before they vanish from memory and tack your initials onto them so that you won't mix your ideas with those of the original author.

As a researcher, you enjoy a tremendous advantage over people like Thomas Jefferson, Charles Darwin, and Winston Churchill. Say, for example, that you run across a few pages full of meaty, relevant information in a book, magazine, or encyclopedia that can't be borrowed. You could easily waste an hour or so copying the pages in longhand. Since almost all libraries have photocopy equipment, use it to save time. Reading important information into a cassette tape recorder can also be a time-saver.

No question, conducting research can be a time-consuming, difficult, and sometimes discouraging activity, but the overall re-

Paraphrase of original paragraph

The mental and physical rewards of swimming are like a deep and long-lasting personal therapy. A high school art teacher, suffering from tension, anxiety, and high blood pressure, tried a regular program of swimming. The results astonished him beyond belief. Within weeks of starting, he pared 30 points off his blood pressure. An overweight friend of his dropped his blood pressure the same amount and streamlined himself by lopping off more than 50 pounds. Both men swim because they enjoy it, not because it is good for them, and for that reason their mental attitudes have changed for the better. They are now more relaxed and easy going, without any inner tension and bursts of temper.

A direct quotation from one of the swimmers

"I work out all my frustrations when I swim. I feel calmer, more at peace. In the water my aggressions disappear. . . ."

Figure 7-4
A paraphrase of an original paragraph and a direct quotation.

Take a few notes.

sults will be most rewarding. Remember the words of Quintilian, who said, "Nature has herself appointed that nothing great is to be accomplished quickly, and has ordained that difficulty should precede every work of excellence."

THINGS TO THINK ABOUT AND DO

1. List a few subjects that interest you but which, because of your lack of knowledge, would require research if you were planning to talk about them.

2. Would you prefer to select your own topics or have them selected for you? Why?

3. List a few speech topics that would apply only to specific audiences. Explain your reasons for choosing them.

4. Select a topic that would interest the class and list some possible sources of information on it.

5. Research some significant events that took place the day you were born.

WHAT DO YOU REMEMBER FROM THIS CHAPTER?

1. After you've decided on a topic for a talk, what should the next steps be?

2. List several ways to find information.

3. Name some guidelines to be used in searching for a topic.

4. What role does the audience play in your selection of a topic?

5. List some sources that would be helpful if you're looking for material on business, industry, public affairs, or education.

6. Name two sources that would provide statistical data.

7. Name two sources that would supply information on people.

8. Name two publications that specialize in word usage.

VITALIZE YOUR VOCABULARY

Business and Finance

assets (n.)   property, equipment, merchandise, and money owned by a business.

balance sheet (n.)   a financial statement showing the condition of a business on a particular date.

bankrupt (adj.)   being unable to pay one's debts.

depreciation (n.)   a loss of value because of age or wear; in financial records, an allowance made for the loss.

discount (n.)   a reduction from the usual price.

distributor (n.)   a person or company that buys products from manufacturers and sells to retail stores; a wholesaler.

dividend (n.)   a share of profits paid to a stockholder.

endorsement (n.)   a signature enabling a check to be cashed.

entrepreneur (n.)   a person who organizes and operates a business.

fiscal (adj.)   pertaining to financial matters.

insolvent (adj.)   being unable to pay one's debts.

inventory (n.)   the supply of goods on hand; stock.

liabilities (n.)   debts or obligations.

liquidation (n.)   paying off debts; closing down a business by paying off debts.

maturity (n.)   the time when a financial note becomes due for full payment.

monopoly (n.)   complete control of producing or selling a product or service.

overhead (n.)   the operating expenses of a business, such as heat, lighting, taxes, insurance, rent; overhead does not include the cost of labor or materials.

partnership (n.)   a relationship in which two or more persons own a business and share the profits and losses.

promissory note (n.)   a written promise to pay a sum of money plus interest by a certain date.

proprietor (n.)   the owner or owner-manager of a business.

prospectus (n.)   a description of a proposed business, sent out to gain financial support.

recession (n.)   a period of reduced economic activity.

repossess (v.)   to take back for failure to pay installments when due.

8

Putting It All Together

Order and simplification are the first steps toward mastery of a subject. . . .[1]

CHAPTER OBJECTIVES

After reading and understanding this chapter, you should know:

- The two principal types of outlines.
- How to prepare an outline.
- The three parts of a talk and how to put them together.
- How to come up with a title for your talk.
- How to use transitions.
- Why practicing your talk is critical.

CHAPTER DIGEST

At this stage you've done your research and you know your subject. Now you must plan or outline your talk. In the long run, a good outline will save you far more time than you will

---

[1]Thomas Mann, *The Magic Mountain* (1924).

devote to preparing it. The two most common outlines, the topic outline and the sentence outline, are explained and illustrated so you can compare them and decide which one is best for you.

When you construct your talk, you may work on the body first and then the introduction or conclusion. A well thought out introduction will usually win audience good will and interest. Numerous suggestions for an effective introduction are given, and all of them appear in introductions quoted from actual speeches. In addition, some ideas for forming conclusions are listed, and excellent examples are included.

Since every talk should have a title, actual titles of many speeches are listed, along with pointers on their distinguishing characteristics.

In every talk you give, the introduction, body, and conclusion should be linked or bridged smoothly to each other by means of transitions. Examples of transitions, together with the conditions that call for their use, appear in a table.

When your introduction, body, and conclusion are organized in outline form and in your mind, you're ready for a practice session, or a rehearsal. This is a necessary step before delivering any talk, and should be done at least a few times, preferably with a critical listener.

NOTE

Everything you learn in this course comes together in this chapter. In other words, the way you organize and practice your talk can "make or break" your overall performance. For that reason, this chapter deserves a great deal of your time and effort.

PREPARING AN OUTLINE

You've done your research, you've uncovered more than enough material — always a wise policy — you've turned the material over in your mind, and you understand it inside out. Where do you go from here?

What you need now is a plan to organize all the information you've gathered. In a sense, you're in the same position as an architect about to envision a building, an airline pilot about to fly the Atlantic, a motorist about to drive from Boston to San Francisco. To accomplish these objectives, the architect needs blueprints, the pilot needs a flight plan, the motorist needs road maps.

By the same token, you need a plan or outline of your talk. Unfortunately, the word *outline* has a high chill factor, probably because the process of outlining is often presented with umpteen cautions and commandments. Here is a useful format.

STATEMENT OF CENTRAL IDEA

I. MAJOR POINT

A. Minor point (supporting data)

These sublevels
should consist of
two or more points.

    1.

    2.

       a.

       b.

B. Minor point (supporting data)

II. MAJOR POINT

  A. Minor point (supporting data)

In this basic speech course you should not have to delve deeper than I.A.1.; in other words, down to the second level of supporting data. If you wish to change this suggested number/ letter system to suit yourself, you may do so. You may use any organizing system you wish, as long as it's logical and coordinate in structure. This means that major point I, in importance or weight, equals major point II, equals major point III, and so on. Similarly, minor point I.A., in importance, equals II.A., equals III.A. If your outline adheres to the principle of coordination, you're on the way to a well-organized speech.

It's possible that your professor may ask you for an outline before you speak so that he can judge how well you've prepared yourself and can see if you actually fulfill your objectives. But even if an outline is not requested, you should prepare one anyway because it will help you perform better.

ADVANTAGES OF OUTLINING

For any talk, no matter how short or long, you should prepare an outline after you've researched and digested your material.

Proper outlining offers you two advantages:

1. It enables you to arrange your major and minor points in logical sequence.

2. It saves you much time by revealing possible gaps or redundancies in your body of information.

You need a plan.

TYPES OF OUTLINES

The principal outlines commonly used are topic and sentence outlines. In the topic outline one or a few key words stand for a topic and should start your thoughts flowing.

In the sentence outline a complete sentence stands for a topic. The sentence outline is more difficult to construct because it calls for thinking through and phrasing a complete idea. This kind of outline is usually more helpful because each sentence stands for a topic that requires one or more paragraphs for development.

You should choose the outline that suits your style. In the following outline (Figure 8-1), based on an actual speech,[2] the introduction and body exemplify a topic outline, and the conclusion exemplifies a sentence outline. Virtually all textbooks on oral communication and English grammar espouse either a topic outline or a sentence outline, but warn you against mixing both in one outline because doing so violates parallel structure.

[2]Noel Annan, "Why Do You Go to a University?" Commencement address delivered by Vice Chancellor of the University of London and member of Parliament, 19 May 1980, at the University of Pennsylvania, Philadelphia. Reported in *Vital Speeches of the Day*, 15 July 1980, pp. 589–591.

Why Do You Go to a University?

THESIS STATEMENT: You can gain many substantial benefits from studying hard at a university.

I. Introduction
  A. Historical anecdote about British judiciary
  B. A youthful American experience of speaker

II. Body — Reasons for going to a university
  A. To acquire knowledge
  B. To make mental efforts under criticism by professors and peers
  C. To express your views and to question your professors
  D. To learn to disagree without being disagreeable
  E. To learn to work against time under pressure; for example, taking exams and meeting deadlines for papers
  F. To learn to speak and write English logically, lucidly, elegantly
  G. To develop self-knowledge and a sense of direction for your life
  H. To appreciate and live a life of the intellect — reading, thinking, studying

III. Conclusion
  A. There are many reasons why the English admire the United States: energetic drive, resourcefulness, enjoyment in meeting a challenge, a sense of justice, technological achievements.
  B. "It is for these reasons, Mr. President, that I am so proud, as the son of an American citizen, to have been chosen by you to salute the class of 1980."

Figure 8-1
Example of an outline combining topics and sentences.

We don't "buy" that rigid, conventional approach. If you're comfortable with mixing topics and sentences in an outline, we say, "Go to it," as long as you know what you're doing.

BODY OF YOUR TALK

Since every talk has a title, an introduction, a body, and a conclusion, your outline must reflect that arrangement of elements. Yet, in preparing your talk, a logical order is to outline the body first and then the introduction or conclusion. The reason for this suggested sequence is that you need to know your message before you can introduce it.

However, if you prefer to work on your introduction first, body second, and conclusion last, then do it your way.

The main points and subpoints that support your thesis statement comprise the body, or main discussion, of your presentation. For short talks such as you'll probably give in this basic course, two or three main points should be enough. For longer efforts, four or five main points should be the maximum number. More than five may confuse an audience, especially one that isn't familiar with the subject matter.

Each main point, when subordinated or broken down, should be supported by two or more subpoints. As suggested earlier, proper development of each subpoint will require one or more paragraphs.

Clearly, it's impossible to know in advance how many main points and subpoints you'll end up with, or, for that matter, how many paragraphs each point will require for adequate coverage. You'll find the answers when you get down to translating all the bits and pieces that form your outline into sentences and paragraphs. You can arrange your main points in various sequences.

- Simple to complex — a much used strategy in teaching.

- Effect and cause, or cause and effect.

- Problem and solution.

- According to space.

- According to time.

Simple to complex. If, for example, you're explaining and demonstrating various tennis strokes to your class, you'd logically start with the basic forehand and backhand. You'd then cover more advanced strokes like the serve and lob. Finally, you'd move into the really difficult strokes like the smash and volley. However, if you had begun with the smash and volley, you would, no doubt, have confused and discouraged most novice players; they'd have lost interest. In other words, when discussing something technical or new to an audience, be sure to start with elementary concepts.

Cause and effect. Reasoning from cause to effect involves a situation, event, or condition that will happen in the future. For example, if you insulate your house or apartment (install storm windows and doors, caulk them, lower the thermostat, use an economical shower head, etc.), your heating bill will decrease substantially. All these causes, but especially insulation, will result in the effect — a lowered heating bill. Here a caution is in order. An effect is usually produced by more than one cause. To win, a football team needs a sharp, hard-driving coach, talented players who are willing to go all the way and then some, cooperative opponents, and a smidgen of luck.

Effect and cause. This kind of reasoning involves an event that has happened. Let's say, for example, that the number of house robberies in your city has doubled in the past two years, and in the same period your police force was cut forty percent. The odds are very high, indeed, that the two events are closely linked. Or you witness an auto accident and notice that one of the two drivers moves unsteadily, slurs his words, and has slightly glazed eyes. You may conclude that the accident was caused by a driver under the influence. These simple cases illustrate kinds of thinking that we do throughout life. Some cases, however, are not so clearcut; because they combine many causes and effects, they will require hard, straight thinking.

Problem and suggested solution.   Air and water pollution is a critical problem in today's industrialized societies. Some of the steps being taken to solve the problem are: improving the internal combustion engine, controlling the exhaust of industrial smokestacks, and restricting the dumping of waste into bodies of water.

According to space.   Let's say that you want to discuss the mountain ranges in the United States. A logical approach would be to start with the White Mountains in New Hampshire and move westward to the Sierra Nevada Mountains in California. Or you could go the other way around. But you would surely not go from New Hampshire to California and then back to the Rockies in Colorado.

According to time.   Suppose you decide to speak on wars engaged in by the United States. There are two logical approaches: start in the 1970s and work your way back to the Revolution, or vice versa. In either case, you are handling your subject according to time.

INTRODUCTION TO YOUR TALK

Now that you know what the substance of your talk will be, you're in a much better position to frame a strong introduction. Such an introduction is vital to the success of your talk because it can win over your audience immediately. Since the first few sentences are crucial, you should consider memorizing them. Rehearse them until you can voice them smoothly and confidently.

Your introduction should serve two major purposes:

- Gain audience good will.

- Arouse audience interest.

To achieve those aims, your introduction may include any one or a combination of the following:

1. Reference to occasion and sponsor

2. Reference to audience

3. Reference to speaker

4. Reference to literature

5. Questions to audience

6. Quotation and question

7. Anecdote and question

8. Anecdote

9. Quotation

10. Startling statement

11. Historical reference

12. Central idea

13. Statistics

All the above suggestions are illustrated in the following introductions from actual speeches.

REFERENCE TO OCCASION AND SPONSOR

Good afternoon. It's a pleasure to be here today. And it's especially appropriate that the YWCA should be sponsoring this seminar on civic responsibility and the corporate woman. Few organizations have put themselves on the line quite the way the Y.W. has in its concern to provide equal opportunities for growth and development to everyone.

Looking back through history, whenever there's been an important women's issue, or relevant needs to be addressed, the Y.W. has been there. This includes being in the forefront in initiating programs for women returning to the labor market after absences of many years; offering career-oriented workshops for teenagers; and using "Y" buildings which were formerly dormitories as shelters for battered women or as senior citizen centers.[3]

---

[3]Mary M. Gates, "The Changing Role of Women in Voluntarism: Individual Growth and Worth," speech delivered to the Y.W.C.A., Seattle, Washington, February 27, 1981.

REFERENCE TO AUDIENCE

I am honored to have been asked to talk at the University of Dayton today. For one thing, while I lecture at a good many places during the average year, I seldom am asked to talk to students at the home school of one of *my* former students. Most of them probably think that if they never again hear me talk, it will be too soon; so, I want especially to thank Professor Juddi Trent, one of my field's queen bees of rhetorical criticism and political communication, for inviting me here. I'm also more than pleased to be lecturing at Dayton, because you are folks who have been forced to use one of my textbooks. You, of course, have my sympathy. That sympathy is especially strong these days, as I am in the process of revising it. I am right now painfully aware of the fact that you are struggling to understand it; I know I am, as I try to improve the prose, clarify the examples, and increase the amount of practical advice it offers on public speaking.[4]

REFERENCE TO SPEAKER

Life, in this world, is a stunning array of paradoxes. The world we live in is a real world, and we must not allow ourselves to dream that it is anything else.

I will be honest and tell you with more candor than the storyteller that in this world happy endings are not automatic: Cinderella does not always win the handsome prince, the gallant knight does not always manage to save the kingdom, the evil witch is not always thwarted, good does not always overcome evil, and everyone does not always live happily ever after.

Although the world is often cruel and bitter, if you have good sense, if you have courage, if you have integrity, if you believe that there is a power greater than your own, and if you work a little smarter than the next person, you will succeed.

I am an American of Afro heritage . . . .
I knew long ago, when I was a youth, . . .
My parents did not believe that nonsense then or now . . . .[5]

---

[4]Bruce Gronbeck, "Oral Communication Skills in a Technological Age: The Power of Mass Media Is Overrated," speech delivered at the University of Dayton, Dayton, Ohio, March 26, 1981.

[5]Benjamin H. Alexander, "Sense, Courage and Professional Competency: Selling Education," speech delivered to the National Industrial Recreation Association, 40th Annual Conference, Chicago, Illinois, May 9, 1981.

REFERENCE TO LITERATURE

Thank you for this chance to keynote Kent State's honors week events. We gather this week to recognize academic achievement. Oddly, the theme of these proceedings is the approach of 1984, the year George Orwell made a metaphor for totalitarianism. I say "oddly" because the central feature of Orwell's *1984* was the mass mind — whole populations thinking in state-imposed uniformity. Such uniformity strikes me as the antithesis of the individual intellectual excellence that we gather to honor this week, the excellence that Rene Descartes celebrated in saying, "I think, therefore I am."[6]

QUESTIONS TO AUDIENCE

Why are we here to discuss the theme "Rethinking the American Economy"? Why are we perplexed? Doesn't our evident desire to "rethink the economy" indicate a form of dissatisfaction? Furthermore, if the economy we have is not satisfactory, how should we change it? What sort of an economy do we want? How would it differ from what we now have?[7]

QUOTATION AND QUESTION

Speaking as "Poor Richard," Benjamin Franklin once asked, "Who is wise?" His answer, as usual, was both definitive and provocative:
Who is wise?
He that learns from everyone.
He that governs his passions.
He that is content.
Nobody.[8]

---

[6]Alton W. Whitehouse, Jr., "The Misinformation Society: Renewing Our Commitment to the Power of Education," speech delivered at Kent State University Honors Week, Kent, Ohio, April 20, 1981.

[7]Robert H. Edmonds, "Appropriate Economics: The Goals of Zero Inflation and Full Employment," speech delivered at Monterey Peninsula College, Monterey, California, May 17, 1981.

[8]Ronald Roskers, "Who Is Wise? To Learn About Caring," speech delivered at Commencement at the University of Nebraska, Lincoln, Nebraska, May 9, 1981.

ANECDOTE AND QUESTION

I am honored by your invitation but somewhat intimidated at the prospect of sharing ideas with so distinguished a group of engineering professionals. I myself was an engineering major in college but I strayed from the fold — and I'm not sure today that I could tell an orifice flange from a purged peduncle pump!

However, I did learn to tell engineers from chemists at a glance, and that's been helpful in my present job.

The other day, for example, one of our young chemists announced at a luncheon that he had discovered a great new solvent capable of dissolving anything in the world — concrete, steel, glass, plastic . . . anything.

I looked around the table, quickly spotted a senior engineer and he didn't let me down.

"Tell me," he asked the chemist, "when it comes time for storing this revolutionary new solvent, what kind of container do you plan to use?"[9]

ANECDOTE

Before starting my talk, I have a humorous story about diplomacy, which is my subject today. Just after the Russo-Japanese War in 1905–06, Admiral Togo, who had defeated the Imperial Russian fleet at the Tsushima Straits, visited Washington, D.C. The Secretary of State, William Jennings Bryan, did not drink. This posed a problem for the festivities. Bryan, a real diplomat, rose to the occasion. He stood up to toast Admiral Togo and declared: "Admiral, you have won a great victory on water, and therefore I will toast you with water. When you win a similar victory on champagne, I will toast you with champagne."[10]

QUOTATION

In the waning days of his exciting, productive life, Samuel Eliot Morison urged us to face the future resolutely and to adapt boldly to a world in which unsettling change was an ever-present reality.

---

[9]John W. Hanley, "Some Old-Fashioned Responsibilities for Business in America's New Beginning: A Second Chance to Earn the Public's Confidence," speech delivered to the Instrument Society of America, St. Louis, Missouri, March 23, 1981.

[10]Ramon H. Myers, "Options for American Foreign Policy in the 1980s: East Asia," speech delivered before the Inland Southern California World Affairs Council Seminar, Riverside, California, November 14, 1980.

"Have faith," he exhorted. "Hang on! In human affairs there is no harbor, no rest short of the grave. We are forever sailing forth afresh across new and stormy seas, or into outer space."[11]

STARTLING STATEMENT

Ladies and Gentlemen: The security of corporations is seriously threatened by the growing incidence of white collar crime. It's a major national problem. Right now, at this moment while you're listening to me, some 60 to 65 percent of the companies you represent are being ripped off. And I'm being generous, not sensational.

White collar crime, excluding computer and industrial espionage crimes, currently costs this country nearly $70 billion a year! And that's only a guesstimate. It has become a high priority with local law enforcement agencies in the country, and ranks as one of the three top programs for the FBI. The Assistant Director of the FBI's Criminal Investigative Division recently reported that there are almost 16,000 white collar crimes — including 1,100 cases of public corruption — now pending nationwide.

The new emphasis is proving effective. Last year the FBI recorded more than 3,000 convictions, recovered $60 million, and prevented almost $1 billion in losses. But white collar crimes are increasing almost as fast as the efforts to combat them.[12]

HISTORICAL REFERENCE

When Henry Barnard was named the first U.S. Commissioner of Education 112 years ago, he had just one assignment to fulfill. His job, according to the law, was to report to Congress on the condition of education in America. They say it took him 18 months and 700 pages to prepare his first report.

This morning my goals are much more modest. I'll spare you my own 700-page report and limit my remarks to some personal reflections about the strengths and weaknesses of public education.

First, since coming to Washington two and a half years ago, I've deepened my conviction that Federal programs in support of education can make a difference.

---

[11]Elliot L. Richardson, "National Security: The Law of the Sea," speech delivered at the launching of the USS Samuel E. Morison, Bath, Maine, July 14, 1979.

[12]Herchell Britton, "The Serious Threats of White Collar Crime: What Can You Do?," speech delivered to the Executives Club of Chicago, Chicago, Illinois, November 14, 1980.

Consider, for example, the impact of *vocational education* legislation enacted over 60 years ago.[13]

CENTRAL IDEA

I welcome this opportunity to speak to the people in the front lines of private sector employment issues. And I am here to stress that the central human resources issue of the 1980s is the issue of equal opportunity.

My thesis is a simple one. It can be summed up briefly.

Black people have suffered discrimination in the past. They still suffer from the effects of past discrimination combined with continuing discrimination based on negative stereotypes and irrational prejudices. That disadvantage must be overcome through vigorous affirmative action programs.

There can be no doubt that such programs are necessary. There are advocates of the proposition that black progress has been so sweeping that special efforts are no longer necessary. They have met with favor from people who want to hear that message, for it is a message that absolves employers from making costly and inconvenient changes in their operating procedures.

But relatively few blacks have made the kind of progress that should induce complacency. And even among those that have benefitted, the jury is still out. Indeed, there is widespread belief among blacks in managerial positions that there is a firm ceiling on their future prospects, that their white peers will move out of middle management and into the upper levels while they remain behind.[14]

STATISTICS

Mr. President, Mr. Speaker, fellow delegates, colleagues and friends: I stand before you today not only as your president-elect, but also as a dean and as a professor. As a professor, I am programmed, once started, to speak for fifty-five minutes. However, I have been reminded that the story of the creation of the world is told in Genesis in 400 words, that the world's greatest moral code, the Ten Commandments, contains only 297 words, that

---

[13]Ernest L. Boyer, "Public Confidence in Education: The Lack of Vision and Ideas," speech delivered at Washington, D.C., May 17, 1979.

[14]Vernon E. Jordan, "Where Is This Black Progress? Negative Stereotypes and Irrational Prejudices," speech delivered at an American Society for Personnel Administration Conference, Milwaukee, Wisconsin, July 18, 1979.

Lincoln's immortal Gettysburg Address is but 266 words in length and that the Declaration of Independence required but 1,321 words to set up for the world a new concept of freedom. I think I get the point.[15]

CONCLUSION OF YOUR TALK

With your main discussion and introduction ready to go, you should be all set to work out a conclusion. Two cautions are in order: (1) A conclusion should not drag on and on. (2) It should not contain any new material.

Here are some ideas to incorporate in your conclusion:

1. Summary of key ideas

2. A prediction

3. A quotation, either emotional or factual

4. A quotation from literature

5. A quotation from an authority

6. An anecdote or question, or both

All the above suggestions are illustrated in the following conclusions from actual speeches.

SUMMARY OF KEY IDEAS

In conclusion, I feel sure that these programs of communication are proving of great benefit to both managers and employees. Even if they were expensive, *which they are not,* it would still be worth it. *The cost of economic ignorance would be much, much greater.* After all, better communication reaps the following benefits for a corporation:

— Employees know decisions and the reasons for them
— Less misunderstandings occur
— The possibility of cooperation with change is greatly increased
— The damaging effects of rumor are lessened
— The role of management is reinforced

---

[15]C. John Tupper, "A New American Revolution: 'Do Your Own Thing vs. Guaranteeism,' " speech delivered before the California Medical Association, Los Angeles, California, March 12, 1979.

Managers, union leaders and rank-and-file employees readily understand the need for these improvements in their relationships. And, as the Japanese have proved, whether working with their own nationals, or American or Australian workers, employee understanding and involvement works for everybody's benefit. Certainly we are experiencing these benefits in some corporations in Australia.

Enterprise Australia is proud to have contributed toward these advancements in employee communication.[16]

A PREDICTION

The Urban Transportation Future

Where does this leave us? I wish I could conclude with a flourish, evoking some grand Tofflerian vision of accelerating future and captivating you with images of exotic technology and effortless movement in the city of tomorrow.

In reality, I believe, we will evolve along a more conventional and prosaic trajectory. Barring some cataclysmic developments on the energy front, the automobile is likely to remain the preferred means of transportation of most Americans well into the next century — although, as we have noted, it will be a vehicle vastly different in design and performance. At the same time, public transportation — or, I should say, *collective* transportation — will assume a much more significant role in our daily lives. Transit of tomorrow will have more varied forms and utilize a wider range of vehicles, service modes, and operating arrangements, as it tries to serve a broader, more differentiated market.

While public transportation will tend to become more flexible and personalized, the automobile will . . . .

Rail transit of the surface variety may . . . .

Finally, pedestrians will have regained some of the territory they lost to the automobile during the last fifty years, as cities and suburbs impose more stringent requirements on the use of cars in congested centers and residential neighborhoods.

And — oh yes — we will still have rush-hour traffic and potholes. They will be there to remind us of the good old days, back in the late 1980's, when gasoline was still only one dollar/

---

[16]J. T. Keavney, "Australia: Turning Away from Socialism," speech delivered to the Board of Trustees of the American Economic Foundation, New York City, New York, January 19, 1981.

gallon, when parking in government buildings was still free, and when one could still afford the luxury of driving to work in one's own automobile.[17]

You might conclude with a prediction for the future.

A QUOTATION, EITHER EMOTIONAL OR FACTUAL

In conclusion, we need to be reminded of the famous words of the Protestant minister who recounted the prevailing attitude during the Holocaust:

". . . They came first for the Communists, and I didn't
    speak up because I wasn't a Communist.
Then they came for the Jews,
    and I didn't speak up because I wasn't a Jew.
Then they came for the trade unionists,

[17]C. Kenneth Ovski, "Urban Transportation: A Profile of the Future," speech delivered at the NASA Colloquium on Profiles of the Future, Washington, D.C., September 11, 1979.

and I didn't speak up because I wasn't a trade unionist.
Then they came for the Catholics,
and I didn't speak up because I was a Protestant.
Then they came for me,
and by that time no one was left to speak."

Thank you.[18]

A QUOTATION FROM LITERATURE

The late George Bernard Shaw once wrote, "Nothing is worth doing unless the consequences could be serious."

By that or any other measure, this is a job worth doing — for this nation's older citizens, for the business community, and for our nation itself.[19]

QUOTATION FROM AN AUTHORITY

I want to conclude my talk by quoting in its entirety a brief but, I think, superb exposition of what I've been trying to say. The author is Leo Rosten, and, believe it or not, I once worked with him too. He called his little essay *The Power of Words*, and it goes like this:

"They sing. They hurt. They teach. They sanctify. They were man's first immeasurable feat of magic. They liberated us from ignorance and our barbarous past. For without these marvelous scribbles which build letters into words, words into sentences, sentences into systems and sciences and creeds, man would be forever confined to the self-isolated prison of the scuttlefish or the chimpanzee. 'A picture is worth 10,000 words,' goes the timeworn Chinese maxim. 'But,' one writer tartly said, 'it takes words to say that.' We live by words: Love, Truth, God. We fight for words: Freedom, Country, Fame. We die for words: Liberty, Glory, Honor. They bestow the priceless gift of articulateness on our minds and

---

[18]R. Y. Woodhouse, "Equality Faces a Dangerous Decade: Defend Our Beliefs and Speak Out," speech delivered at the Naval Supply Systems Command Human Resource Management Conference, Seattle, Washington, November 18, 1980.

[19]M. H. Beach, "Business and the Graying of America: Opportunities for Older People," speech delivered before the National Council on the Aging Annual Conference, Nashville, Tennessee, March 29, 1981.

hearts — from 'Mama' to 'infinity.' And the men who truly shape our destiny, the giants who teach us, inspire us, lead us to deeds of immortality, are those who use words with clarity, grandeur and passion. Socrates, Jesus, Luther, Lincoln, Churchill."

The power of words . . .[20]

AN ANECDOTE OR QUESTION, OR BOTH

And I'll close with a true story to illustrate how we *are* set apart and what our values really are. During the days of the Soviet triumph with their first Sputnik, a grade school class in Russia was discussing that remarkable feat — eclipsing the whole world in scientific genius. The teacher asked the class if they were thrilled with the prospect of a Russian satellite probing space and perhaps some day landing a Russian on the moon.

The class smiled with pride and agreed it would be a great achievement to go to the moon. But one thoughtful student broke the silence and spoke a different kind of response.

"Yes, it would be wonderful to go to the moon," he said. "But I would like to know — when may we go to Vienna?"[21]

THE TITLE OF YOUR TALK

Just as every book has a title and every newspaper story a headline, so every talk should have a title. Your title is an ad, a billboard for your speech. And audiences generally appreciate knowing immediately what they are about to hear rather than waiting to find out what the message is. If you can imagine a movie without a title, you can appreciate the importance of a title.

Usually, the most propitious time to consider a title is after you've developed the main ideas of your speech. It's possible, however, that during the process of building the introduction,

---

[20]Melvin J. Grayson, "The Last Best Hope: Words," speech delivered to the Society of Consumer Affairs Professionals in Business, New York, New York, April 3, 1981.

[21]Harvey C. Jacobs, "Finding Your Way Through the Words: It's a Lifelong Challenge," speech delivered at the Defense Information School, Fort Benjamin Harrison, Indianapolis, Indiana, January 24, 1981.

body, and conclusion of your talk, a striking title may suddenly appear, seemingly out of nowhere. If it does, you're lucky. If it doesn't, try to create one that meets these criteria:

1. It should be provocative enough to pique your listeners' interest.

2. It should be short and simple, say from three to ten words.

3. It should indicate the purpose and content of your talk.

A striking title may suddenly appear.

Following are titles from the journal *Vital Speeches* as well as from talks given by some of our students. These titles are preceded by a listing of their most unusual traits.

Trait	**Title**
Questions	"Who's Got the Energy?" "Where Is This Black Progress?" "What Can American Industry Learn from the Japanese?"
A new twist on a book title	"Braving a New World"
A new twist on an ad slogan	"Pave Now, Pay Later" "Come to Where the Favor Is. Come to High Tech Country."
Fairy tale opener	"Once Upon a Time"
A sentence	"A Humanist Views the World Hunger Problem." "Despite Everything We Have Reason for Confidence."
Startling statements	"Here Comes World War III" "Raising Corn and Beans and Hell" "Higher Education Is a Fraud"
Alliteration	"Women and Work" "Change and Challenge" "Communication and Credibility"
Brevity	"Welcome Home" (Pres. Reagan to former Iranian prisoners) "What Now?"
An unusual statement	"Can't Nobody Here Use This Language?" "Almost Nobody Writes Silence Anymore" "How the Truth Becomes a Lie"
Words that rhyme	"Town and Gown" "Taxation Without Representation" "TV's Jiggle and Wiggle"
Words from a foreign language	"Whatever Happened to Ceteris Paribus?"

A play on words

"Today's Dollar Doesn't Make Much Cents"

"How Secure Is Our Social Security?"

"If You Don't Think <u>Dieting</u> Is Serious Business — What Do Its First Three Letters Spell?"

TRANSITIONS OR CONNECTING LINKS

Just as a brick wall needs cement to hold it together, so a speech needs something to hold it together. That "something" is transitions — statements, questions, or phrases that connect the introduction to the body and the body to the conclusion. Transitions also show the relationships between ideas.

You use transitions in daily interpersonal communication, but when you speak to a group, you may tend to forget them. Don't. They help your listeners follow your train of thought and thus make your communication task easier. Below is a list of some transitional phrases and conditions that call for their use:

To Indicate	Use These Transitions
Place	Adjacent to, on the opposite side, diagonally across, diametrically opposite
Time	After a few hours, meanwhile, in the meantime, afterward, immediately, earlier, later, then
Purpose	For this reason, to this end, with this goal
Concession	Of course, to be sure, naturally
Comparison and contrast	On the other hand, nevertheless, on the contrary, in contrast, in the same way, conversely, however, in like manner, similarly, whereas
Summary or repetition	In other words, to review briefly, in short, on the whole, to sum up, as previously noted, here again, in summary, in brief, if I may repeat
Explanation	For example, in particular, more specifically

Addition	Furthermore, in the second place, besides, moreover, again, in addition, equally important, finally, also
Cause or result	On that account, therefore, as a result, thereupon, for this reason, consequently, accordingly, under these conditions, hence
Conditions	Although, because, even though, since, if, unless, under these circumstances, nevertheless, otherwise, this being so

When you complete your introduction, the right connecting links can help you move smoothly into the body of your talk. The same principle applies when you cross over from the body to the conclusion. Remember, also, that asking a question or two can lead you and your listeners comfortably into the next phase of your speech.

Summing up, then, transitions afford you the means to "telegraph" to your audience that:

1. The introduction is over and you're swinging into the body.

2. The body is over and you're moving into the conclusion.

3. The conclusion is almost over and you're ready to answer questions or to sit down.

"PRACTICE IS NINE-TENTHS"

You've just studied the major steps in preparing a talk, but one critical step still remains before you face your audience — rehearsal.

Facing an audience is not theory. It's your moment of truth, and there's no better way to prepare for that moment than to practice aloud beforehand. Many beginning speakers skip this exercise and then regret it. Ralph Waldo Emerson, the "Sage of Concord," struck the bull's-eye when he said, "Practice is nine-tenths."[22] He knew the truth of that aphorism because he made outstanding speeches in public for fifty years.

---

[22]Emerson, "Power," *The Conduct of Life* (1860).

Preparation and practice are the keys to successful speaking. In 1962 President John F. Kennedy made a historic speech in Berlin (see Appendix B). The following four words in that address helped to win over the Germans: *"Ich bin ein Berliner"* ("I am a Berliner"). JFK practiced at least ten minutes to master the German accent in its two-second delivery. And a half-million Berliners exploded with tumultuous approval during the speech.

Try to give your talk to at least one person who will listen and offer a suggestion or two. If you can't find a volunteer, use a tape recorder (a videotape recorder is even better because you see and hear yourself as an audience does), and then listen to the playback. It's a sobering and educational experience. Another idea is to speak in front of a mirror; you'll benefit from this once you get over feeling self-conscious about doing it.

You have three choices for practice — a live audience, a tape recorder (audio or video), or a mirror. In fact, why not use all three? Whichever method you choose, PRACTICE before you face your audience.

If you can't find a volunteer . . . .

THINGS TO THINK ABOUT AND DO

1. Give the class an example of a sentence outline and a topic outline. Explain why you prefer one over the other.

2. List several titles of speeches you consider outstanding. Explain why you consider them as such.

3. Prepare a short talk on any subject you may give in class and then write an outline. Don't forget the title.

4. Share with the class a very effective speech introduction you've recently heard and explain why it was so effective.

WHAT DO YOU REMEMBER FROM THIS CHAPTER?

1. Why should you outline your talk?

2. Describe the two principal types of outlines.

3. List a few ingredients of a good title.

4. What are the chief purposes of an introduction?

5. List several approaches you can use in your introduction.

6. Explain the main parts of a speech.

7. List some ways you can arrange your main points.

8. Mention a few ways to prove your main points.

9. What elements should be present in a conclusion?

10. Why should you use transitions?

VITALIZE YOUR VOCABULARY

Computers and Data Processing

access time (n.)   the time it takes a computer to locate a bit of data and deliver it to the user.

alphanumeric (adj.)   indicates a coding system consisting of letters, numbers, and punctuation symbols; a contraction of "alphabetic" and "numeric."

binary (adj.)   a numbering system based on 2's (rather than 10's) that uses only the digits 0 and 1.

block diagram (n.)   a chart showing sequences of computer operation as represented by boxes and interconnecting lines; same as flow chart.

bug (n.)   a mistake in the design of a program or computer.

central processor (n.)   the computing center of a computer; also called central processing unit (CPU).

COBOL (n.)   (COmmon Business Oriented Language) a programming language using basic English phrases and designed for business applications.

debug (v.)   to find and correct mistakes in the design of a program or computer.

downtime (n.)   the period when a computer is malfunctioning.

flow chart (n.)   see block diagram.

FORTRAN (n.)   (FORmula TRANslation) a programming system that converts mathematical statements into computer language.

hardware (n.)   the mechanical, magnetic, electrical, and electronic components of a computer system.

input (n.)   information fed into a computer; may be instructions to direct the computer, or data to be processed by the computer.

language (n.)   a system of communication between computer and user.

magnetic disk (n.)   a flat circular plate with a surface that can be magnetized to store information in binary form.

magnetic drum (n.)   a rotating cylinder with a surface that can be magnetized to store information in binary form.

magnetic tape (n.)   metal or plastic tape coated with a surface that can be magnetized to store information in binary form.

microsecond (n.)   one-millionth of a second, a measurement of computer operating speed.

millisecond (n.)   one-thousandth of a second, a measurement of computer operating speed.

output (n.)   information passed by a computer and fed to external devices that produce tape, cards, etc.

peripheral equipment (n.)   physically independent machines that work with the central processor, such as high-speed printers, card reader-punches, magnetic tape units, etc.

program (n.)   a series of instructions that tell the computer how to process data; (v.) to prepare such a program.

real-time processing (n.)   data processing performed during a business transaction, i.e., an airline ticket agent may consult a computer about available seats while you wait.

software (n.)   programming techniques developed for the most efficient use of a computer.

time sharing (n.)   using a computer to process requests of many independent users at the same time.

9

Know Your Listeners and Speak Their Language

You will be successful only to the extent that you cast your thought in accordance with the make-up of your forum.[1]

CHAPTER OBJECTIVES

After reading and understanding this chapter, you should know:

- Some ways to research your audience.
- Some differences between oral and written communication.
- How to use words that motivate people.
- How to improve your oral style.

CHAPTER DIGEST

The words and sentences that flesh out your thoughts, feelings, and opinions critically influence your total impact on your audience. For that reason, audience analysis should rate top priority in preparing for any oral interpersonal situation. Several ideas are given to help you with that analysis.

---

[1]Cicero, *Paradoxa Stoicorum* (46 B.C.).

Your career can be helped or hindered by the way you use words in speech. Some examples of the power of words are sprinkled throughout the chapter. Many different kinds of words are discussed: specific and abstract words, short and pretentious words, loaded words, clichés, and slang.

Next, oral communication and written communication are compared. They share traits such as clarity, accuracy, and appropriateness, but you should always be aware of differences between the two methods.

As for sentences, some suggestions are advanced regarding their length, structure, and human warmth. Again, real-life examples spice up the text.

The chapter closes with several steps for developing your use of language to its full potential.

AUDIENCE ANALYSIS

The level of language you use in a speech should reflect to a great degree the kind of audience listening to it. The more you know about the audience, the better you will communicate. There are several questions to ask about it and to try to answer.

Is the gathering large or small? Is it all male, all female, or mixed, and what percentage mixed? Is it a random audience, or do they all belong to one organization? What's the average age — twenty, forty, or sixty? Age is a very important factor to consider. You would not use the same language to twenty-year-olds as you would to senior citizens.

What about social, economic, and educational strata? If you were talking to a group of unemployed high-school dropouts and to a group of successful business people, your language, to be effective, would have to be geared to their educational back-grounds.

Religion, political affiliation, race, and national origin are crit-ically important elements to evaluate when you face the challenge of speaking your listeners' language. To an American audience the word *bloody* is just another adjective; to an English audience, it is tasteless profanity.

Know your audience and speak their language.

SOME WAYS TO RESEARCH YOUR AUDIENCE

Remember that the reason you're seeking audience information is to be better able to communicate your message in language they understand. The more you know of your audience, the better you'll be able to adapt what you have to say. (For more on audience analysis, see Chapter 12.)

If you don't have this firsthand knowledge of your audience, here are several suggestions for rounding it up:

- Contact officers or members of the group either by mail or telephone. Talk to the person who invited you to speak.

- Contact other people who have spoken recently before the group. A wealth of information can be obtained in this manner.

- Perhaps you have a friend in the organization who may invite you to attend a meeting. In this way you can experience the group firsthand.

- Sometimes you may acquire information from newspapers, magazines, or newsletters.

No greater opportunity exists that will enable you to analyze an audience than that right here in your speech class. Recall Chapter 4, "Your First Talk," in which everyone talks about himself or herself for a few minutes. There is no better way to get to know your class members than through this exercise.

LANGUAGE AND YOUR FUTURE

You can have a powerful delivery, an expressive voice, an attractive appearance, and thorough knowledge of your subject, but if your words are poorly chosen, your speech will fail to communicate.

With the right words, you can communicate your thoughts, your feelings, and your emotions. With the right words you can teach people, give them understanding, entertain them, persuade them to change attitudes, and even persuade them to do your bidding. But before you can do any of that, you should learn as much as possible about words.

Words are double-edged tools of communication that can both help you and hurt you. They can make you happy or miserable, they can inspire you or depress you, they can propel you toward a full, useful life, or they can hinder your progress. Whoever said, "Sticks and stones may break my bones, but words will never hurt me" lived in a world of fantasy, not in the real world of men and women, of love and hate, of success and failure, of hope and despair, of honesty and crookedness.

In the 1976 Democratic presidential primaries, Governor Jimmy Carter said: "I see nothing wrong with ethnic purity being maintained" (in the suburbs). The expression "ethnic purity" outraged millions of black and liberal voters, and it shook up his smoothly functioning campaign. Carter later apologized for those words.

Eight years earlier, a similar incident occurred in the Republican presidential primaries. This time, however, it ended in a shambles for George Romney, governor of Michigan and a powerful candidate. Powerful, that is, until he said that the White House had "brainwashed" him regarding Vietnam. That one word torpedoed Romney's campaign for the nomination, because anyone who could be brainwashed is not shrewd enough and not strong enough to be president of the United States.

The way you use words will peg you in people's minds. From your words people will form opinions of your education, intelligence, and character as well as your economic and social status. You may be highly intelligent, but if you trample on the English language, almost all intelligent, educated listeners will probably write you off as someone who's not going anywhere, someone who's a loser. And that can hurt you.

Mangling the language will place you in a predicament similar to that faced by Commodore Cornelius Vanderbilt, a nineteenth-century American shipping and railroad tycoon. Because he had little formal education, he was embarrassed when he had to deal with "all them British lords. I know I am smarter than they are," he said, "but they sound smarter." Tape-record yourself sometime, and consider how your language sounds.

Before discussing words and their ways, let's first compare the oral and written word.

"Sorry, we don't need no grammar books."

COMPARING AND CONTRASTING ORAL AND WRITTEN COMMUNICATION

There are many differences between communicating in writing and communicating in speech — one to one or one to many. Because talking is face-to-face and personal, it is much more direct than writing. Hand and body gestures, facial expressions, and vocal variety help greatly to support face-to-face communication. It is also reinforced by instant feedback from listeners in the form of smiles, frowns, applause, catcalls, clenched fists, and so on. An alert speaker who is sensitive to feedback can "shift gears" and adapt to changing circumstances.

Writing, however, depends solely on words and punctuation to deliver the message. There are no gestures and no voice, and if there is any feedback, it takes time to reach the writer.

Good talking is wordy, repetitive, and far less structured than efficient writing. (Perhaps that's why so many more people find talking well easier than writing well.) A good speech, reproduced word for word on paper, usually does not read well because it rambles and repeats words and thoughts. It is not nearly as disciplined and organized as good writing.

Effective talking is aimed at people's minds and hearts through their ears, and ears prefer short, direct, conversational sentences. Long, involved sentences are acceptable in writing for two reasons: (1) The eye can absorb many more words in an instant than a speaker can say. (2) If a reader stumbles on a marathon sentence, he can reread it at leisure. Not so with the spoken words — once uttered they're gone, especially in a speech. If a listener misses a sentence, both she and the speaker have lost part of the message; there is no going back, except perhaps during the question-and-answer period. In a conversation, of course, the listener can ask the speaker to repeat. The following table summarizes and adds insight into the differences between speaking and writing.

Speaking	Writing
Wordy, repetitive	Concise, seldom repetitive
Tends to wander around topic	Better organized, sticks to topic, more relevant
Sentence length — roughly 5 to 20 words	Sentences usually longer

Speaking	Writing
Sentence structure — usually simple S-V-O (subject-verb-object) sequence	More compound, complex, compound-complex sentences
Style — often informal, may be spiced with slang, contractions, sentence fragments	More formal — very little slang, if any; few contractions and sentence fragments, if any
Depends heavily on personal pronouns — we, us, you, they, them, I, me	Depends less on personal pronouns
Is reinforced with facial and vocal expressions; hand, arm, body gestures	Depends on words and punctuation to get message across; format or layout may help
Feedback — usually instantaneous	Feedback may take days, weeks, or longer
Transitions — verbal are same as in writing; pauses and change in body position can signify a new topic coming up	Verbal transitions — same
Can be marred with vocalized pauses — "er, ah, like, ya know"	No equivalent distractions
Planned strategic pauses can produce a powerful effect	No verbal equivalent
Words — uses more concrete words and shorter words	Tends to be more abstract and polysyllabic
Tends to repeat and restate more	

Now let's focus on three standards that apply equally to talking and writing — clarity, accuracy, and appropriateness.

CLARITY

If the audience doesn't understand the message instantly, then the speaker has, to some extent, failed. Thus, every possible measure must be taken to ensure that all her words and thoughts are perfectly clear to the audience.

Throughout your talk, words are your prime means for helping your audience understand your message. And to harness the profound power of words, you should use a dictionary and a thesaurus. If you do not exploit these resources, you will fail to achieve your full potential as a speaker and conversationalist. (Words are discussed later in this chapter.)

Other devices that will help you achieve clarity in your talk are summaries and transitions. If your talk consists of three well-researched major points, list those points in your introduction so your audience will know at once what ground you will cover. Discuss them in depth, summarize them at the end of your talk, and emphasize any conclusions that they lead to; an example of such an ending is given in Chapter 8.

Another aid to clarity is the use of transitions — words that indicate the connections between ideas — which show whether you are continuing in the same vein or are about to shift to another topic. (Transitions are covered in more detail in Chapter 8 and many are tabulated there.)

A common speaking fault is failing to define technical terms or jargon. For example, one of my students (AJV) gave what could have been an interesting talk on his profitable hobby. He is a disc jockey and conducts record hops for colleges and various organizations. During his presentation he frequently used esoteric terminology like pots, cans, fade, segue, equalizer, DBs, mixer, and control board. As a result, very few students understood what he was talking about.

Most hobbies, professions, trades, and sports have their own language, vernacular, shop talk, or jargon. Whether your subject is plumbing, carpentry, auto mechanics, sports, journalism, cooking, ceramics, or law, you must realize that the audience may not be familiar with your subject. You should, therefore, be prepared to explain uncommon terms and also to ask if they understand your language.

Confucius, the Chinese philosopher, said it all 2400 years ago: "In language clearness is everything."

ACCURACY

As a conscientious speaker, your information should be as current and as accurate as research can make it. The surest and quickest way for you to damage your credibility is to spew forth misinformation.

How many times have you seen a story, a name, an important fact, or a charge against some person retracted in newspapers? Unfortunately, the damage was done when this misinformation first appeared in print. Such unwarranted embarrassment and mental anguish could have been avoided if someone had taken the time to recheck facts. If your talk is on a current or crucial topic, do your homework and come armed with quotations and sources to fortify your facts.

"In language clearness is everything."

APPROPRIATENESS

In addition to being precise, the language should also be suitable to the subject, audience, and occasion. For example, a speaker who's addressing a Parent-Teacher Association should avoid the statistical and psychological jargon of advanced educational researchers. By the same token, she should not indulge in teen-age slang. Any speaker worth her salt will analyze her audience first and adapt her language accordingly. (See Chapter 12 and the introduction to this chapter.)

COMMAND OF THE LANGUAGE

We are concerned here with one goal — to catch, capture, and condense some insights and practices of the best oral communicators. From them we can learn a great deal about using words to get results.

What follows is not the Ten Commandments on using language, but rather guidelines or suggestions on how to generate maximum power in your command of the language.

CONCRETE, SPECIFIC WORDS VERSUS ABSTRACT WORDS

For informative speaking, there is no question that concrete, specific words carry a message most effectively. Concrete words stand for things that we can see, hear, touch, taste, and smell. When you're hungry, what does the mouth-watering aroma of a Thanksgiving turkey and stuffing simmering in the oven do to your appetite? And at the dinner table when your eyes feast on the golden brown bird glistening and dripping in thick, rich gravy, is your appetite cranked up?

If parallel construction can be built into a sentence of such words, the emotional impact can be intensified.

Here are two statements composed of concrete, specific, vivid words strengthened and made immortal with parallel construction. In 1933 President Franklin D. Roosevelt said to the Depression-battered American people:

> I see one-third of a nation ill-housed, ill-clad, ill-nourished.

Early in World War II, Prime Minister Winston Churchill declared to the English people, staggering under military setbacks and facing conquest by Hitler's Germany:

> . . . we shall fight on the beaches, we shall fight on the landing grounds, we shall fight in the fields and on the streets, we shall fight in the hills; we shall never surrender.

Note the striking force of these sentences. Note that the words are short and specific and that they permit instant understanding. Not even one abstract, nebulous word emasculates those sentences.

Here are some examples of concrete and specific words:

Flood	Drought	Life
Politician	Hot	Death
Taxes	Cold	Sickness
Famine	Mortgage	Harassment
Gun	Bomb	Crash
Rent	Shoot	Burn

You cannot, of course, avoid abstract words in interpersonal communication. Sometimes they're necessary and serve a worthwhile purpose, but remember that they're subject to various interpretations and arguments depending on people's backgrounds, religions, education, nationality, and so on. For example, when you speak of our democracy, you mean a particular kind of government. When citizens of the German Democratic Republic (East Germany) speak of democracy, they mean another kind of government. Yet, you're both using the same word — democracy.

Democracy — whose?

Abstract words stand for ideas or concepts, things that you cannot touch, taste, see, hear, or feel. Here are some examples:

Freedom	Fascism	Morality	Compassion
Liberty	Justice	Character	Love
Democracy	Patriotism	Goodness	Beauty
Communism	Honesty	Sin	

SHORT, SIMPLE WORDS VERSUS SHOWY $5.00 WORDS

Again, for the purpose of informing your listeners, the simple, one- or two-syllable words are usually better suited. A notable exception is Lincoln's Gettysburg Address. He delivered it, not to inform people but to inspire them. Of its 265 words, 195 consist of one syllable.

Yet, some audiences prefer longer, more elegant words. The more you know about your audience, the better you can judge what kinds of words to use. Here is a sample listing of what some people refer to as pompous and pretentious words, together with their simple, direct equivalents:

Showy, polysyllabic words	Short, direct equivalents
Ablution	Washing
Ameliorate	Improve
Assimilate	Absorb, digest
Cognizant of	Aware of
Conflagration	Fire
Consolidate	Unite, combine
Contiguous with	Touching
Delineate	Describe
Designation	Name
Effectuate	Carry out
Enumerate	Count, list
Facilitate	Make easy, simplify
Expedite	Speed up
Incombustible	Fireproof
Initiate, institute	Begin, start
Innocuous	Harmless
Modification	Change
Optimum	Best
Progenitor	Forerunner
Subsequent to	Later, next
Termination	End

A glaring example of pompous, inappropriate language was given by the former United States ambassador to Great Britain, Walter H. Annenberg, when he was presented to Queen Elizabeth. She asked him a simple question about his housing arrangements and he replied: "We are in the ambassadorial residence subject, of course, to some of the discomfiture as a result of the need for elements of refurbishing and rehabilitation." He might have said, "We're redecorating now so the house is a bit messy."[2]

Another striking example of pedantic verbosity appears below in a letter from a Houston, Texas, high school principal to a student's father:

> Our school's cross-graded, multi-ethnic, individualized learning program is designed to enhance the concept of an open-ended learning program with emphasis on a continuum of multi-ethnic, academically enriched learning using the identified intellectually gifted child as the agent or director of his own learning.
>
> Major emphasis is on cross-graded, multi-ethnic learning with the main objective being to learn respect for the uniqueness of a person.

The parent wrote the principal:

> I have a college degree, speak two foreign languages and four Indian dialects, have been to a number of county fairs and three goat ropings, but I haven't the faintest idea as to what the hell you are talking about. Do you?[3]

LOADED WORDS

Some words that concern race, religion, politics, and personal character can provoke heated and sometimes overpowering reactions. Loaded words can either infuriate or humiliate people, and they can induce people to commit irrational acts. Loaded words are like a loaded gun; they can cause devastating damage. Here are examples of words that spell potential *danger* to you and to others:

Race or Religion

Whitey	Nigger	Chink	Hebe
Honky	Oreo	Jap	Kike
Racist	Uncle Tom	Wasp	Fish-eater

---

[2]Barbara Walters, *How to Talk with Practically Anybody About Practically Anything* (Garden City, N.Y.: Doubleday, 1970), p. 136.

[3]*Boston Sunday Herald American*, 6 Feb 1977.

"Conflagration!"

Nationality

Gringo	Frog
Spic	Hun
Harp	Polack
Wop	Slant-eyes
Dago	

Political Philosophy

Radical	Nazi
Anarchist	Fascist
Revolutionary	Communist
Imperialist	Right wing
Reactionary	Left wing

Whereas the above words are extreme in their potential for trouble, there are other words and their synonyms that can either be complimentary or belittling. Here are some examples:

Slender — skinny	Cocktail lounge — bar
Inexpensive — cheap	Discriminating — finicky
Imported — foreign	Deliberate — indecisive
Prudent — stingy	Courageous — reckless
Pre-owned — used	Overweight — fat

In some situations your choice of words can either make or break you. Think before you speak.

CLICHÉS

Clichés are expressions that have been kicked around so often that they are now shopworn, threadbare, and meaningless. Since they reflect a sparse vocabulary and a pallid imagination, avoid them at all costs. Below are a few examples:

Tough as nails	Goes without saying
Leave no stone unturned	By leaps and bounds
Last but not least	Lean over backward
In the final analysis	Equal to the occasion
Sweet as honey	Slept like a log

SLANG

The use of slang depends largely on the occasion of your talk and on the relationship between you and the audience. At a formal or even semiformal affair, slang would violate good taste even if you know almost all the guests. In any case, it's important to resist the temptation to overuse slang; too much of it will degrade any talk.

VOCALIZED PAUSES, OR THE PAUSE THAT IRRITATES

Far too many speakers can't endure a moment of silence. Either from nervousness or habit or both, they fill pauses with sounds like "er, ah, um, OK, right, you know, or something." Very often they're not even aware that they're making these sounds.

If you tend to sputter during pauses, don't despair. Become conscious of it, concentrate on conquering it, and try to keep your mouth closed during pauses. Here again, perseverance pays off. (For more on pauses, see Chapter 5.)

WHAT ABOUT SENTENCES?

The subject of sentences received some attention in the comparison of oral and written styles. What else need be said about spoken sentences? By all means, they should be of different lengths, mostly short, say from five to twenty words. These figures are merely estimates that stress the vital importance of short, conversational sentences.

Varied structure is another vital aspect. Try to avoid composing all your sentences in the same form. More than half your sentences can follow the conventional *subject-verb-object* pattern, but if *all* of them are structured like that, you may lull your listeners to sleep.

In his immortal Gettysburg Address, Abraham Lincoln pointed up a third valuable lesson, that of the personal, human approach. Even though the occasion was most solemn, the dedication of a national cemetery, he reached out and touched his listeners with noble ideas clothed in personal pronouns and nouns in every sentence: ". . . our fathers, we, us, they, the brave men, living and dead, who struggled here, of the people, by the people, for the people . . ." These words breathe life and humanity into communication; use them.

Your thoughts and the way you phrase them are often influenced by context, by surrounding circumstances, and by events preceding your talk. A relevant example is the attention-getting introduction often used by Jimmy Carter in the 1976 Democratic presidential primary campaign. In 1976, Watergate, the worst political scandal in United States history, dominated American newscasts and newspapers. And the principal perpetrators of that shame were mainly lawyers based in Washington, D.C. Here are the opening remarks of many of Carter's campaign speeches:

> Hi, I'm Jimmy Carter and I'm running for president. I am not a lawyer. And I am not from Washington, D.C.

Also, in his vote-winning speeches Carter said something that struck a responsive chord among Americans wearied and angered by deceit in high office:

> I will not lie to you.

He communicated — and the voters sent him to the White House.

Short personal sentences can be very convincing.

One more outstanding introduction comes to mind, the one used occasionally by President Harry S. Truman in the nip-and-tuck presidential campaign of 1948. The pollsters tabbed him as a loser to Republican nominee, Thomas E. Dewey, governor of New York. Here is Truman's no-nonsense, no-doubletalk introduction:

> My name is Truman, I'm President of the United States, and I'm trying to keep my job.

He communicated — and the voters sent him back to the White House.

A third example of a blockbusting one-liner, was Governor Reagan's closing question to the voters in the televised debate with President Carter:

> On election day ask yourself, "Am I better off today than I was four years ago?"

He communicated — and the voters sent him to the White House.

HOW TO IMPROVE YOUR ORAL STYLE

If you feel, as many people do, that great speakers are born and not made, consider Ralph Waldo Emerson's words, "All the great speakers were bad speakers at first." Unique proof of his words was the acceptance speech delivered by then President Gerald Ford at the Republican National Convention in August, 1976. It was "the best speech of my life." It electrified the delegates and gave them hope of victory. It changed Ford's lifelong image of a bumbling, stolid, lackluster speaker to a powerful, dynamic, fighting-mad speaker who could inspire an audience.

How did he do it?

First of all, the speech was planned for many weeks. President Ford spent more time rewording and polishing it than any speech he had ever given in his thirty-seven-year political career. For two weeks, with the aid of a speech coach, he practiced delivering it. In addition, he went through two complete videotaped rehearsals, always concentrating on delivery. As a result of all this work, he was able to maintain almost constant eye contact with his audience and to use powerful, spontaneous gestures at the right moments.

But the main ingredients that made the speech a smashing success were Ford's own efforts, the importance he placed on it, and his emotions of the moment. No wonder he was interrupted with cheers more than sixty-five times.

Great speakers are made, not born. If Gerald Ford could do it at age sixty-two, you can do it at twenty-two, thirty-two, or whatever.

Now, for another example of a speaker being made, let's flash back to Boston in 1947. Sometime in that year at the Hotel Kenmore, I (HKM) was in a small audience of World War II veterans listening to a speech on foreign policy by freshman Congressman John F. Kennedy. He was witty and knowledgeable, but his voice lacked depth and variety, his language contained er's and ah's, his Boston accent was strong, and his hands were stuck in his pockets much of the time.

JFK was aware of his limitations. He knew that great speakers are made, not born. He knew that President Franklin D. Roosevelt and Prime Minister Winston Churchill struggled for years before they reached their full potential as speakers. He knew what he had to do and he did it.

Kennedy gave speeches often, read good literature to strengthen his vocabulary, and received coaching from a Boston University speech professor. In addition, he rehearsed his speeches beforehand, used a tape recorder to improve his voice and dilute his Boston accent, observed competent speakers, and wrote newspaper articles on social and political problems. He spoke before live audiences, on radio, and on television. As a result of his strenuous efforts, by 1960 he was ready for the crucial television debates with Vice-President Richard Nixon. Many historians agree that Kennedy's performance won the presidential election for him.

Granted, JFK had many things going for him — wealth, education, family contacts, a brilliant mind, a sense of humor, good looks, personal drive — but if you do half what he did, you will improve as a communicator.

To summarize, below are ways to speed up the development of your own personal speaking style:

1. Speak at every opportunity.

2. Observe able speakers and learn from them.

3. Read good literature.

4. Use a dictionary and thesaurus to strengthen your vocabulary.

5. Practice writing (including your talks).

6. Rehearse your talks with a tape recorder and a critical listener.

THINGS TO THINK ABOUT AND DO

1. Tell the class about a recent experience in which you felt that the speaker either talked over the heads of or talked down to the audience.

2. Bring to class an example of a talk in which short sentences with one- or two-syllable words proved to be very effective.

3. Give a few examples of the power of words and how they've affected people's lives.

4. Ask a public speaker or lecturer to explain his method of audience analyzing. Ask if he is always successful. Discuss.

WHAT DO YOU REMEMBER FROM THIS CHAPTER?

1. Explain the importance of researching and analyzing an audience.

2. Explain several differences between oral and written communication.

3. List several examples in which language directed at one audience will not be effective with another audience.

4. What type of words carry the message more effectively in informative speaking?

5. What is a danger in using abstract words in communication?

6. What are loaded words? Give several examples.

7. What is a cliché? Give an example.

8. List some ways to help develop your speaking style.

VITALIZE YOUR VOCABULARY

Education

accreditation (n.)   recognition held by a school certifying that it meets prescribed standards.

alma mater (n.)   the school that one attended, usually a college.

alumnus, alumna (n.)   a man or woman who has graduated from a specific school, college, or university.

baccalaureate (n.)   a bachelor's degree awarded after completion of four years of college.

curriculum (n.)   courses of study offered at a school.

doctorate (n.)   the highest degree awarded by a graduate school.

elective (n.)   an optional course, in contrast to a required one.

emeritus (adj.)   retired but holding an honorary title like the one held before retirement.

extracurricular (adj.)   school activities outside regular course work.

intramural (adj.)   carried on between groups in a school and involving no outsiders.

liberal arts (n.)   the course of instruction at a college comprising the arts, natural sciences, social sciences, and humanities.

matriculate (v.)   to enroll as a student at a college.

orientation (n.)   a program to acquaint new students with school procedures.

Ph.D. (n.)   Doctor of Philosophy.

prerequisite (n.)   a requirement that must be met before a certain course can be taken.

registrar (n.)   a college official responsible for registering students and keeping their records.

syllabus (n.)   a description of the main points in a course or lecture.

valedictorian (n.)   the highest ranking student in the graduating class and the one who delivers the farewell address at commencement.

varsity (n.)   the best team representing a school or college in competition.

10

First Aid on Audiovisual Aids

In one of the most famous and fateful incidents in the Bible, the Lord summoned Moses to the top of Mount Sinai. There he appeared to Moses in the form of a fiery cloud, and there – to the appropriate accompaniment of thunder and lightning – he presented Moses with the Ten Commandments. That, so far as I know, is the earliest recorded use of audiovisual techniques for mass education. [1]

CHAPTER OBJECTIVES

After reading and understanding this chapter, you should:

- Understand the value of utilizing audiovisual aids to enhance and complement your talk.

- Be more familiar with the various types of audiovisual equipment and what to be aware of when using them.

- Be able to think of a topic and present a demonstration talk on it.

CHAPTER DIGEST

Specialists in modern educational psychology agree on at least one principle: the more senses involved in learning, the greater the learning. That is a convincing reason to use audiovisual aids when you think that they will enhance your presentation.

---

[1] Harold Howe II, former U.S. Commissioner of Education, addressing the National Audio-Visual Association.

Aids discussed in this chapter are the movie projector, slide projector, opaque and overhead projectors, tape recorders, easels, record players, scale models, maps, charts, and photographs. Several pointers on how to use and operate these aids (hardware) are presented.

In 1962 aerial photographs helped avert nuclear war between the United States and the Soviet Union. This earth-shaking emergency is briefly reviewed below.

In October 1962 the world teetered on the brink of nuclear war. The United States and the Soviet Union, the super-powers, found themselves headed on a collision course. Had they collided, hundreds of millions might have been killed and civilization might have been turned to ashes.

But an East-West nuclear holocaust did not engulf the world, thanks to the ability of man to reason and thanks to the power of pictures to persuade.

Why was there a confrontation of titans? Because the Soviet Union, in utmost secrecy and in violation of our Monroe Doctrine, had set about establishing in Cuba bases for intercontinental ballistic missiles (ICBMs). Once completed, those bases, only ninety miles off the Florida coast, could serve as launching pads for ICBMs. In a potential surprise attack masterminded by the Kremlin, some of our key cities — Washington, D.C., Chicago, Atlanta, Cleveland, and New York — could have been destroyed in minutes. Indeed, even our capability of striking back might have been paralyzed.

THE POWER OF PICTURES

Never underestimate the power of pictures to persuade. In fact, pictures were our "secret weapon" in preventing nuclear war in 1962. Briefly, here is how war was averted in the Security Council of the United Nations. Our ambassador there, Adlai Stevenson, a forceful, eloquent speaker, formally accused the Soviet Union of building offensive missile bases in Cuba. He supported his charges with reconnaissance photographs, taken from U-2 planes, of Russian missile bases.

The Russian ambassador to the UN, Valerian Zorin, refused to look at the photographs and when he branded them forgeries fabricated by the Central Intelligence Agency, the following exchange crackled between Stevenson and Zorin (see Figure 10-1).

UPI Telephoto

Figure 10-1
Ambassador Stevenson and Soviet Deputy Foreign Minister Valerian Zorin trade verbal punches during the heated UN Security Council session, October 26, 1962.

Stevenson: All right, sir, let me ask you one simple question: Do you, Ambassador Zorin, deny that the USSR has placed and is placing medium- and intermediate-range missiles and sites in Cuba? Yes or no? Don't wait for the translation. Yes or no?

Zorin: I am not in an American courtroom, sir. . . .

Stevenson: You are in the court of world opinion right now!

Zorin: . . . and therefore I do not wish to answer a question that is put to me in the fashion that a prosecutor does. In due course, sir, you will have your reply.

Stevenson: I am prepared to wait for my answer until hell freezes over, if that's your decision.

Although Zorin turned his back on the photographs, other UN delegates studied them meticulously and were convinced. So was world opinion. While this confrontation was raging at the UN, several communications were exchanged between President Kennedy and Chairman Khrushchev. As a result of their cool judgment and the Stevenson presentation, the Soviet Union dismantled the missiles and bases. And the world breathed easier.

ADDING SIGHT TO SOUND

After speaking with numerous business executives and managers, I (AJV) learned how amazed they are at the huge number of sales presentations that miss the mark. Yet, with a little more effort and imagination in the use of audiovisual aids, these presentations could have convinced associates at a business conference, won over potential clients to the speaker's viewpoint, or closed a crucial sale.

Fortunately, more and more companies are realizing the critical importance of making presentations with audiovisual aids and are establishing in-house media departments. Some of the larger insurance, utility, and industrial companies have media production studios that rival commercial radio and TV stations.

Although you may not have access to such a first-class team of media production professionals, there's no reason why, with some preparation, imagination, and knowledge of visual aids, you can't offer a successful audiovisual presentation or demonstration talk.

Because of the increasing impact of TV viewing habits, visual aids are, to some extent, replacing reading habits. This fact is substantiated by the dismally low reading scores in public schools. In fact, most high school graduates have seen 15,000 hours of TV and, as a result, expect speakers to use visual aids. Furthermore, a recent study by psychologists shows that 85 percent of what we learn comes through your eyes, and only 11 percent through your ears.[2]

With a few graphs (see Figure 10-2), charts, pictures, models, film strips, movies, videotapes, projectors, tape recordings, cassettes or records and a dash of creativeness, an average presentation at a sales meeting, business conference, or in the classroom can be transformed into an exciting, highly motivating event. This is the essence of a demonstration talk.

---

[2]Robert L. Montgomery, *A Master Guide to Public Speaking*. (New York: Harper & Row, 1979), p. 36.

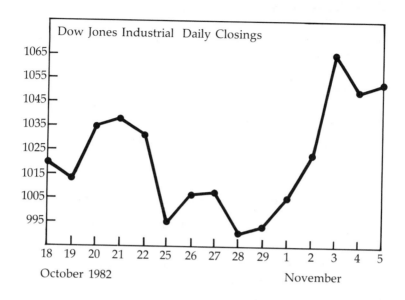

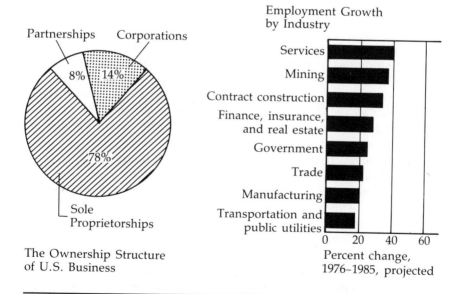

Figure 10-2
Graphs like these make very effective visual aids. A line graph, a circle or pie graph, and a bar graph are shown here.

DEMONSTRATION TALK

One of your talks during the semester will probably be the demonstration (demo) speech. Its objectives are:

1. To actually show the class how to do something. For example:
    - How to read music
    - How to develop black and white film.
    - How to change a flat tire.
    - How to make cherries jubilee.
    - How to perform CPR (cardio-pulmonary resuscitation)

2. To explain to the class how something operates. For example:
    - How a solar panel creates energy.
    - How a radar oven works.
    - What an automobile clutch does.
    - How an off-shore oil drilling platform operates.
    - How a nuclear power plant operates.

Without question the demonstration talk ranks number one among students. In most cases it truly adds up to a genuine learning experience. You should plan your topic to take between ten and twenty minutes. A shorter time will not give you worthwhile experience in using audiovisual aids, and your audience may just be getting warmed up to your subject when — poof, it's all over.

If appropriate, have someone from the audience help in your demo.   Whenever you can get a member or members of your class to participate in your demonstration talk, your effort will involve your audience more deeply. For example, if you were to demonstrate how to manicure fingernails, use a volunteer as a model. If your topic is sketching, instead of drawing from a picture or photo, use a student from the class as your model. I (AJV) had one student who showed the Heimlich maneuver of aiding a choking victim. Following the lecture portion of her presentation, she demonstrated the method on a class volunteer. She then had the entire class pair off, and every member performed this life-saving technique on another. The class selected this talk as its favorite. So remember, if possible, involve members of the audience.

If you need a volunteer.   If you're planning to use a volunteer as a part of your demonstration talk, arrange this in advance. Why? For several reasons. First, you want to be sure you have a volunteer when the time arrives. Second, you need to know that a volunteer will cooperate. And third, you'll prevent the potential embarrassment of someone trying to upstage you. Most professionals who need a volunteer for their presentation "plant" one in the audience.

USING AUDIOVISUAL AIDS

The use of audiovisual aids is supported by an established principle of psychology: that people learn far more through two senses — hearing and seeing, for example — than either through hearing alone or seeing alone. If some of your aids, for example, models or small objects, can be handled by your audience, then the sense of touch reinforces hearing and seeing. The more senses involved, the greater the learning. (This principle is also discussed in Chapter 11.)

Another powerful reason for utilizing visual aids is that they arouse and maintain audience interest. There's no question that the right aids can turn a good speech into an excellent presentation.

Try to avoid displaying visual aids before you refer to them in your presentation. If you're going to use charts, graphs, photos, etc., keep them covered or out of view so that your listeners will not get a sneak preview and not be distracted.

Let's now discuss some of the more common types of audiovisual aids you may use during your presentation.

TYPES OF PROJECTORS

Movie projector, 8 or 16 millimeters (mm), sound or silent. When you use sound, be sure to check the volume before the audience arrives. Having the volume too low is as annoying as having it too high. If you use silent film, remember that operation of the equipment produces a hum and that you must speak loudly enough to overcome the hum. Have the film already threaded so that all you have to do is flick the switch to start the film.

Slide projector. Be sure that the slides are arranged numerically and locked in trays or in a carousel. If you don't, you'll waste time holding slides up to the light to try to figure out how to place them in correct sequence. Just remember that color slides are more compelling than black and white ones. Slides also combine well with audio aids.

Opaque or overhead projectors. These projectors enable you to show either published material or your own material. They are fairly easy to operate, but be sure to set them up beforehand to ensure that you're at the right distance from the screen or wall for the size of projection desired. If the machine is placed at the back of the room, you may find it helpful to have someone operate it for you so that you can give your talk at the front of the room.

CAUTION

When you use either the opaque or the overhead projector, place it either in the front or the back of the room. If it is placed in the middle of your audience, it could be distracting.

Be sure the slides are locked in.

EASELS

Easels may be utilized in two ways: to display large cards (3 feet by 4 feet) bearing information, or to hold a large pad of paper (3 feet by 5 feet) upon which you may write information and then flip upward onto the next page.

To display large cards.   Cards that are prepared in advance are usually about 3 feet by 4 feet. You place all your cards on the easel, and as you cover the material on each card, you take it and place it on the floor. When preparing these cards, be sure to number them in case they get out of sequence. Also, instead of using just one color, use two or more. Not only will the presentation be more eye-catching, but you can use different colors for headings, sub-headings, and overall emphasis. To prevent the possibility of blocking people's view, use a three-foot pointer. In that way you can remain at arm's length from the cards and still reach the material comfortably with the pointer.

To hold a large pad of paper.   The pad of paper you would use is approximately 27 inches by 33 inches and normally contains about fifty pages. Just as in using the chalkboard, be sure you don't talk to the pad of paper when writing on the pad. Keep your attention focused on the audience. Again, the information you're putting on the pages can be made more interesting and emphatic by using two different colored magic markers.

THE CHALKBOARD

Before you write on the chalkboard, be sure that it is completely erased. If possible, write before you give your presentation and cover your material so that the audience is not distracted by it. When you're ready to discuss what you've written, use a pointer and stand sideways so that you can look at your listeners.

   If you must write while you're giving your presentation, don't speak while you're writing on the board; talk either before or after. Try to avoid long periods of silence because silence causes interest to lag. Remember to write clearly and large enough for all to see — and try to write on a straight line. Be sure to hold the chalk at a sharp angle (30 to 40 degrees) to the board; otherwise, the moving chalk will cause nerve-wracking squeals.

OBJECTS

Displaying objects (for example, tools, pieces of equipment, etc.) is excellent when you're explaining how something operates. If you can't bring in lifesize objects (for example, an auto engine or 747 aircraft), bring in scale models, but be sure that they are large enough to be seen. Always stand behind or beside the object, never in front of it or between it and the class. If you're using more than one object, display and discuss them one at a time so that all the attention will be focused on the one under discussion.

HANDOUTS

Passing objects around the class can be tricky. If all the listeners receive the same objects at the same time, they'll be better able to follow you than if you passed around several different objects at different times. Audiences can become more engrossed in looking at objects in their hands than in what you're saying.

Plan how to use handouts for maximum effect. For example, be sure to have enough copies for each member of the class and distribute them just before you discuss them. Allow the class enough time to become familiar with the contents — and then resume speaking.

Some common handouts are maps, charts, photographs, and diagrams. Be sure that they are large enough for all to see and are clearly depicted so that they can be easily understood. After your talk, you might consider displaying them on a table so that your audience may inspect them closely.

TAPE RECORDERS AND RECORD PLAYERS

Tape recorders and record players can add another dimension to your presentation; for example, you can use a recorder in conjunction with a silent film or slides.

Make sure that the physical surroundings are adequate for your audiovisual aids. If a table is needed to hold your models, be sure one is there. Be sure that an electrical outlet for your tape recorder is within reach or that you have an extension cord.

Always rehearse your presentation a few times using the same equipment you plan to use in your talk. The key to a flawless performance is practice, practice, practice. It's the only way to veto "Murphy's law": If anything can go wrong, it will. Nothing is more embarrassing in the middle of a presentation than forgetting how to operate a piece of equipment because you haven't practiced using it.

If you plan and practice, you'll not only be able to put on a performance that will be a credit to you, you will also reinforce your self-confidence. If you're required to give a presentation that involves using visual aids, you'll probably find it challenging and rewarding because it is informative and, in some cases, entertaining, even though it might not start out that way. It will afford you a rich opportunity to further develop your self-confidence, for it will place you in the role of expert lecturer.

Many schools have audiovisual departments that are well-stocked with various pieces of equipment and that usually are staffed by professionals. In a short time, staff members can teach you to operate the equipment. Knowing your audiovisual staff and the equipment can be very helpful.

If anything can go wrong, it will.

SELECTING A TOPIC TO DEMONSTRATE

You're probably scratching your head now and wondering, along with many others in the class, what you can demonstrate. This is a common reaction, but from years of experience we've found that those who encounter difficulty in selecting a topic usually end up with a highly satisfactory one. If you're having a problem, tell your professor; a five-minute chat with him may turn up an answer for you.

You can approach this talk from one of two directions. You can either select a topic that you know or one that you know little about but would be willing to research. If you choose the latter way, you'll become involved in a solid learning experience.

A TOPIC YOU KNOW

The natural choice is a topic you know something about. You should take inventory of your knowledge, experiences, and skills to decide which topic you will present. Did any of your jobs, full-time or part-time, require special skills? Were you in the service? Did anything unusual happen? What about your hobbies? Have you done any traveling? Have you collected slides or made movies? Do you sky-dive, scuba-dive, sail, play tennis, soccer? Do you like to cook or bake? If you give yourself half a chance, you'll probably be astonished at some of the things you've done that would make a worthwhile presentation. Don't sell yourself short.

Below are some topics that resulted in successful presentations by students whose initial reaction was "there's nothing I can do."

- A student who had worked in an ice-cream parlor demonstrated how to make several types of sundaes.

- A football enthusiast gave an excellent presentation and explanation of the various signs and signals that a referee makes. He even wore the official black-and-white striped shirt.

- A young woman intrigued the class with her talk and demonstration of various positions in yoga.

- A young woman, in a presentation on self-defense, effortlessly flipped several men students on the mat.

- A police officer student demonstrated the art of fingerprinting by using classmates for subjects.

- A class in which there were many women was astonished to be invited outside to the parking lot by a student who demonstrated the safe way to change a flat tire.

A TOPIC YOU KNOW LITTLE ABOUT

If you're ambitious about learning, you may select a topic that you're not too familiar with, conduct research on it, probably receive instruction, and then give the presentation. This approach requires considerable preparation, but it will be rewarding, indeed.

Need some ideas? Below are some topics that have been successful:

1. Forecasting the weather.

2. Types and use of sporting equipment.

3. Photography.

4. Collections (coins, stamps).

5. Playing musical instruments.

6. Firefighter and police equipment.

7. How to play games (chess, backgammon).

8. Assembling terrariums.

9. Making animals from balloons.

10. How to identify counterfeit money.

11. Some basic exercises in Yoga.

12. How to pack a parachute.

13. What to look for when reading a wine label.

14. How to make an antipasto.

15. How to communicate by sign language.

16. Basic self-defense for women.

17. Some basic carpentry tools and how to use them.

18. How to gift-wrap a package and make bows.

19. How to pack a suitcase.

20. How to coordinate a wardrobe. (male or female)

21. Applying makeup.

22. Card tricks.

23. Handcrafts (knitting, macramé, découpage, crocheting).

24. Cooking.

25. Types of artificial respiration.

26. Art (sketching, collage).

27. How to read the stock market page.

28. Taking your own blood pressure.

29. Scuba diving.

30. Giving first aid to a choking victim (Heimlich maneuver).

31. Making a lamp out of a bottle.

With some thought, you'll be able to come up with many more ideas and topics. (See more topics at the end of Chapter 11.)

The practical value of using audiovisual aids in some of your presentations is beautifully expressed in an ancient proverb, a masterpiece in three short lines:

What I hear, I forget.
What I see, I remember.
What I do, I know.

THINGS TO THINK ABOUT AND DO

1. Visit your audiovisual department and become familiar with its equipment.

2. Tell about a recent talk in which audiovisual aids were used, for example, a talk given by a TV pitchman or a door-to-door salesperson, a class lecture, etc.

3. List some professions or occupations in which audiovisual aids play an important role.

4. Select a topic you'd like to talk about and explain what audiovisual aids you'd use and how you'd use them.

5. List a few topics for which the use of audiovisual aids would be a must. Explain.

6. Can you think of a few topics for which the use of audiovisual aids would not be effective? Explain.

WHAT DO YOU REMEMBER FROM THIS CHAPTER?

1. How can the use of audiovisual aids help to get your message across to the audience?

2. Is it permissible to use more than one aid in a presentation? Explain.

3. Explain the "power of pictures to persuade."

4. What must you be careful of when you use handouts?

5. What should you keep in mind when you write on the chalkboard?

6. What's a good technique to employ when preparing large cards to be placed on an easel?

7. What is good advice to remember when planning to use an 8- or 16-millimeter projector?

8. If you show objects or scale models, where should you stand in relation to the audience?

9. What's a good thing to remember if you're planning to use a volunteer during your demonstration talk?

10. Explain the ancient proverb:
    What I hear, I forget.
    What I see, I remember.
    What I do, I know.

VITALIZE YOUR VOCABULARY

Stages of Life

adolescent (n.)   a male or female teen-ager.

callow (adj.)   immature and inexperienced.

crone (n.)   a withered old woman.

forebear (n.)   ancestor, forefather.

geriatrics (n.)   scientific and medical study of the biological processes and diseases of old age.

infantile (adj.)   childish, like a baby.

juvenile (adj.)   immature, youthful, young.

matriarch (n.)   a woman who rules a family, clan, or tribe.

mature (adj.)   fully developed or grown.

octogenarian (n.)   a person in his eighties.

patriarch (n.)   a man who rules a family, clan, or tribe.

pediatrics (n.)   the medical care of infants and children and treatment of their diseases.

posthumous (adj.)   occurring after death.

puberty (n.)   physical beginning of manhood (at about age 14) and womanhood (at about age 12).

puerile (adj.)   childish, immature.

senile (adj.)   showing the weakening of mental or physical abilities due to advanced age.

septuagenarian (n.)   a person in his seventies.

sexagenarian (n.)   a person in his sixties.

venerable (adj.)   worthy of respect because of age, position, or wisdom.

11

Inform
Them

Whatever the calling students may later pursue, their effectiveness will depend mightily on ability to express views clearly.[1]

CHAPTER OBJECTIVES

After reading and understanding this chapter, you should know:

- The purposes and kinds of informative talks.

- Four principles of learning.

- How to use statistics effectively.

- How to prepare the introduction, main discussion (body), and conclusion of an informative talk.

CHAPTER DIGEST

In this age of widespread college education, of national computer networks, and of endless research into the unknown, information has evolved into a critical national resource. By the same token,

---

[1]Kingman Brewster, Jr., former president, Yale University, "The Report of the President," September 1, 1976, p. 11.

information has become an invaluable asset to the individual who can absorb it and share it through talking with her peers. In other words, speaking to convey knowledge and understanding can help you to advance your career.

Adapting the knowledge level of your talk to the knowledge level of your audience is of supreme importance. Three kinds of audiences are described from this viewpoint and to meet their needs, various types of informative talks are explained.

Certain principles of learning that help you are discussed briefly. If you apply them, your informative talks will get better results, but applying these principles is not enough. First you need to acquire knowledge, information, and understanding in order to flesh out your talk. And that means doing your homework.

Many down-to-earth suggestions are given for the introduction, body, and conclusion of your informative talk. After you finish your presentation, a question-and-answer period is an excellent way to tie up loose ends.

Because the words *information* and *knowledge* appear throughout this chapter, let's define our terms:

information (n.)   facts, data, news; knowledge communicated by others or obtained from study, instruction, or investigation.

knowledge (n.)   comprehension, learning, information, an organized body of facts, or ideas inferred from those facts.

From the earliest days Americans have set a high value on knowledge. We believe that democracy functions best when its citizens are armed with sound knowledge on which to base intelligent decisions. Because of this belief, the United States has developed the most extensive system of public education that the world has ever known. Because of this belief, the United States has more colleges and universities than do England, France, East and West Germany, and the Soviet Union combined. Because of this belief, the United States has more newspapers, magazines, book publishers, radio stations, television channels, computer networks, and public libraries than those same five countries all put together.

All these media, both here and abroad, have created a revolution in the handling of information and an explosion of knowledge in countless specialized areas. As a result, information is now regarded as "a new basic resource that supplements the familiar re-sources of matter and energy."[2] The crucial difference between these three resources is that matter and energy are degraded or destroyed with use, but knowledge is not. On the contrary, the more that knowledge is shared and used among people, the more valuable it becomes; for example, the knowledge needed to produce and use penicillin and other miracle drugs.

PURPOSES OF INFORMATIVE TALKS

In this age of information revolution and knowledge explosion, much of your talking has one major objective — to present information so that it will be understood and remembered. Briefly, you want to open new horizons for your listeners, give them new perspectives and an understanding. In regard to knowledge and understanding, most audiences fall into three categories that may overlap:

- Not informed
- Generally informed
- Well informed

With listeners who are not informed, deal in elementary matters and explain any jargon or specialized concepts. Here's where relevant comparisons and statistics (discussed later in this chapter) can help your audience understand your presentation. Just be careful not to talk down to them and not to cover too much ground at one time.

With a generally informed audience, use fundamental knowledge sprinkled with advanced material. The perplexing question is this: how much of each is appropriate? (For ideas on researching your audience, see Chapter 9.) Since some of your listeners may resent basic information as an onslaught against their egos, you may explain that you're simply laying a foundation on which to build deeper understanding. Another diplomatic "out" for you is that you're reviewing fundamentals for a few people whose memories may need refreshing.

---

[2]*Encyclopaedia Britannica* (1973), 12, 244A.

Be careful not to talk down to your audience.

With well informed listeners, you're home free to skip fundamentals and plunge into advanced information in depth. Listeners
armed with knowledge are usually easy to handle, but a warning
belongs here — know your subject.

No matter what type of listeners you're trying to inform, it is
wise to assume that they are intelligent and to strengthen your talk
with audiovisual aids (see Chapter 10).

When it comes to listening and observing to gain understanding, several kinds of audiences may be involved, for example:

- Classes in school.

- Decision-making individuals or groups on the job.

- Voters assessing candidates at an open forum.

- Consumers listening to purchasing experts for tips on
  stretching the dollar or conserving energy.

- People listening to radio and television newscasts,
  documentaries, etc.

- People listening to their religious leaders for wisdom and emotional reinforcement.

Someday at school or on the job or in your community, you may find yourself giving an informative talk to one of the above audiences and attempting:

- To describe a person or a place

- To report an event, a problem, a situation

- To explain a concept, a device, a process, a theory

KINDS OF INFORMATIVE TALKS

Among the major categories of speeches — to entertain, to inspire, to persuade, to actuate, to inform — the most used, by far, is the speech to inform. What does this mean to you? Simply that the way you handle your storehouse of information and share it with others can have a significant impact on the direction of your career.

Let's clarify those major categories of speeches. Because a speech is labeled "informative" doesn't mean that it's boxed in a neat compartment called "information." An informative speech may contain elements of persuasion or entertainment or both, and those extras will, very likely, make it a more effective speech. The point is that, although speeches belong primarily to one category or another, they often include elements of other categories as well as the use of audiovisual aids.

The general objective in the speech to inform is to convey understanding and knowledge, because humans have an instinctive need to understand themselves and their surroundings. From that general objective we may focus on various types of speeches to inform: reports, instructions, demonstrations, and lectures.

Reports. A chief function of committees in business, education, politics, Armed Forces — you name it — is to give reports on projects and problems. A neighborhood committee, for example, may investigate the need for traffic lights at a dangerous intersection, report its findings, and make a recommendation for or against traffic lights. At the other end of the spectrum, the President of the United States reports on the State of the Union. Oral reporting goes on in all walks of life.

Instructions. Today you may tell an out-of-state tourist how to find the new shopping mall at the other end of town. Tomorrow your professor may explain how to do a research paper. He may even supplement his oral instructions with handouts containing specific steps to follow. Very often, written instructions help to clarify the oral how-to-do-it phase and, when possible, are worth utilizing.

Demonstrations. When you show someone how to use a camera or how to perform a card trick or how to operate a computer terminal, you are demonstrating. This kind of informative speaking is so important that it rates a chapter all by itself — Chapter 10.

Lectures. In addition to class lectures, this type of informative speaking embraces talks at professional seminars, talks on travel and politics on radio and television, and book reviews at club meetings. These talks are often given after luncheon or dinner, with the prime purpose being to enhance the listeners' knowledge and appreciation of a particular subject.

PRINCIPLES OF LEARNING

Before you embark on your first informative talk, let's review some findings on how people learn. Teachers in the past few thousand years and psychologists in the past hundred and fifty years have discovered that the following principles, when applied, speed up the learning process.

People learn better when you, as a speaker, involve as many of their senses as possible. For example, suppose that you're demonstrating how to make a new kind of spaghetti sauce. You cut and mix the ingredients (seeing), fry them or whatever (smelling), explain the procedure (hearing), and then hand out samples to your listeners (tasting). With their four senses involved in this learning experience, your listeners will remember far more than if you used only words to convey the message.

Of course, this example is an extreme case because you'll not often be able to intermingle four senses in the same talk. Often, however, you'll be able to involve the sense of seeing (movies, filmstrips, photographs, maps, models) along with the sense of hearing (the spoken word).

Involve as many of their senses as possible.

People learn better when salient points of information are repeated a few times or are restated in different words. Here is an example of this principle:

> Doctors and dieticians tell us that breakfast is the most important meal of the day. Yet, millions of Americans skip this crucial meal daily, to save time or to pare off pounds or both. After seven to nine hours in bed, these people may be rested sufficiently, but physically and mentally they need the energy — "fuel," if you don't mind — that a well balanced breakfast can provide. Without that energy, their bodies and minds cannot take off and operate at top efficiency through the morning. That is why, for most people, a good breakfast is a key element in nutrition that can lead to a healthy life.

Notice that the significant idea (underlined) in the preceding paragraph is mentioned seven times.

People learn better when they're motivated to do so. Your listeners pay close attention to you when you answer the often unspoken question that most people ask: "What's in it for me?" Tell them how to get a better job, reduce their income taxes, be healthier, live longer, be more attractive to the opposite sex, and you can be sure that they will hang onto every word you utter.

People learn better when new, relevant information is presented in small, well-organized amounts. If you're explaining the basic causes of World War II to an audience that knows little about the subject, you should present political, economic, and military causes. You should discuss each category separately but not deeply, and in your conclusion you should point out how all three causes combined to trigger the most devastating war in the history of mankind.

GETTING INTO YOUR INFORMATIVE TALK

To inspire, persuade, entertain, and activate people, you don't need a great deal of information or knowledge. But the talk to inform, by its very nature, dictates that you do your research and that you know your subject cold. After all, your primary purpose is to convey information and understanding to your listeners that they didn't have before. Hopefully, you will know more about your subject than anyone in the audience.

Because a strong introduction is crucial to any talk, before you plan your opening remarks you should review the ideas listed in Chapter 8. Just about all those ideas apply to introductions to all kinds of talks. At the very least, in the introduction to your informative talk you should:

- State the purpose of your talk.

- List the main points orally and, if possible, write them on a chalkboard. However, if writing takes unduly long, your listeners' attention may wander. You may consider highlighting the main points on a poster. Doing this is excellent visual reinforcement for the oral listing.

- Stress the subject's importance to your listeners; if it will save them time or money or make their lives easier, say so immediately.

MOVING INTO THE MAIN DISCUSSION

You're now ready to launch into your two, three, or four main points mentioned in the introduction. As you know from Chapter 7 (doing research) and Chapter 8 (organizing your information), each main point requires subpoints for support: facts, examples, quotations from authorities, incidents, anecdotes, comparisons, statistics, and so on. Ample research should provide you with many of these supports (these supports, except comparisons and statistics, are illustrated in Chapter 8). Now let's look at comparisons, statistics, audiovisual aids, and questions.

COMPARISONS

Whether you're explaining concepts or things that are new to an audience, try to compare them with something familiar to the audience. A few apt comparisons can bring your explanation to life. For example, assume you tell your speech class that the fastest speed attainable by Olympic swimmers is approximately four miles per hour. Compared to dolphins, which swim at 35 mph, the Olympic speed is nothing special, and some students may snicker at 4 mph. Then, after saying that this speed is a brisk walking pace, ask how many of them do a mile in 15 minutes.

Below are two concise comparisons, one dealing with money and the other with science; both can be grasped with no difficulty:

1. The greatest real estate deal in history is Seward's purchase of Alaska from Russia for $7,200,000 — *less than two cents for an acre.*

2. Sun flares sprayed streams of particles into space, sweeping the solar system *like streams of water from a revolving lawn sprinkler.*

STATISTICS

The use of statistics supplies concrete information that may perk up your audience's interest and, at the same time, may prove your point. Below are some cautions to observe in using statistics:

- Don't throw reams of figures at your audience; they're too difficult to remember.

- In addition to giving statistics orally, write the key figures on a chalkboard.

- Repeat the most important figures at least once.

- Round off long figures. Instead of saying "$1,000,359," say "a little over a million dollars." Your audience will appreciate it.

Notice how the following example dramatizes the total cost of President Carter's 1979 budget. He requested more than a half trillion dollars.

One trillion dollars has 12 zeros. It looks like this:

$1,000,000,000,000.

If you put that much money in a line of dollar bills end on end, it would stretch around the earth more than 1,800 times. It would reach to the moon and back 250 times.

Carter's budget would have provided $6.50 to every human being who has lived and died in the past 600,000 years.[3]

AUDIOVISUAL AIDS

Be sure to use audiovisual aids, for example, recordings, movies, photographs, charts, maps (see Chapter 10). Say, for example, that you're discussing old whiskey bottles. The most compelling visual aids would not be word pictures or photographs or replicas of bottles, but the actual bottles themselves, if possible. Reality "grabs" people.

QUESTIONS

A foresighted tactic to carry out while researching and preparing for your speech would be to figure out some relevant questions that your listeners may want to ask at various stages of your talk. Tossing out occasional questions often stimulates your audience to think along with you.

---

[3]*Boston Herald American*, 24 January 1979, p. 1, cols. 3 and 4.

WINDING UP YOUR INFORMATIVE TALK

At the end of your main discussion, you might pause a few seconds and move a step or so to either side. The pause and movement signal that your talk is about to end. Then you may say something like, "In conclusion, . . ." or "To summarize my principal points, . . ." Again, you may stress the importance of the subject and the benefits that the listeners may derive from the knowledge you've shared with them. Remember that a conclusion should be brief and to the point. Don't drag it out or trail off by muttering, "Well, I guess that's about it."

Another idea for your conclusion is to encourage listeners who want to learn more about the subject. For them you can list, on the chalkboard, relevant titles of magazine articles or books, or better still, prepare this information as a handout that you can distribute on the spot. Most people like handouts because they're free, and can be useful.

A conclusion should be brief.

Where other categories of talks seldom require a question-and-answer period, the informative talk does, and for these practical reasons: (1) If your treatment of a particular topic was foggy or incomplete, you now have an opportunity to clarify it. (2) If you omitted a facet of the subject that concerns some of the listeners, you can supply the missing information.

President Harry S. Truman summed up the value of the question-and-answer session in these words: "I know of no way of communicating more information in shorter time than the question-and-answer method."

Sometimes question-and-answer periods begin with a resounding silence that embarrasses both speaker and listeners. Almost everyone shies away from being the first to ask questions for fear of sounding stupid. In that case, planning can avert this silence. Ask a few questions, thought out beforehand, and answer them yourself if nobody in the audience cares to try.

Or you can do what many professional speakers do — "plant" a question or two with a friend in the audience; it's perfectly legitimate. If nobody speaks up, your friend can "break the ice." Then other listeners will very likely pop questions at you.

If you've done enough research, you'll be able to answer almost all queries, which should give you a feeling of accomplishment for a job well done. If a question stumps you, don't try to bluff around it. Admit that you don't know the answer, but that you will try to find it. Many, and possibly almost all, of your listeners will appreciate that you're an honest human being who doesn't pretend to be a know-it-all.

SUGGESTED TOPICS FOR INFORMATIVE TALKS

1. What is stagflation?

2. What causes a depression?

3. Is the demise of public education approaching?

4. How to manage your checkbook.

5. Why the voters should be able to recall public officials.

6. The effects on children of living with just one parent.

7. Why we should limit public school attendance to students who wish to attend.

8. Why Japanese cars require fewer repairs than American cars.

9. Some of the best ways to invest your money.

10. Are we headed for an economic disaster?

11. Should we withdraw our support of the United Nations?

12. Should we abolish the electoral college?

13. How safe are nuclear power plants?

14. Why we should (should not) reinstitute the draft.

15. What the ERA is all about.

16. Alternative ways to heat or cool your home.

17. What is the meaning of "détente"?

18. How a bill becomes a law.

19. Sexual harassment — an occupational hazard.

20. Are colleges doing their job in preparing students for work?

21. The herpes epidemic in the United States.

22. The startling increase of teen-age pregnancies.

23. Who said that crime doesn't pay?

24. How to plant a productive garden.

25. How to get better mileage from your car?

26. How to shop and save.

27. Why this course should be mandatory for all students.

28. Why more marriages are failing.

THINGS TO THINK ABOUT AND DO

1. Prepare an informative talk that explains one of the following: a concept, device, process, or theory.

2. List a topic for an informative talk that reports an event, a problem, or a situation.

3. List some principles which, when applied, speed up the learning process. Give examples of these principles.

4. Prepare a short talk (a minute or two) giving specific directions on how to get somewhere. Be as concise and explicit as possible. Should you use visual aids?

5. Prepare a five-minute talk on the organizational structure of a business, educational facility, political campaign, or law enforcement agency. Would visual aids enhance your presentation?

WHAT DO YOU REMEMBER FROM THIS CHAPTER?

1. What are the prime purposes of informative talking?

2. List several categories of speeches. Which one is used most often?

3. List some principles which, when applied, speed up the learning process. Give examples of these principles.

4. What are some elements that should be included in the introduction of your informative talk?

5. What cautions should be observed when you use statistics?

6. It it a good idea to follow an informative talk with a question-and-answer period? Explain.

VITALIZE YOUR VOCABULARY

Because thousands of English words are derived from Latin words, there's no question that the study of Latin would strengthen your English vocabulary, but you don't have to study that ancient language in order to benefit from it.

To increase your word power, we suggest that you learn the meanings of dozens of Latin prefixes and hundreds of roots. By doing this, you'll improve your command of the English language in four ways: in speaking, writing, reading, and listening.

To get you moving, below are a few Latin prefixes, along with their meanings and some sample English words:

Prefixes	Meanings	Sample words
Ambi	Both	Ambidextrous, ambiguous
Anti	Against, opposite	Antifreeze, antibiotic
Circum	Around, on all sides	Circumference, circumlocution

Equi	Equal	Equidistant, equilibrium
Intra, intro	Within	Intramural, intrastate, introvert
Sub	Under, beneath	Subcontract, subhuman, submarine
Super, supra	Above, over	Superhighway, supersonic, supernatural

Now let's do the same with some Latin roots:

Roots	Meanings	Sample words
Aqu	Water	Aquarium, aquatic, aqueduct
Aud, audit	Hear	Audio, audience, auditorium
Ben, bene	Good, well	Benefactor, benefit
Cid, cis	Cut, kill	Homicide, incision, suicide
Cred	Belief, trust	Credible, credit, creed
Flu, fluct	Flow	Fluctuate, influence
Leg	Law	Legal, legislate, legitimate
Medi	Middle	Medieval, mediocre, medium
Nov	New	Innovate, novelty, renovate
Tors, tort	Twist	Contortion, distort, torque
Viv	Life, lively	Vivacious, vivid

If some of the above sample words are not clear to you, then poke your nose into that dust-covered dictionary.

12

Persuade Them

People are generally better persuaded by the reasons which they have themselves discovered than by those which have come into the minds of others.[1]

CHAPTER OBJECTIVES

After reading and understanding this chapter, you should:

- Appreciate the importance of persuasive speaking.
- Know the purposes of speaking to persuade.
- Be familiar with methods of analyzing an audience.
- Understand various strategies to help you convince an audience.

CHAPTER DIGEST

A form of interpersonal communication crucial to the achievement of your career goals is persuasive speaking. Several examples of persuasive speaking are listed to show how practical and how valuable it can be to you.

---

[1]Pascal, *Pensees* (1670), 10, tr. W. F. Trotter.

Persuasive speaking has three purposes: to convince people to take action that you want them to take, to change their attitudes or beliefs, and to buttress their current attitudes or beliefs.

Before you can persuade an audience to change its stance and do what you want, you must analyze the audience. Several questions relevant to analysis are asked and if you can find answers, you'll stand a far better chance of winning your audience to your side.

Armed with some understanding of your audience, you're now in a position to plan strategy. Two types of audiences are considered: friendly and neutral or passive.

Authorities on persuasion, starting with Aristotle 2,200 years ago and continuing to the present day, agree on three ways to persuade:

1. Through logical argument.

2. Through speaker credibility.

3. Through basic social, biological, and psychological needs and desires.

The discussion of each method is highlighted and specific examples are given.

IMPORTANCE OF PERSUASIVE SPEAKING

Is the ability to persuade important to you and your career? Instead of answering "yes," we'll simply list examples of persuasive speaking that occur all around you. Then you can answer the question.

- A job applicant selling himself to a department manager.

- People who speak for public interest organizations (Common Cause, Sierra Club, League of Women Voters) recruiting members or testifying for or against pending legislation.

- A real estate agent selling a house to you.

- Leaders of charity drives appealing to you to open your purses and wallets.

- An attorney pleading to a jury to acquit his client.

- Political candidates asking you to mark the big X in the ballot box.

"How about going away for the weekend?"

- A corporation president persuading stockholders that his policies will boost the value of their shares.

We're sure that you get the point that persuasive speaking is a highly valuable skill that you can develop. Although there are no magic formulas or rules of thumb to transform you overnight into an accomplished persuader, there are several suggestions in this chapter to help you sharpen your ability. Of course, before you can convince anybody of anything, your body, your voice, your facial expressions, and your gestures should reflect the fact that you yourself are convinced. Audiences sense when a speaker is convinced of the truth of his arguments or is faking it.

The Stanford University Graduate School of Business, perhaps the foremost school of its kind in the world, conducted research on successful managers and found that they have five major characteristics in common. "Oral persuasiveness" leads the list because "the successful manager is primarily an effective speaker . . . he is interested in persuading others to his point of view."[2]

[2]*Nation's Business* (June 1976), p. 6.

PURPOSES OF PERSUASIVE SPEAKING

All the examples of persuasive speeches listed above have one aim in common: to convince people to take some form of action. That's why they're called speeches to *actuate* or to *motivate*.

Two other purposes underlie talks to persuade: One is to change people's attitudes and the other is to reinforce or strengthen their existing attitudes. Let's say, for example, that you favor court-ordered busing of school children and you're to speak to a pro-busing group. Here you would simply repeat a few powerful arguments in order to reassure your listeners and to harden their position.

If you are speaking to a neighborhood group that is neutral and open to discussion, tailor your approach differently. In your introduction, try to capture their goodwill immediately (see the section on introductions in Chapter 8). You could describe how, in some places, busing achieved its aims of equal educational opportunities and satisfied teachers and parents.

AUDIENCE ANALYSIS

It is crucial that you learn as much as possible about your audience's beliefs and attitudes toward your topic and your position. If your listeners' beliefs and attitudes are hard and fixed, perhaps you should settle for a chance to speak your piece and hope that they'll give you a fair hearing. Realistically, you cannot expect to change their minds with just one speech, no matter how convincing you are. If, however, your listeners are open-minded, you may be able to swing some moderates among them to your banner.

Figure 12-1 shows the range (from strongly opposed to strongly favorable) of audience feelings, attitudes, and beliefs toward any speaker and subject. Sometimes an audience is polarized at one inflexible position, especially on emotional issues that cut deeply into their lives, such as unemployment, busing, gun control, abortion, and the high cost of energy. At other times an audience may be so fragmented that its members span the entire spectrum from strongly opposed to strongly favorable.

No question about it, audiences deserve to be studied — beforehand. (Refer to Chapter 9.)

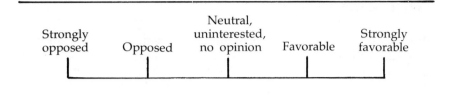

Figure 12-1
The range of beliefs and attitudes of many individuals.

Turning an audience around is a devilishly difficult task, much tougher than selling an automobile or a house. Even convincing an audience to make a slight change in direction requires a carefully planned approach anchored in a shrewd assessment of the audience. Before you can make that assessment, however, you should try to answer the following questions and any others that pertain to your particular situation:

1. What are you trying to accomplish? In other words, what is your specific purpose in speaking?

2. How does your audience feel toward your purpose and position?

3. What emotional or psychological appeals will move these people?

4. What logical reasoning will "reach" this particular group of people?

5. Are they willing to accept new ideas?

6. Why should this audience listen to you?

7. Do you know anyone who has had previous experience with this audience, and can that person help you answer these questions?

After you've analyzed your audience in terms of these questions, you will better understand its attitudes, feelings, and motives. Only then will you be prepared to plan your overall strategy.

SPEECH STRATEGY

Because this is a basic speech guide, we will delve into strategy just deeply enough to help you cope with some typical situations, for example:

- If the audience agrees with your position, discuss a few major issues so that you will reinforce your audience's position and erase any doubts that may plague it.

- If the audience is interested but undecided, use a few of your strongest arguments, both logical and emotional, to nudge it over the line into your territory. For an audience that is "sitting on the fence," sometimes only a gentle prod will spur it to make a decision favorable to your point of view.

- If your audience is not interested in your subject, try to link the audience to some aspects of its self-interest (discussed later in this chapter).

- If your audience disagrees with you, don't be aggressive in the introduction. Instead of using a strong, positive statement, phrasing your proposition or solution in the form of a question or two may be a more tactful approach. Let's say that you're to speak to hard-pressed taxpayers (is there any other kind of taxpayer?) in your town about raising taxes to finance a cleanup of the town's polluted lake. You might start by asking, "Do you want your children to have a safe, healthful place to swim, fish, and sail? Or do you want them to hang around street corners, pizza parlors, pool parlors or video game arcades?

- Under the same circumstances, another approach would be to discuss areas of agreement first — if there are any — and then move to areas of disagreement. Here you might start like this: "We taxpayers all agree on the need for a family recreation area in town. Fortunately, we have a lake and we should use it for family fun. After we clean up the lake, our taxes will return to normal. In other words, this proposed tax increase will last only as long as the cleanup project lasts."

- If your audience understands the problem, spend less time on it and more time on your solution. Let's continue with the lake situation. Since your listeners, the taxpayers, understand the problem, you should devote practically all your efforts to describing the benefits that they will enjoy from the restored lake. Be sure to stress that the tax increase is temporary and will stop when the lake is cleaned up.

- Try to anticipate questions and objections. Plan your answers beforehand. This tactic applies to all speech situations, not just to persuasive speaking, and it can spare you many a headache.

- Spot your most convincing arguments at the beginning and end of your speech. Arguments in the middle tend to be forgotten. Playwrights know this, which is why the best plays usually open with a bang and close with a crash.

- Group participation, such as questions and answers, may win over some hostile listeners. If you've studied your audience, you know who its influential members are. While you're speaking, focus special attention on them, because the other members tend to follow their lead.

WAYS TO PERSUADE PEOPLE

Speech authorities, psychologists, politicians, trial lawyers, and master salespeople know that there are three principal methods of changing people's attitudes or actuating people into doing what you want:

1. Persuading through evidence and reasoning (the formal term for this action is *argument*).

2. Persuading through speaker credibility.

3. Persuading through basic social, biological, and psychological needs, wants, and desires.

In almost all cases of successful persuasion, all three methods are mixed in varying degrees, depending on the speaker's analysis of his audience, on his character, and on his style.

PERSUASION THROUGH EVIDENCE AND REASONING

Let's consider these methods, starting with argument and moving through evidence and reasoning. Evidence, as you know, consists of facts and expert opinions. A fact is information that can be proved or verified. That there is no human life on the moon is a fact. That there is no human life in outer space is not a fact because we don't know.

Opinions may be either your own or those of other people. As with facts, some opinions are convincing and others are not, depending on their sources. Your opinion of the causes and probable cure of inflation will carry weight only if you're an expert economist who has a reputation for sound thinking. Therefore, if you're using opinions in your speech to persuade, identify the sources and their qualifications.

In the presidential TV debate, watched by 90 million people in October 1980, President Carter committed a gaffe that cost him dearly. During the exchange on whether or not to increase our stock of nuclear arms, he mentioned his daughter Amy's fear of nuclear proliferation.

That statement not only turned people off, but it made President Carter the butt of countless cutting comments. The voters didn't give a damn about eleven-year old Amy's opinion on nuclear weapons. The President should have quoted a world-famous nuclear physicist; that opinion would have been credible.

Governor Ronald Reagan showed us, at the conclusion of the debate, how to use people's own opinions to win votes by asking questions that hit Americans where it hurt most — in their pocketbooks: "Is it easier for you to go and buy things in the stores than it was four years ago? Are you better off than you were four years ago?"

That masterful use of questions to persuade an audience helped catapult Governor Reagan into the White House.

Types of reasoning. If you have your facts and authoritative opinions, you're in a position to carry out some reasoning. The three types of reasoning — deductive, inductive, and causal — are discussed below.

Deductive reasoning means making deductions or drawing conclusions. It involves moving from a general principle to a specific principle, as illustrated in this example:

People who speak in a monotone tend to bore their audiences.
Mr. White speaks in a monotone.
Mr. White tends to bore his audiences. (Conclusion)

Here's another example of deductive reasoning:

Under the Bill of Rights, all Americans have free speech.

Armen Khoylian, a refugee from Iran, has become an American citizen.

Armen now has free speech and can say anything, without fear of imprisonment.

Inductive reasoning, the reverse of deductive reasoning, starts with specific *examples* or *cases* and ends with a general *conclusion* based on the examples or cases. For instance, much American food lacks taste and food value; canned produce and bread are notorious in this respect. Compared to European breads, most American bread is flat, tasteless, spongy mush. In addition, almost all our canned fruits and vegetables are "embalmed" with chemical preservatives and additives that may cause serious health problems years later. Almost all these foods are produced, processed, and packaged by giant farm corporations. From these examples, we may draw the conclusion that these farm corporations are impairing the health of the American people.

Here's another example of inductive reasoning:

Some federal laws and regulations promote clean air and water.
Clean air and water are essential to good health.
Therefore, we should support these laws and regulations.

A common weakness in inductive reasoning is illustrated in the following generalization. The Professional Air Traffic Controllers Organization and another union went on strike in violation of their contracts. Therefore, all unions are bad and should be outlawed.

That generalization is weak and invalid because it is based on a very limited number of examples. There is no rule about how many examples you need, but the more you can cite, the stronger your case will be.

Causal reasoning, also discussed in Chapter 8, moves from cause to effect (result). For example, studies have demonstrated that the 55 mph speed limit has reduced the number of fatal auto accidents throughout the United States. The conclusion based on that finding is compelling and clearcut — speed kills.

Would you like another common-sense case? Doctors and scientists have proved, through thousands of experiments, that if you smoke heavily — more than a pack daily — you will shorten your life by x number of years.

The danger in causal reasoning is to oversimplify, to rely too heavily on one cause; in the real world of people, almost all effects are usually brought about by a few or even several causes. Regarding heavy smoking, other factors, such as heredity, environment, and life-style, also influence longevity.

To avoid oversimplification in causal reasoning, keep the following two questions in mind:

1. Did the alleged cause, in fact, result in or contribute to the effect?

2. Is the alleged cause the only cause of the effect?

If you use these three types of reasoning — deductive, inductive, and causal — you should be able to handle your evidence (facts and opinions) effectively.

PERSUASION THROUGH SPEAKER CREDIBILITY

During the Watergate crisis, White House credibility plummeted to its lowest ebb in American history. The word "credibility" was bandied about daily — in newspapers, in magazines, on television, on radio, in conversations everywhere. The scandal had reached such alarming proportions that people no longer believed any statements issued from the White House. Its credibility, an intangible but vital resource, was utterly destroyed.

When an audience believes a speaker and has faith in him, the speaker enjoys credibility. Credibility doesn't just happen; it has to be earned. It evolves from such personal characteristics as:

- Sincerity and concern for listeners

- Tact and friendliness

- Reputation and character

- Self-confidence and poise

- Experience and special knowledge of the subject

PERSUASION BY APPEALING TO SOCIAL, BIOLOGICAL, AND PSYCHOLOGICAL NEEDS, WANTS, AND DESIRES

What are some of these basic human needs, wants, and desires? In part, they are the following.

Self-preservation.   All of us need food, clothing, and shelter. We want to escape accidents, fires, violence, and other risks to our well-being and to our families' well-being. These needs are reflected in the escalating sales of fire and smoke detectors. In the same vein, the demand for burglar alarms and other security systems in motor vehicles, as well as in homes and industry, has prompted manufacturers to include them as standard equipment.

Sexual attraction.   Most of us want to be admired and fulfilled by the opposite sex. It's a normal desire that lasts a lifetime. The

He really enjoys credibility.

growing popularity of nude dancing (female and male), massage parlors, and R- and X-rated movies available to cable TV subscribers and owners of video playback machines reflects this desire.

This sexual need is responsible for the multi-billion dollar a year cosmetic and apparel industry supported by both sexes. And how else can you explain the popularity of such services as mate-matching, computer dating, singles clubs and trips, and male and female escort services?

Feeling good and looking good.   Again, this is a universal want and if you can unlock the secrets of good health and grooming, you will not lack an audience. Today more and more men go to hair stylists, enjoy facials, and seek the services of plastic surgery, once patronized mainly by women.

You may also be aware of the dynamic growth of health clubs and weight salons patronized by both sexes and the rising consumption of fresh and natural foods, herbs, and vitamins to improve health and looks. Interest in nutrition has never been higher.

Social acceptance.   Almost everyone craves acceptance by his peers at school, at work, and in social activities. Some people continually strive for acceptance and don't "make it"; other people bask in acceptance without appearing to exert much effort. Some individuals would go to any length to become a member of an exclusive club, society, or organization, or to have their child attend a "very" private school.

This strong desire for social acceptance is probably the reason why so many people are taking self-help courses and purchasing record numbers of self-development books.

Acquisition of wealth.   Just about everyone wants wealth in some form — jewels, stocks, land, real estate, art objects, or just plain old cash. Tell your listeners how to acquire wealth and you'll have them eating out of your hand.

Many books which have enjoyed best-seller status have targeted the subject of financial security. Titles such as: *How to Make a Fortune in Real Estate, How to Invest Wisely, The Fortune to Be Made in Penny Stocks, Investing in Gold and Other Precious Metals,* and *Create Your Own Treasure With Paintings and Other Artifacts* are not only being gobbled up by a hungry public, but many of the authors are attracting SRO audiences at their public lectures and seminars.

Curiosity.   People are curious about many topics — science, business, sports, government, entertainment, other people, and especially themselves. If you can answer their questions and, in particular, predict events, audiences will be mesmerized by your every word.

This curiosity accounts for the high popularity of such people as psychics, numerologists, tea and palm readers and of such fields as astrology and biorhythms. Radio and TV talk shows, as well as newspaper and magazine columns featuring these topics, enjoy large participatory audiences.

Altruism.   This is the generous urge to help others without any motive of self-gain. It is on this basic urge that the United Fund, Heart Fund, the Salvation Army, and the various cancer research funds base their appeals for financial aid, and the Red Cross bases its appeal for blood donations. It also explains why such programs as the Peace Corps and VISTA have been so successful.

Many people feel a compulsion to help others — to do something for mankind.

Patriotism. Many people who don't respond to other appeals may react generously when asked to help their country. This is especially true in times of war or other national disasters.

Although our sense of patriotism reached a low ebb during and after the Vietnam War, a noticeable reversal of the anti-patriotic mood has been reported since the election of Governor Ronald Reagan as President. This fact is further documented by the increasing number of public and private colleges offering ROTC military training programs.

Identification of speaker with audience. Let's say you're going to speak to a gathering of farm workers about joining a union. If you once spent a summer picking lettuce or grapes, you should mention that experience in your introduction. Then you could relate to the farm workers, and they would more likely feel that you understand their day-to-day problems, and that you're concerned about their welfare. They would be far more inclined to accept your ideas than if you had never experienced their long hours, meager pay, and spartan housing.

Belonging. All of us belong to families and feel loyal to them as well as to friends, schools, social clubs, political parties, and neighborhood organizations. Most of us feel a very strong loyalty to our profession and place of employment. These networks of loyalties and interrelationships strongly influence our actions and attitudes. Most people need the feeling of belonging.

Desire for adventure. Traveling to faraway, exotic places or experimenting with a new sport (scuba diving or hang gliding) are examples of the desire for adventure.

Some people feel a compulsion for adventure laced with clear-cut danger. For example, climbing a challenging mountain or exploring a fearsome glacier, big game hunting in Africa, diving perilously deep for ship wreckage or treasure, or sailing across the Atlantic singlehandedly. Our history is distinguished by families and individuals with a penchant for adventure — from our early pioneer settlers to our pioneers in space travel.

Since all the above motives (needs, wants, desires) affect people in different ways, when you speak to persuade, you should try to appeal to your listeners through as many motives as possible.

Another phase of your overall strategy is to make it easy for your listeners to take the action you advocate. For example, if you're speaking to a neighborhood organization about better street lighting, don't ask them to send letters to their selectmen or mayor, because they probably won't. Instead, make it easy for them: have a typed petition ready, circulate it immediately after you talk, and push them to sign it.

This very basic discussion of human needs, wants, and desires merely touches the surface of the vast, tremendously complex subject of human motivation and persuasion. It is a fascinating area with endless frontiers.

Who would imagine, for example, that even the *locale* (where the speech is given) of a persuasive speech could possibly influence the outcome of the speech? Yet, this happened in the 1976 presidential primary campaign. Governor Jimmy Carter, a Southerner born and bred, won the black vote consistently, except in Maryland, and thereby won some crucial primary elections. One tactic distinguished Governor Carter from all the other Democratic candidates — he spoke to black audiences in their churches.[3]

Remember this — to convince people, you should appeal to their minds and emotions; one reinforces the other.

> When listeners are convinced in their minds that what the speaker says is right, and when they feel in their "guts" (glands, muscles, nerve endings, viscera) that they very much want to engage in the action or movement he is urging, the combination of intellect plus emotions is all but unstoppable.[4]

SUGGESTED TOPICS FOR SPEECHES TO PERSUADE

1. Examinations for public school teachers should be mandatory as part of their evaluation process.

2. A public school education should not be for everyone.

3. There is (is not) an equitable solution for the Mideast crisis.

---

[3]*Boston Sunday Globe*, 11 July 1976, p. 33.

[4]Communication and Leadership Program, Toastmasters International, Inc. Santa Ana, California, p. 69, 1971.

4. Will there be a Social Security program when we retire?

5. Women should have the right to decide on a possible abortion.

6. Have we learned anything from the last energy crisis?

7. Can Detroit compete with Japan?

8. Is the strength of American unions beginning to wane?

9. All educational grants should be replaced by loan programs.

10. Most welfare programs should be replaced with workfare ones.

11. Why we must (must not) reinstitute the draft.

12. Why (why not) a basic speech course should be required for graduation.

13. We should (should not) withdraw from the United Nations.

14. Prisons should be for punishment, not for rehabilitation.

15. There should be a recall petition for all elected officials.

16. All millionaires should pay some income tax.

17. X-rated movies should (should not) be permitted on late-night TV.

18. Criminals are getting away with murder.

19. Why entrapment should (should not) be illegal?

20. Since liquor and tobacco are legal, why not marijuana?

21. Everyone should be fingerprinted at birth.

22. In national elections, all polling places should close at the same time.

23. Grade inflation is watering down higher education.

24. Why public employees should (should not) have the right to strike.

THINGS TO THINK ABOUT AND DO

1. List a few topics for a persuasive speech that would affect members of your class. Explain what methods you would use to win their sympathy and motivate them to react the way you want them to.

2. Excluding the topics previously listed, give two topics for speeches to persuade.

3. Evaluate three TV commercials as to their intended audience and the persuasive appeal(s) used. Did the commercials accomplish their purpose?

4. Prepare a five-minute gripe talk about something at your school or place of employment. Present a solution to the situation and conclude by suggesting some form of action for your audience to take.

WHAT DO YOU REMEMBER FROM THIS CHAPTER?

1. List a few purposes of talks to persuade.

2. Why is audience analysis critical?

3. What is the benefit of anticipating questions and objections?

4. Name a few ways to persuade people.

5. List several traits of a speaker's credibility.

6. Is credibility the sole requirement to persuade people? Explain.

7. Name several basic needs of individuals.

VITALIZE YOUR VOCABULARY

Present-day English embraces thousands of words based on roots taken from the ancient Greek language. Here is a sampling of roots, along with their meanings and some relevant English words:

Roots	Meanings	English words
Anthrop	Man, mankind	Anthropology, philanthropy
Bio	Life	Biology, biography
Chron	Time	Chronicle, chronology, synchronize
Geo	Earth	Geology, geography, geometry
Gon	Angle, corner	Pentagon, trigonometry
Hydr	Water	Dehydrate, hydrant, hydroplane
Metr, meter	Measure	Diameter, metronome, geometry
Onym	Name, word	Anonymous, pseudonym, synonym

Orth	Straight, correct	Orthodox, orthodontist, orthopedic
Phil	Like, love	Anglophile, bibliophile, philanthropic (see *anthrop* above)
Phon	Sound	Euphony, phonetics, telephone
Pod	Foot	Tripod, podium
Scop	Look at, watch	Microscope, periscope, telescope
Tele	Distant, far	Telegram, telephone, telescope (see *scop* above)
Tom	Cut, split	Appendectomy, atomize

13

Saying a Few Words

*Let thy speech be short,
comprehending much in a
few words.*[1]

CHAPTER OBJECTIVES

After reading and understanding this chapter, you should be able to:

- Make an announcement.
- Introduce a speaker.
- Present an award.
- Give a thank-you talk after receiving an award.
- Make a nominating speech.
- Give an installation speech.
- Propose a toast.
- Utilize a public address microphone.

[1]Ecclesiastes 32:8.

CHAPTER DIGEST

Since many of you belong to or may join an organization, you may be called upon sometime to introduce a speaker, present an award, nominate someone for office, make an announcement, or give a report. You may even be asked to propose a short toast. If you're lucky, you may be elected toastmaster or function chairman, and in that position you may present some or all of the special types of speeches explained in this chapter.

As an active member of your organization, you may also be called upon to respond to any of the above speech situations.

This chapter briefly touches upon these special-occasion talks from the standpoints of the introducer (function chairman, toastmaster, master of ceremonies) and the person giving the response. Some examples of these talks are included.

Once upon a time, in the days of the Roman Empire, a mob was gathered in the Coliseum to watch as a Christian was thrown to a hungry lion. The spectators cheered as the wild beast went after its prey. But the Christian quickly whispered something in the lion's ear and the beast backed away with obvious terror on his face. No amount of calling and foot stomping by the audience could get the lion to approach the Christian again. Fearlessly, the Christian walked from the arena.

The Emperor was so amazed at what had happened that he sent for the Christian and offered him his freedom if he would say what he had done to make the ferocious beast cower in fear. The Christian bowed before the Emperor and said, "I merely whispered in the lion's ear: 'After dinner, you'll be required to say a few words.' "[2]

GIVING A SHORT TALK

The odds are in your favor that as you mature and as you start your ascent in the business or social community, you may be called upon "to say a few words." Industry executives agree that there is

---

[2]S. H. Simmons, *New Speakers' Handbook* (New York: Dial Press, 1972), pp. 22–23.

"After dinner, you'll have to say a few words."

no surer way for an employee to make her mark in the company than to display the ability to communicate effectively before an audience. The same holds true for your fraternal, civic, or other social activities, and you'll be amazed at the respect and admiration you earn when you can comfortably stand up to give a short talk.

There is no specific set of rules that encompasses all the situations that may surround a special-occasion talk. Many factors impinge upon the talk: your personality and position, circumstances of the occasion, time element involved, type of audience, the main speaker, and the reason for the particular talk. All these factors must be considered.

The most important qualification of all these talks is brevity. Usually the talk ranges from one to five minutes except for the toast, which is usually less than a minute. If you're the chairman, your function is to be an intermediary between head table and audience. You're not expected to give a long-winded speech about yourself or to poke fun at the guest of honor. Your job is to move the proceedings along, quickly and smoothly, with dignity and a sense of professionalism.

There are many types of special-occasion talks ranging from announcements to sales talks to welcomes. This chapter deals only with talks that might be of immediate concern to you.

MAKING AN ANNOUNCEMENT

At almost all organizational meetings, time is usually set aside to ask for help with a future event and announce its time and place. Announcements should be short and carefully prepared, and they should include all pertinent information.

It's amazing how many announcements exclude an important bit of information, for example, the date or time of the event. Perhaps you can recall attending a meeting in which a committee chairman announced an upcoming event, only to be asked, "What was that date again?"

GETTING THE FACTS

If you're responsible for gathering information for an announcement, seek an authoritative source (the president of your organization, the chairman of a committee, the member designated by the chairman). Get the source's phone number so that you can double-check information or any changes that may occur before the announcement has to be made. In preparing your announcement include as many of the five W's (who, what, when, where, why) as possible and the H (how).

When you've prepared the announcement, check it for all details. Ask yourself:

1. What is being planned?

2. When and where will the event be held?

3. Will tickets be necessary? If so, how much will they cost?

4. Is the event open only to members?

5. What is the reason for the event?

6. Where will the proceeds go?

7. Who is responsible for the event?

8. Are volunteers needed? If they are, who should be contacted?

9. Do the day and date of the event coincide on the calendar?

10. If there's to be a speaker, who will she be?

Gather as much correct information as possible and present only vital information. Almost all organizations publish newsletters or bulletins that will include more details of a particular event. Because of this, your announcement need not give telephone numbers of people to contact.

DELIVERING THE ANNOUNCEMENT

Delivering your announcement with enthusiasm can bolster interest and positive reaction from your audience. You may conclude your announcement by repeating key facts.

Example of an Announcement

The Boston College High School Parents' Club will hold its annual May Festival, Saturday, May 18, from 9 a.m. to 4 p.m. on the school grounds. As you know all the proceeds will go toward the scholarship fund.

We can still use some volunteers for an hour or two. Please check in with one of our volunteer coordinators, Mr. Joseph Robert or Ms. Deborah Grilli right after this meeting. We would appreciate a little of your time and effort.

Remember, our annual May Festival will be held all day Saturday, May 18, right here on the B.C. High School grounds and we need more volunteers. Thank you.

INTRODUCING A SPEAKER

The main problem with introducing a speaker is that, all too often, the introducer talks far too long. This situation was highlighted in an anecdote told by the late Chief Justice and President William Howard Taft.

Once he presided at a meeting at which a number of distinguished guests were to give five-minute talks. The chairman of the event, a young man, rose to say a few words and proceeded to ramble on for forty-five minutes. After he sat down, Chief Justice Taft stood up and said: "I remember once when I was in politics,

we had a meeting at which there was to be one of these prelimi-
nary addresses. One guest captured and held the platform and
when he finally finished, I remarked, 'I will now present Mr. So-
and-So, who will give you his address.' Mr. So-and-So arose and
stated, with some heat, 'My address is 789A 22nd Street, New
York City, where my train goes in fifteen minutes. Good night.' "

If you're responsible for introducing a speaker, consider the
following Be's:

Be aware of your responsibility   Your primary function is to prepare and motivate your audience for the featured speaker. If you
can instill an interest in listening to her, you've done your job.

Be familiar with the speaker and the topic.   As soon as you know
who the speaker will be, find out as much as possible about her
background and the subject of the speech. If she is well-known,
information on her will be available through the speaker's press
office or in newspapers. If she is not well-known, a phone call
could bring you a profile.

If possible, try to meet the speaker before the event to ensure
that your information is accurate and current and that you know
the topic she will discuss. You don't want her to have to correct
you during her opening remarks. Sometimes the title of the speech
will suffice; at other times it may be appropriate to mention the
subject matter.

Be brief.   How often have you heard an MC (master of ceremonies) say, "Our speaker this evening needs no introduction,"
and then proceed to extol her from birth to the present? If she
needs no more than a short introduction, then give a short introduction and let her take over.

Your introduction should not exceed two or three minutes. No
better example exists of brevity and simplicity than the introduction
you've heard many times, "Ladies and gentlemen, the President of
the United States."

Be careful not to embarrass the speaker.   Sometimes a chairman
can go to extremes in praising the speaker as one of the most brilliant, eloquent, and humorous orators of the day.

This is embarrassing for three reasons: (1) the speaker may not
be able to live up to such an introduction; (2) she probably *realizes*
that she cannot match the introduction; (3) the chairman may be
preparing the audience for a resounding letdown.

Be brief in your introduction.

Be natural. If you're good at telling anecdotes and jokes or at being humorous, great. Nothing sets an audience more at ease and in a receptive mood than a few laughs. It is of benefit to you if you can spice your introductory remarks with humor that directly links the speaker, her subject, and the occasion. However, if you're not a naturally humorous person, *don't try to be.* Humor in the wrong hands can be disastrous. As any professional comedian will admit, there's nothing funny about trying to make people laugh. It's a very serious business.

Be informative. It's important to have a balanced blend of the following ingredients: the speaker's background, the subject of the message, the specific occasion, and the audience. Ponder each of these items separately and completely when you're preparing your introduction.

Be careful not to make personal comments about the speaker's subject. This is not the time and place to editorialize. When you introduce the speaker's topic to the audience, don't spout off on the topic. That is why the speaker is there. You may mention the importance of the subject, its relationship to the audience, and the speaker's knowledge of it, but leave the contents to her.

Be sure to pronounce the speaker's name correctly.   The most famous slip of the tongue was uttered by radio announcer Harry Von Zell when he proclaimed to the nation, "Ladies and gentlemen, the President of the United States, Hoobert Heever." Clearly, the announcer knew how to pronounce the name, but it just didn't come out that way.

If you're not positive about the exact pronunciation of the speaker's name, ask her how to pronounce it. Failing to make an effort to ascertain the correct pronunciation is inexcusable. If you have to, write it down phonetically.

Present the speaker to the audience.   If you feel that the speaker is not well-known to the audience, you may mention her name several times during the introduction. If she is known to the audience and you want to use a dramatic approach, you may announce her name at the very end of your introduction. After you've presented her, face her, and in a warm, welcoming manner, wait until she arrives at the speaker's stand; then return to your seat. (You start the applause.)

Example of a Speech to Introduce a Speaker

It is, indeed, a rare privilege for me to have the opportunity of introducing our guest speaker for this evening.

Dr. Tardanico has been an active member of our state society for almost twenty years. He graduated from Palmer College of Chiropractic with the highest honors. He has served on many committees and has been elected to the four highest offices of the profession in our state society. He served in all these positions with great distinction and acclaim.

His reputation as a brilliant practitioner and eloquent speaker has taken him throughout most of the United States lecturing and conducting seminars. He has achieved a national reputation as a spokesman for the chiropractic profession and has appeared on many national radio and television talk programs.

Last year he was the recipient of the "Chiropractor of the Year" award — a most coveted honor since it represents the love, respect, and admiration of the entire membership . . . his peers.

It is a great personal honor to present to you our esteemed colleague and guest speaker this evening, Dr. Philip A. Tardanico.

PRESENTING AN AWARD

In planning to present an award you should:

Refer to the award itself.   It is important in your opening remarks to call attention to the award that is about to be presented. What is its significance? When and why was it founded? Who was its first recipient? Is it presented annually or only on special occasions? These are some questions to consider, and you may think of others.

Refer to the occasion.   This will prepare your audience for what is about to take place. You will attract the audience's attention and interest.

Refer to the recipient.   This is a very important part of your talk. Explain why this individual or group was selected and how the selection was made. Be sure to point out to the audience the recipient's achievements which led to this honor.

Refer to those whom you represent.   If this award is being presented in behalf of a lodge, council, club, or company, mention this fact. The source of the award is of vital interest not only to the recipient but also to the audience. The source certainly deserves praise. Express the sincere good will of the source and its satisfaction with the person chosen.

Make the actual presentation.   For the sake of building interest and including an element of mystery, you may wish to mention the name of the recipient last. Then, if the award can easily be handled, hold it up for all to see, read the inscription on it, present it, and congratulate the recipient. Then allow the recipient the opportunity to respond.

Example of a Speech to Present an Award

The award I'm about to present is a very special one. It is the "Outstanding Athlete Award." What makes it very very special is that not only does it represent the student's ability and accomplishments in athletics, but perhaps even more significant is the fact that the winner is chosen, by vote, by his fellow students.

In the four years he's* been here, he's excelled in soccer, track, and baseball, helping to bring championships in those sports to this school.

He's been active in various school activities and if that weren't enough, he is graduating with a 4.0 average. Many of his colleagues know him as a "regular" guy who was always ready to help someone.

Next year he will be a freshman at Stonehill College. I'm sure it won't take them very long to realize what a quality young man he is. I'm very proud to present "The Outstanding Athlete Award" to someone we're all going to miss . . . Albert James.

RECEIVING AN AWARD

Sometimes when an award is presented, no formal reply is needed or expected. If that's the case, a simple sincere "Thank you" will be sufficient. At other times a reply might be appropriate or called for by "speech, speech." If you're going to a function and there is the slightest possibility that you may be given an award, prepare a thank-you statement. It is much better to be ready to say something and not be presented with an award than to be presented with it and not be ready to speak.

In preparing a speech of acceptance:

Be honest.   If the award comes as a total surprise, your facial expression may attest to the fact, but don't hesitate to express your surprise orally. The audience will be more appreciative and delighted. You should have no difficulty expressing your sincere feelings of gratitude. Sometimes a sincere "thank you very much" will suffice.

Call attention to the award.   Explain what the award means to you. (You might want to refer to others who have received the award previously.)

Be generous in your praise.   If you're accepting an award in behalf of a group or team, be sure to share the honor with them. If it was a singular effort and someone inspired you, don't keep it a secret. If appropriate, mention the future and how this honor may

---

*This contraction for he is is acceptable in speech but not in most formal writing. For a detailed comparison between written and spoken communication, see the table on page 156.

affect your efforts and plans. Don't forget to thank those responsible for presenting you with the award. It may also be appropriate to thank the individual who made the presentation.

Example of a Speech to Accept an Award

You know, I can honestly say that I can't remember a single instance in my life when I was really at a loss for words.

There are two things I will always remember this evening for. One, I'm at a loss for words, and two, I'm deeply moved to receive this plaque naming me the recipient of your "Outstanding Member of the Year Award."

I know what this award represents, because I have actively participated in the voting for our first two recipients. It is indeed a thrill for me to join their elite company.

The honor you have presented me with this evening will always remain very special. I wish to thank the members of the nominating committee and each and every one of you for your most generous expression of recognition.

I will always cherish this award and the precious moments of this evening. Thank you very much.

Be generous in your praise.

MAKING A NOMINATING SPEECH

As you become more involved in organizations, whether scholastic, business, or political, the opportunity may present itself to nominate someone for an office. If you belong to an organization, perhaps you recall a meeting when nominations for offices were called for. Someone from the floor, after being recognized by the chairman, may say, "I would like to place in nomination the name of Mrs. Marcia Driscoll" or "I would like to nominate Mr. Vincent Shea." What you heard were *names* placed in nomination. Following are some suggestions to use if you want to nominate more than just a name but a person worthy of the office.

Describe the responsibilities of the office.   Mention the specific requirements attached to the office. Include its duties, importance, and broad responsibilities. (Remember that you want to build a powerful case for your nominee.)

Name the candidate.   In a voice so that all can hear *clearly*, announce your candidate and then explain to the gathering why she is the right person for the office. Mention the candidate's background, experience, and other offices held. How long has she been a member and did she serve on any committees? Now's the time to fire all cannons.

Place the name in nomination.   You now conclude your nomination talk by formally announcing the full name of your candidate. For example, "Therefore, ladies and gentlemen, it is with a great deal of pride that I place in nomination for the office of president of local 2259 the name (loud and clear) of Jim Hurley." At this point your fellow supporters should explode with approval.

Example of a Speech to Nominate a Candidate

I am very proud to place in nomination for president of our alumni association the name of one of our most active members, Mr. Andrew Aloisi.

We all know the demanding responsibilities that this office bears . . . leadership qualities, the talent to select chairmen of important committees, the ability to look ahead, the gift to motivate and certainly the love of his alma mater.

Mr. Aloisi possesses all these attributes and more. During the last few years he has "answered the call" many times from this organization, and with distinction. As chairman of the membership committee, he was responsible for significantly increasing our active rolls. As program director, he brought many new and interesting events to this organization. Last year he was chairman of the Fund Raising Committee, and our coffers were swelled by the most successful year ever enjoyed by our association. He has also served with credit on our travel committee.

Mr. Aloisi is a successful businessman and, at the request of this association, has generously made himself available many many times to talk and meet with recent graduates and help them in launching their careers.

He is an executive with understanding and compassion and that special talent of being able to get things done. Those of us who have had the good fortune of working with Andrew know only too well his executive ability and devotion to his duties.

This coming year we will be celebrating our 100th anniversary. It is a special occasion that promises to attract renowned educators and political leaders from all parts of the world. This special time warrants special leadership, and with that in mind I take great pleasure to place in nomination for the office of president of our alumni association . . . Mr. Andrew Aloisi.

GIVING AN INSTALLATION SPEECH

Congratulations, you've been elected to office. Now your headaches really begin. Not really, because you've worked hard for the victory and you deserve it. However, you must now plan to make your first speech before the group. Below are some helpful ideas.

Express your gratitude.   The first order of business is to express your sincere thanks for the vote of confidence bestowed upon you, particularly by your supporters. You should also ensure your non-supporters that you will represent them fairly.

Accept the challenge.   You may wish to mention what the office is all about and enumerate some significant responsibilities. Explain that you accept all the challenges the office has to offer and look forward to the coming term.

Admit that it's not a job for one person.   Tell the group that getting the job done requires more than one person and you're looking forward to working closely with the other officers and various committees. It's also appropriate (and could win goodwill) to refer to the past president in a complimentary fashion and indicate that you would like to call upon her occasionally for advice.

Look ahead. A very important part of your installation address is now at hand. The group will be anxious to hear something about your future plans. You can motivate your audience by outlining some of the steps you plan to take in the coming term. It is not necessary to detail every program, plan of action, or all you hope to accomplish. Again, brevity is important. You'll have many other opportunities to address the group.

Example of an Installation Speech

I wish to express my sincere thanks for the honor you have bestowed upon me this evening. Our association is well-known in the community not only for its active membership, but also for the many acts by its members in and for our community. It is a privilege to have been elected to its highest office.

This organization — and we are all proud of it — achieved many milestones during the past year. It comforts me to know that I will have the full support and cooperation from our now past president, Stephen Rowley, as I begin my new term.

Shortly, I will be calling upon you for your assistance . . . to head committees, become committee members, and to fulfill other important duties. I know your response will be as generous as it always has been.

This organization, as any organization, is only as effective as the involvement of its members. We have one of the largest memberships of any organization in the state. And we have a record of accomplishments that speaks for itself.

The two major goals I have established for the coming year are to increase our membership and to become more involved in our community. A high-priority item on our agenda will be the establishment of a special fund-raising committee to help us further meet special community needs.

This will be a year of commitment, challenge, and participation. I will furnish that commitment. I will accept that challenge. I now ask for your participation.

Again, I thank you for your vote of confidence and the opportunity to serve you.

WARNING

Be careful not to say anything critical of the preceding year that will reflect unfavorably on your predecessor. Remember that you've just been complimentary to your predecessor.

PROPOSING A TOAST

There are many occasions when proposing a toast is appropriate and desirable: births, birthdays, graduations, bar mitzvahs, weddings, anniversaries, promotions, and so on. The occasion could be a large gathering or an evening with a companion. No matter what the occasion, the toast should be brief, meaningful, and sincere.

A good exercise is to try to write down as many short toasts for as many situations as possible and keep the list handy for various occasions. Whenever you hear a clever toast, jot it down, perhaps rewording it to fit your own personality.

The following are examples of toasts for various occasions:

Births

To Brian . . . may you have the strength of your father, the patience of your mother and, until that time, may you be as quiet as your kitten.

Birthdays

May the joy of this day be the forerunner of the many, many more to come, happy birthday.

Graduation

For all your studies which brought much achin'
May they make it easier for you to bring home the bacon.
Congratulations.

Bar Mitzvah

May the helping hand of God be always near as you leave boyhood and enter manhood. Shalom.

Weddings

To two beautiful people who have found each other, Frank and Barbara, . . . may life shower upon both of you torrents of love, health, and happiness.

Anniversaries

May the happy memories of yesterday and today be multiplied tenfold for all your tomorrows. Congratulations.

Job Promotion

To one of your company's wisest investments from which it's bound to reap substantial dividends — your promotion. Good Luck.

A Toast to You

Here's to the student who may be called upon to say
    A few meaningful words on someone's special day
Be the request from a friend, a loved one, or boss
    When you open your mouth, may you never be at a loss.

TESTING 1 . . . 2 . . . 3 . . . 4

The chances are slim that you'll ever appear before a radio microphone (mike) or a television camera to express your views. It's far more likely that you'll appear before a public address (P.A.) microphone before a school, fraternal, taxpayer, or social gathering. Let's discuss some testing and speaking techniques you may find helpful.

Before you speak, you should test the mike to be sure it's working and at the proper level (volume). To test a mike, *speak* into it. The most common testing phrases are, "Testing 1 . . . 2 . . . 3 . . . 4" or "Hello, testing. Can you hear me OK in the back of the hall?"

Above all, never test a mike by slapping it or blowing into it because it is a very delicate, sensitive instrument. Doing either may damage it and also may annoy your audience.

Being the right distance from the mike is important. If you're too close, your voice will boom at everyone and your P's and B's (*plosives*) will sound like explosions. If you're far away from the mike, the audience will have to strain to hear you and may then tune you out.

The best way to know the correct distance from the mike is to try it out. If the level (volume) has been set correctly, your mouth should be 3 to 5 inches away from it. If your voice is strong, move back from the mike. If your voice is soft, move closer. It's important to listen to yourself and to look at your audience. You can hear yourself from the loudspeakers in the hall, and you can receive feedback from observing your audience.

When speaking over a P.A. system mike, be sure to slow your delivery so that every word can be heard clearly and distinctly. Otherwise, your words may sound all jumbled. Because you'll hear yourself over the loudspeakers a split second after you've spoken, you shouldn't speak too rapidly.

Be sure you speak directly into the mike. Don't move your head from left to right, or the audience will miss half of what you're saying. This movement applies particularly to MC's who may be introducing head table guests. After you've introduced someone, you may look in her direction for a second or two, introduce the next person and speak directly into the mike, then glance at her. Face the person you're introducing only if you can speak directly into the mike at the same time.

And above all, speak in your natural voice. For many people this is the hardest thing to do. It seems that whenever people appear before a microphone, they either try to lower their voices, or sound dramatic, or start to over-e-n-u-n-c-i-a-t-e. Speak as you always do. Remember, the microphone is like a magnifying glass and will detect and amplify flaws in delivery.

Always treat a microphone with respect and always assume it is "on" (live). Otherwise, you could experience an embarrassing and humiliating few moments.

If you have to sneeze, cough, or blow your nose, be sure to turn your head as far away as possible from the mike.

Finally, don't grab or hold onto the mike that you're speaking into. Doing so could produce a hum or static over the loudspeakers that could annoy your listeners.

THINGS TO THINK ABOUT AND DO

1. Get some news of an upcoming event either from your school newspaper or from the student activities center, and make an announcement of the event to the class.

2. Introduce one of your classmates who's prepared to give a talk.

3. Prepare and deliver a two-minute talk to present an award.

4. Prepare and deliver a two-minute talk after receiving an award.

5. Make a two-minute nominating speech.

6 Give a two-minute installation speech.

7. Give a short toast for a wedding, birthday, job promotion, bar mitzvah, or christening.

WHAT DO YOU REMEMBER FROM THIS CHAPTER?

1. What information should be included when you make an announcement?

2. Mention several valid sources of information for an announcement.

3. What is a common problem when someone introduces a speaker?

4. When you introduce a speaker, why should you be careful not to overpraise her?

5. Why should you try to inject some humor in your comments?

6. Name several elements to include when you present an award.

7. Name the important elements of a speech to nominate.

8. What information should an installation speech contain?

9. List several occasions when a toast would be appropriate.

10. How should you test a microphone for operation and level?

11. While speaking into a P.A. mike, how can you be aware of the right volume?

VITALIZE YOUR VOCABULARY

When you communicate, you often use number words or number ideas, but did you ever wonder where the numbers come from? Nearly all the number words in English derive from either Latin or Greek (L or G). For example:

Source words	Meaning	Number words
Uni, from unus (L)	One	Unit, union, unison, unilateral
Primus (L)	First	Primary, primate
Monos (G)	Single, solitary	Monarch, monocle, monogamy, monolog
Semi (L)	Half	Semicircle, semicolon
Hemi (G)	Half	Hemisphere
Bi, bin (L)	Two	Bigamy, binary, binocular
Tri (G)	Three	Tripod, triad, trilogy
Quadr, quadri (L)	Four	Quadrangle, quadrant, quadrille
Penta (G)	Five	Pentathlon, Pentagon, Pentateuch
Quin, quint (L)	Five	Quintet, quintuplets
Decem (L)	Ten	Decade, decathlon, December
Deca, Deka (G)	Ten	Decalogue
Decimus (L)	Tenth	Decibel, decimal
Centum (L)	100	Centennial (see Bi above), centipede
Mille (L)	1,000	Millennium
Kilo (G)	1,000	Kilometer, kiloton
Mega (G)	1,000,000, extremely large	Megaton, megabuck

Myriad (G)	A large indefinite number	Myriad is used as an English word
Micro (G)	1/1,000,000, extremely small	Microscope, microeconomics

14

Let's Meet and Discuss It

Men are never so likely to settle a question rightly as when they discuss it freely.[1]

CHAPTER OBJECTIVES

After reading and understanding this chapter, you should know:

- The characteristics of a panel discussion, symposium, lecture, round-table discussion, and forums.
- The characteristics of brainstorming and buzz sessions and committees.
- The responsibilities of a panel moderator.
- The responsibilities of a panelist.
- The responsibilities of the audience.

CHAPTER DIGEST

The environment, the consumer movement, health care, and education are just a few areas of public concern in which

---

[1]Thomas Babington Macaulay, *Southey's Colloquies*, 1830.

Americans are demanding and getting a voice. They are not only serving on more and more committees, forums, panels, and symposia, they are also speaking up more. In other words, they are interacting in groups to hammer out decisions and to carry them out.

This chapter explains the more common types of group discussion: panel, symposium, lecture, roundtable, brainstorming, committees, and buzz sessions. These various groups consist of moderators, chairpeople or leaders, panelists or participants, and sometimes audiences. The significant responsibilities of these people are listed in detail. Also included in this chapter are diagrams of suggested seating arrangements for these major types of group discussions.

More and more Americans are becoming involved in the affairs of their communities. For example, in the past decade the consumer movement, spearheaded by Ralph Nader, has emerged as a vibrant force in our lives. As a result, consumers are being appointed to state and local regulatory boards and commissions. Parents are participating in advisory councils involving the operation of their children's schools. Concerned citizens are being selected as trustees and advisers to state-supported colleges and universities.

Perhaps never before have people shown more determination to "have a say" in events that affect them, their families, and their pocketbooks. They are a powerful force that can help return big government to grass-root levels.

More than just being present at hearings or large meetings in which they might ask a question or two, citizens are now becoming members of symposia, panels, and committees to communicate, interact, and make decisions.

In the business and professional worlds you may be asked, or may wish, to participate in a convention, conference, department or committee meeting, seminar, brainstorming or buzz sessions, or any one of the many other types of group communication.

Most small-group communication is either *public* (open) or *private* (closed). The *public* discussions take place before an audience, which may or may not be allowed to participate, whereas *private* ones are open only to group members. (See Figure 14-1.) You should realize, however, that increasing federal and state legislation tends to favor public or open meetings.

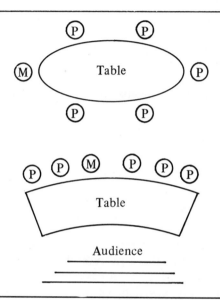

Figure 14-1
A Private/Closed group discussion (top) and a Public/Open group discussion (bottom) with suggested seating arrangements. M signifies moderator and P signifies participants.

The group's private or public status will depend on certain considerations:

- How many group members will participate?
- What is each member's rank and influence?
- What is the subject to be discussed?
- Is the subject confidential?
- How soon must a decision or solution be reached?

- Will the decision affect a small or a large group of people?
- When and where will the meeting be held?

Since this is a basic, practical text, let's discuss the situations in which you're likely to become involved, in or out of class:

- Panel discussion
- Symposium
- Lecture
- Round-table or group discussion
- Brainstorming
- Buzz sessions
- Committees

PANEL DISCUSSION

The panel discussion is perhaps the most popular type of group intercommunication and the one you'll most likely become involved in, either as a moderator, a panelist, or member of the audience. A panel usually consists of four to six members and a moderator seated at a table and facing the audience. Figure 14-2 shows the customary seating arrangement for a panel discussion.

The primary purpose of a panel is for each panelist to state his views on the topic under discussion, to interact with the other panelists, and then to answer questions from the audience. Whenever the audience is allowed to participate in the discussion, regardless of the type of discussion, it becomes a *forum*. Examples of forums are: a *panel discussion forum*, a *symposium forum*, and a *lecture panel forum*.

RESPONSIBILITIES OF THE PANEL MODERATOR

As a panel moderator, you have in your grasp the power to conduct a smooth, meaningful discussion or one fraught with chaos.

1. Be sure that each panelist has a card, with his name clearly printed on it, on the table in front of him so that the audience will know his name. If the class is large and those

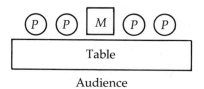

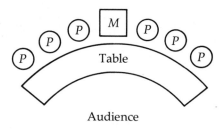

Figure 14-2
Suggested ways to set up a panel discussion. A semicircular seating
arrangement is preferred so that panelists may easily see each
other. This face-to-face arrangement leads to a more effective interpersonal experience. M signifies moderator and P signifies panelists.

in the rear have difficulty reading the names, you might put
each panelist's name on the chalkboard directly behind him.

2. Greet the audience and introduce yourself.

3. Briefly tell the audience the topic to be discussed.

4. Inform the audience when they can question the panel.

5. Introduce each panel member. You may also mention
   whether the panelist's position is pro or con.

6. Allow each panelist to make an opening statement, say, of a
   minute or two.

7. After the opening remarks, allow the panelists to talk and
   question each other.

8. If interaction isn't immediate, be prepared to throw a
   question or two at the panelists to trigger discussion.

9. Remain impartial but be ready to question individual
   panelists if the discussion starts to lag, veer off course, or if
   an opinion needs clarification.

Be tactful, but firm.

10. Be sure to give each panelist a chance to express his views.

11. Be tactful but firm if you have a panelist who's monopolizing the floor. Try to spark some response from the more reticent members.

12. When you feel that the discussion has just about run its course, or if your professor has established a time limit, have each panelist summarize his views in a minute or two.

13. Present a summary of major ideas or concepts expressed from both viewpoints.

14. Open the discussion to the audience.

15. Call only upon those who raise their hands. Again, be aware of time monopolizers. Accept only one question per student so that as many students as possible may speak.

16. Don't hesitate to pronounce anyone out of order if the situation warrants.

17. When the time is up, thank the audience and the panel.

Being a moderator is a responsible assignment that can be extremely rewarding when the result is a smoothly run interactional experience, followed by a spirited but orderly response from the audience.

Be aware of the time element.

RESPONSIBILITIES OF THE PANELISTS

As a member of a team, your attitude and participation are vital to the overall success of the discussion.

1. Be informed and prepared to become totally involved in the discussion. In other words, do your homework.
2. Keep your opening remarks and summary to a minute or so.
3. If a panelist starts to falter, come to his aid immediately by picking up the discussion and sustaining it. Perhaps the panelist just needs a minute or two to regain composure.
4. Have supporting material with you and be prepared to quote the source.
5. Don't monopolize the floor. Give others a chance to speak.
6. Don't interrupt a speaker. Let him finish before you start.
7. Be tolerant and understanding. Don't be overpowering and overbearing.
8. Be brief and to the point. Don't ramble.
9. Don't become personal and sarcastic.
10. Always respect the moderator and the other panelists.
11. Keep cool, no matter how heated the exchange becomes.

Keep cool, no matter how heated the exchange.

RESPONSIBILITIES OF THE AUDIENCE

Psych yourself for a learning experience and be prepared to take notes to use during the question-and-answer period.

1. Give undivided attention to the discussion and to the participants' views.

2. When you wish to ask a question, raise your hand and wait for recognition by the moderator.

3. Keep an open mind until you've heard all the views. Remember the words of engineer-inventor-author Charles F. Kettering, "Where there is an open mind, there will always be a frontier."

4. You may direct your question to the panel in general or to a specific individual.

5. Keep your question short and to the point; don't make speeches.

6. Don't question or enter a discussion with another member of the audience.

7. Don't antagonize or embarrass anyone.

8. Remember that you can disagree without being disagreeable. "We owe almost all our knowledge not to those who have agreed, but to those who have differed."[2]

SYMPOSIUM

A symposium usually consists of three to five members and a moderator. It differs from the panel discussion in that each participant of a symposium covers only one specific phase of the question being presented. The remarks should be well planned, prepared, and practiced before the discussion (just as you would prepare a talk as discussed in Chapter 4).

The symposium is very common at large conventions or business meetings in which experts are invited to speak on specific phases of a question or problem. The moderator introduces the participants and the subject and maintains control over the presentation. He informs the audience of the procedure to be followed and whether or not there will be a forum after the talks. He should also be very much aware of the time element so that he does not interfere with other presentations on the program.

The seating arrangement of a symposium is similar to that of the panel discussion, except that the moderator may sit or stand on one side of the participants instead of in their midst. Figure 14-3 shows the arrangement.

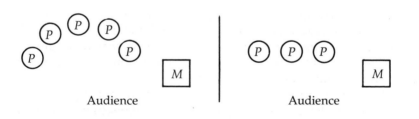

Figure 14-3
Examples of symposia seating arrangements. M signifies moderator and P signifies panelists.

[2]Charles Caleb Colton, *Lacon* (1825).

LECTURES

The lecture panel is one form of public discussion in which a recognized authority on a specific subject presents a lecture and then is questioned by a panel. A variation is the *lecture panel forum* in which the audience is allowed to participate once the lecture and questions from the panel are over. There is also the *lecture forum* in which the audience is allowed to ask questions of the lecturer after he finishes.

A chairman presides over the lecture and introduces the guest lecturer, his subject, and the panel if there is one. He also states the format to be followed. Figure 14-4 illustrates the seating arrangement.

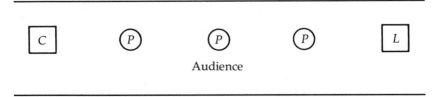

Audience

Figure 14-4
Example of a lecture seating arrangement. C signifies chairman; L, lecturer; and P, panelist.

ROUND-TABLE OR GROUP DISCUSSION

The round-table or group discussion method is most prevalent in classes where discussion and total group interaction are emphasized. The unique feature of this discussion is that there are only participants; there is no audience. Circular seating allows for maximum informality and a sense of closeness.

The leader introduces a subject or question, calls upon individuals for their views, and then invites all members to express themselves freely. This is perhaps the most intimate form of interpersonal communication. The seating arrangement for a round-table discussion is shown in Figure 14-5.

The discussion should be a learning experience for all participants if they make the effort to prepare and participate, keep an open mind, and be ready to inquire. The words of Joseph Joubert, French moralist and essayist, sum up this topic: "The aim of argument, or of discussion, should not be victory, but progress."

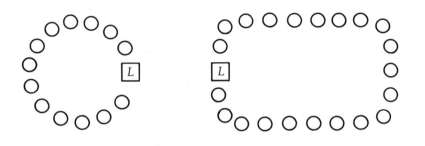

Figure 14-5
Seating arrangements for round-table or group discussion. The choice of arrangement depends on the number of participants. L signifies group leader.

BRAINSTORMING

Brainstorming is a creative, free-wheeling, no-holds-barred approach to solving problems. Participants — usually five to ten in business and up to twenty in a class — should be given a few minutes of silence to think and unleash their imaginations. They should spout anything and everything that comes to mind, and a recorder should list all the ideas on paper or on a blackboard. Quantity of ideas, not quality, should be emphasized.

The crucial principle behind brainstorming is this: no matter how preposterous or "wild" an idea may sound, there must be no criticism or evaluation of it or its contributor. Participants must be free to say anything.

After about fifteen minutes of brainstorming, screen the ideas, then evaluate, expand, and refine them. Next, sift through the surviving list, focusing on the advantages and disadvantages of each, then finalize the list to the best two or three ideas.

Incidentally, brainstorming can be an excellent way to find speech topics.

There should be no criticism of the idea or its volunteer.

BUZZ SESSIONS

This problem-solving process demands a knowledgeable discussion leader who is thoroughly familiar with the problem and who can conduct the entire discussion process. He explains the discussion procedure and the problem to the audience, and divides the group into clusters of four to six individuals. Each group functions independently of the other and may take ten to fifteen minutes to come up with solutions. Someone in each cluster should record them.

At the end of the discussion period, the leader calls time and has each cluster recorder present a one- to two-minute summary of the group's recommendations. The responses are then combined and written on the blackboard. The results are finally discussed by either a pre-selected panel or by the entire audience.

Buzz sessions are an outstanding mode of group communication because everyone usually contributes; some participants tend to clam up in big groups. These sessions may have various formats depending on the people and problems involved, the time constraints, and the location.

COMMITTEES

If you are an activist (and we hope this course helps you become one), you enjoy getting involved. You probably belong to a business, political, religious, educational, civic, or fraternal organization. Such groups have many committees in which you may participate. You may find committees on:

Entertainment	Health and safety
Fund raising	Building
Scholarship	Retirement
Membership	Ward and precinct
Political action	Insurance
Budget and finance	Taxation
Awards	Education

A committee is usually a small group, five to ten members, headed by a chairperson who establishes an agenda (what is to be discussed) and keeps its members on course. Committee members are usually chosen for one or more of these reasons:

Commitment.   They are dedicated members who can place the group's objectives and best interests above their personal feelings. When given an assignment, you know it will be professionally performed. And they will always be prompt for meetings.

Intelligence and experience.   They are knowledgeable persons who know how to track down information, digest it, and present it so everyone can understand it. They can be counted on to have more than one perspective on the subject, and to make positive contributions.

Personality.   They are even-tempered individuals who can take a little "ribbing" and constructive criticism. They can disagree without becoming personal or disagreeable . . . and their friendliness allows them to get along easily with the other committee members.

Integrity.   They have a sense of fair play. They can joke as well as take a joke, but will never belittle or degrade a colleague or his opinions. They can be counted on for their honesty and straightforwardness.

SUGGESTED TOPICS FOR DISCUSSION

1. The electorate should have the power to recall public officials.

2. Judges and/or parole board members should be held accountable for the actions of criminals on probation or parole.

3. Juveniles arrested for serious crimes should be tried as adults.

4. More money should be spent on domestic programs and less for foreign aid.

5. Able-bodied welfare and unemployment recipients should be required to work.

6. Financial aid to students should involve only loans and not grants.

7. Should we curtail our financial support of the United Nations?

8. Capital punishment, yes or no.

9. The Equal Rights Amendment.

10. Is our Social Security program obsolete?

11. Taxes on the middle class have reached confiscatory levels.

12. What to do with the surplus of teachers.

13. Should corporal punishment be reintroduced in the public schools?

14. Should the United States eliminate mandatory public education?

15. Are our colleges and universities suffering from grade inflation?

16. Can we attain full employment?

17. Are we headed for economic disaster?

18. Presidents of the United States should serve one six-year term.

THINGS TO THINK ABOUT AND DO

1. Weigh the advantages and disadvantages of a strong discussion leader.

2. Assume the responsibility for selecting a small group and prepare a fifteen-minute panel discussion. Then, as moderator, present it to the class.

3. List a few topics that would be appropriate for each of the group discussion types mentioned in this chapter.

WHAT DO YOU REMEMBER FROM THIS CHAPTER?

1. List several of the more common types of group discussion.

2. What is generally considered to be the most common type of group discussion?

3. How should a panel be set up for maximum impact?

4. Explain at least five responsibilities of a panel discussion moderator.

5. List and explain at least five responsibilities of a panelist.

6. List and explain at least five responsibilities of the audience.

7. What is it called when the audience is allowed to participate?

8. Briefly explain the symposium.

9. How does the symposium differ from the panel discussion?

10. Explain the differences between a public and private small-group discussion.

11. What is brainstorming?

12. What is a buzz session?

13. Name three qualities that a committee member should have.

VITALIZE YOUR VOCABULARY

Aviation and Space

aeronautics (n.)   the science and engineering involved in flight and in the design, construction, and operation of aircraft.

altimeter (n.)   an instrument that measures altitude.

amphibian (n.)   an airplane that can land and take off on land and water.

anemometer (n.)   an instrument that measures wind speed and force.

asteroid (n.)   any object that orbits the sun.

ceiling (n.)   the top limit of visibility for flying.

cosmic (adj.)   pertaining to the universe, as distinct from the earth.

fuselage (n.)   the body of an airplane.

gyroscope (n.)   a device that helps to keep aircraft on course.

interplanetary (adj.)   between planets.

NASA (n.)   National Aeronautics and Space Administration.

orbit (n.)   the path of a celestial body or artificial satellite in space, especially a closed path around another body.

radar (n.)   a device for locating distant objects by reflecting high-frequency radio waves off them.

reentry (n.)   the return of a spacecraft to the earth's atmosphere.

retrorocket (n.)   a rocket fired from a spacecraft to slow down or stop its forward motion.

satellite (n.)   a celestial body or man-made object that orbits another body.

stratosphere (n.)   an upper layer of earth's atmosphere.

supersonic (adj.)   faster than the speed of sound.

tachometer (n.)   a device that measures engine speed.

thrust (n.)   forward force created by the high-speed discharge from the rear of a jet or rocket engine.

15

"What Do You Say After You Say Hello?"

To listen closely and reply well is the highest perfection we are able to attain in the art of conversation.[1]

CHAPTER OBJECTIVES

After reading and understanding this chapter, you should know:

- Some keys to good conversation.
- Some preconversational elements (factors, tips).
- How to improve your conversational ability.
- How to start a conversation with most people.

CHAPTER DIGEST

Almost all oral communication is speaking face to face with one or a few persons. It's a daily activity in which you can improve a great deal if you try.

One of the keys to becoming a good conversationalist is to be genuinely interested in people. This interest is reflected outwardly by your attitude, eyes, smile, and handshake. Another

---

[1]La Rochefoucauld, *Maxims* (1665).

key is to have many activities or hobbies and to be able to discuss them knowledgeably. Keeping up with the daily news in various fields by means of newspapers, magazines, and radio and TV broadcasts is a third way to help make you a more vital person to be with.

Unquestionably, you can develop your conversational ability if you practice many of the suggestions given. For example, you should be sincere and listen attentively, you should not interrupt, monopolize, offend, complain, or pry, and you should not be a know-it-all.

There are also suggestions for initiating a conversation and keeping it moving, for example, how to introduce people and yourself, how to compliment people sincerely, how to discuss politics and religion, and how to ask provocative questions.

Since many people have trouble remembering names, we briefly discuss some psychological principles that will help you remember names.

Lastly, in today's fast-paced world, making contacts is a significant aspect of getting ahead, so there are suggestions that should help you advance your career.

So far, our major emphasis has focused primarily on how to prepare and deliver a talk confidently on a specific topic. Another more common, critical aspect of communication is one that you engage in daily and one that you should master, namely, the art of conversation.

You will engage in conversation countless times each day for the rest of your life. As far as making an impact on your daily life, there is perhaps nothing more critical than the way you converse with people. Whether at home, at work or at school; at a business, social or community gathering; dealing with your spouse, your roommate, your children or your neighbor; interacting with your bank, utility company or IRS agent; whether in person or over the telephone, conversation plays a vital role in your life. How you converse and the impression you make will have a significant influence on your life and how you live it.

Think for a moment. Can you recall conversations that you wanted to leave or actually did leave because you felt the experience was a waste of time? Perhaps the person who spoke the most was boring and conceited and monopolized the conversation. Perhaps she was a tedious know-it-all or engaged in gossip.

SOME KEYS TO GOOD CONVERSATION

You may recall conversations with people who were interesting and captivating, people who made you feel that you were part of the action, and who listened to you with as much interest as you listened to them. We emphasize this point because, if you're genuinely interested in others, the conversation stands an excellent chance of being interesting. There's nothing like a stimulating conversation. A good conversationalist is usually popular and seldom lacks friends or attention. She knows how to communicate confidently with others. To be well-liked, admired, respected, and to feel honestly that you're making a contribution to society, no matter how infinitesimal, is an unequaled experience.

You can become a better conversationalist, a more interesting person, and a more respected and admired individual. You can if you have the determination to work at it. And what's even better you're not on a stage or under a magnifying glass but among

You're not on stage or under a magnifying glass.

friends. Every day you'll have a multitude of opportunities to practice, to experiment, and to evaluate yourself.

If you blunder, so what? In a few moments you'll have another chance. You won't be graded, criticized, or evaluated. You're free to progress as much as you want, at your own pace. You have your friends, even strangers, classrooms, home, work, the beach, social clubs, and meetings. The world is your laboratory. Are you ready to start experimenting? Let's go!

Conversation begins even before you speak. As we mentioned in Chapter 4, your physical presence and expression transmit impressions, favorable or unfavorable, to those around you. Before engaging in conversation, consider the four following nonverbal elements:

Your attitude.   You must look forward to the conversation. It can be challenging, rewarding, and informative if you allow it to be. Have an open, unbiased mind and be ready to listen to all. Be eager to see what you may derive from this experience and what you may contribute to it.

Your eyes.   If you're genuinely interested, your eyes will reflect it. "The eyes have one language everywhere,"[2] and it's understood everywhere. Look people in the eye to communicate your friendliness and sincerity. If you're not interested, your eyes may transmit a negative impression.

Your smile.   Can you think of a better way to communicate nonverbally with someone than with a sincere smile? Smiling can be contagious. Try it on the next acquaintance you see; you both may be surprised at the results.

Your handshake.   If you're offered a hand or if you offer yours in greeting, shake hands with a grip firm enough to convey a meaningful expression. If you're a person of strength, don't use it for squashing knuckles. By the same token, people don't like a lifeless, dangling handshake.

When you can greet someone with responsive eyes, a friendly smile, and a warm, meaningful handshake, you've mastered the first step in learning to communicate interpersonally.

---

[2]George Herbert, *Jacula Prudentum* (1651).

SUGGESTIONS TO IMPROVE YOUR CONVERSATIONAL ABILITY

Are there any secrets, special formulas, or rules that can make you a more effective conversationalist? No, but you must have a burning desire and a total commitment to effort. Let's look at some suggestions that could help you sharpen your conversational ability.

Be interested.   The right attitude is a prerequisite in participating in conversation. Be interested not only in all the topics but also in each participant. If you're not interested in the participants, they'll respond in the same way. So, when someone is speaking, focus your entire attention on that person.

Be interesting.   One of the secrets to being interesting is to have varied interests and to be knowledgeable about them. A good conversationalist can discuss (with reasonable confidence) local, state, and national politics and knows something about the economy, sports, and the social, educational, and entertainment world. She reads the daily newspaper and a weekly news magazine, listens to news on radio and TV, sees movies, and reads books and magazines. She talks with people and *listens critically.*

Hobbies, travel experiences, sports, jobs, military service, and people you've met or work with are all possibilities for stimulating conversation. If you make the effort to expand your horizons you can become more interesting to others.

Be sincere.   In conversation, don't try to put on airs and don't bluff, lie, or brag. An insincere person usually ends up with himself as his only audience. There is no substitute for sincerity.

Who said, "You can fool some of the people all of the time, all of the people some of the time, but not all of the people all of the time"? Abraham Lincoln? Right.

Be a good listener.   There is no greater compliment to a speaker than your being completely absorbed in what she is saying. Listen with your eyes, your ears, your mind — your total self — with intensity. You'll be amazed at how much you can get wrapped up in an individual and how much information you can acquire which may ultimately enhance your contribution to the exchange. Listening is as important as speaking because one cannot function without the other.

President Franklin D. Roosevelt once received an official visitor who immediately commented on one of the ship models on his desk. FDR took the bait and devoted most of the thirty-minute visit to discussing ships and the Navy. When the visitor left, the Chief Executive said to his secretary, "That man is one of the best conversationalists I have ever met."

Don't interrupt.   An easy way to turn people off or to anger them is to interrupt them often while they're speaking. It's a rude thing to do, and the person guilty of it usually can't wait to finish someone else's story, to correct a speaker, or to announce the punch line prematurely. Interrupting is justified only when a speaker is boring his audience, is becoming offensive (uses profanity, is bigoted or insulting). If you must interrupt, be as tactful as possible to avoid a scene.

Don't have a one-track mind.   We all know one-track people who can discuss only one or two topics: their job, their hobby or sport, their house, car, or boat. It might have been interesting the first or second time, but the third time it becomes boring.

Family and relatives can be boring topics, especially from the person who can't wait to extract a wallet bursting with children's pictures. Winston Churchill felt that the subject of children was inappropriate for adult conversation. At one particular gathering an ambassador said to him, "You know, Sir Winston, I've never told you about my grandchildren." The old warrior chomped on his cigar, dragged deeply, and exhaled, "I realize it, my dear fellow, and I can't tell you how grateful I am."

Don't drag on.   Once your turn has come to talk, don't act as though it may be your last chance on earth and go on and on and on. If you have something to say, say it; that's the essence of conversation. Then give others the opportunity to express themselves, listen to them, and respond.

Unfortunately, long-winded speakers have always assailed our ears and taxed our patience. Early in the nineteenth century General Alexander Smythe was noted for congressional speeches that droned on and on. Once he said to his rival, Senator Henry Clay, "You, sir, speak for the present generation, but I speak for posterity." Senator Clay, a brilliant orator, replied, "Yes, and you seem determined to speak until the arrival of your audience."

Family and relatives can be boring topics.

Don't be offensive. There are many ways to offend people, for example, by making derogatory remarks about their dress, physical appearance, voice, accent, religion, or politics. These remarks cause two negative results: They anger the recipient and they brand the offender as a person to shun. It's far better to say nothing than to rub people the wrong way.

Don't be a constant complainer. Everyone has problems and, as a rule, would rather not hear yours. Briefly introducing your problem might be acceptable to your listeners, but don't dwell on it for the entire conversation. Then there are those who always complain, no matter what the subject is. Since their negative attitude can be contagious, you'd be wise to avoid them.

Don't pry. Nobody can be more offensive than one who persists in prying for personal information. Following are some typical questions:

- Why don't you have any children?
- Your drapes are beautiful. They must be expensive.
- And how old might you be, my dear?

A super reply was once returned by my wife (Mrs. AJV) when a busybody asked about her husband's income. My wife leaned toward the social intruder and whispered, "Are you good at keeping secrets?" "Oh yes, certainly," was the reply. To which my wife answered, "So am I."

Don't be a know-it-all. An obnoxious person in conversation is the expert on everything — politics, labor problems, social problems, religion, family affairs. No matter what the topic of discussion may be, she has the answers. Being knowledgeable is a tremendous asset when you participate in conversation, but sometimes discretion and good taste are higher virtues.

Disagree without being disagreeable. Nothing is more stimulating than a conversation sparked with disagreement, provided it remains on a rational, friendly level. There is much to gain from hearing out opposing viewpoints, plus the challenge of converting or being converted. Whenever disagreement is introduced into a conversation, everybody's interest perks up. Don't holler or lose your cool if someone gets the better of you. If you feel embarrassed at losing an argument, perhaps you could have been better prepared. There'll be a next time. No one likes to lose, but accepting it gracefully could earn you respect.

Remember the old proverb, "We owe almost all our knowledge not to those who have agreed, but to those who have differed."[3]

Don't exclude anyone. When you're involved in conversation, be sure to direct your remarks to everyone, not just to one person. Look at each one as you make your points. In this way you include everyone in your conversation. Then they'll be more apt to pay attention to you and to respond. Interest shown by eye contact, by a nod of the head, and by an occasional gesture toward an individual will do it.

---

[3]Charles Caleb Colton, *Lacon* (1825), 2.121.

Don't be shy.   In every conversation there are speakers, listeners, and speaker-listeners. Perhaps you're the kind who'd rather remain in the background and just listen to what's going on. But that's only half the fun. If you tend toward shyness, you probably belong to the majority of mankind.

TV commentator Barbara Walters was one of that majority. Some years ago she and her husband attended a Fourth of July party where they were introduced to novelist Truman Capote. His book, *In Cold Blood*, had just been published and was zooming to the top of the best-seller list. ". . . I was yearning to talk with him about it," she confessed, "but I couldn't cross the barrier of my own shyness and my fear that Capote must be fed up with people asking about his work."[4]

If you're a listener or a speaker-listener, you may find that small groups (four or five people) are easier to break into than large groups (ten or more). The important thing is that you must *want* to engage in conversation. A good exercise is to observe good talkers in action and to adopt some of their methods.

As we said earlier, since the whole world is your laboratory, experiment with these techniques. You have a great deal to gain, and when you start to participate more in conversation, it will become easier and it will do wonders for your self-confidence. Since improvement depends on your active participation, the sooner you start, the better.

STARTING A CONVERSATION

Let's now look at some ways to help you start a conversation and keep it going.

"I'd like you to meet . . ."   Assume that you're being introduced to a small group. Your introducer, if she's sharp, will mention something about you, your background, experience, or job and perhaps even tell you some unusual tidbits about individuals you're meeting. During this time you can decide to whom you would like to return for conversation because of a possible common interest.

---

[4]Barbara Walters, *How to Talk with Practically Anybody About Practically Anything* (Garden City, N.Y.: 1970), p. xiii.

"Hello, I'm . . ."   If there's no one to introduce you, you should introduce yourself. Since nearly everyone at a gathering enjoys meeting the other guests, take a deep breath, approach someone and introduce yourself. In addition to your name, give some information that might be interesting to the person and that might allow her to respond in kind. After the handshake, repeat her name aloud. Then you might say something about the host and hostess, your work, your home, sports or the latest headline news. Then toss the ball to the other guest and see what she does with it.

"Excuse me, but didn't I hear you mention . . . ?"   On occasion you may overhear a topic of interest from someone in a small group. Nothing could be more complimentary, at your first opportunity, than to approach the person with something like, "Excuse me, but I couldn't help hear you mention . . . ? That sounds fascinating. Could I ask you . . . ?" The mere fact that you're interested in someone enough to pursue her line of conversation will open the door for you, and a lively meeting could ensue.

"Say, I like your . . ."   Nothing is easier to take than a sincere compliment. Perhaps you admire someone's jewelry, shirt, blouse, hairdo, suit. If you do, say so. Again, since bringing positive attention to someone's abilities or possessions is highly satisfying, you're almost guaranteed an interested listener. Paying a genuine compliment is an excellent springboard for starting a conversation.

"Crummy weather we're having, eh?"   Discussing the weather can serve two purposes: It can fill in a silent period between people, and it can be an interesting subject if you're on top of the news. What about the drought in the midwest, its effect on food prices and possible forest fires? What about the sinkholes caused by drought in Florida, the mudslides in California, and the torrential rains and dam burst in Colorado? How about the weather satellite? Is it doing its intended job? Don't forget hurricanes and their awesome power. Can man harness that power?

"I never discuss politics and religion."   Although some people will not discuss politics and religion, these subjects can lead to a stimulating, informative give-and-take. For that to happen, however, the participants must not become hot-headed, irrational, or belligerent. There perhaps has never been a time in our country's history when so much controversy surrounds so many political and religious issues. For that reason alone, we should talk over those subjects more than ever. Exploring them intelligently can be a beneficial experience that could lead to better understanding among people.

"How do you like the weather?"

Play the role of interviewer.   Although some of you may find this technique difficult, it can be most rewarding. It requires discovering someone who has an unusual background or profession, someone who may be quietly sitting in the background. Get the person to talk. This technique involves asking questions (how? what? why?), and could result in an exhilarating experience for you and for many of those present.

A few years ago we (the AJV's) attended a large social gathering where we knew only the host and hostess. From talking with the hostess, I learned that one guest — and the hostess pointed him out — was a senior design engineer in a company that produced and tested missiles. She added that he was not only brilliant and had a sense of humor, he could also translate difficult scientific concepts into layman's language.

At the first chance I introduced myself to the engineer and started questioning him about his early start in mechanics and electronics, about some design challenges and solutions, about his travel overseas, and so on. As the conversation warmed up, more and more guests began to ask questions and contribute comments. When a lull occurred, I revved up the proceedings with another pertinent question.

By the time the conversation ended three hours later, practically every one of the forty guests had participated in this informative and sometimes entertaining experience.

An excellent way to learn this technique is to listen to radio and TV talk shows and to read interviews in the news media. Notice how questions are begun and followed up, how they're developed from answers, and how they're phrased so that they don't elicit one-word answers. Notice how interviewers leave a particular line of questioning and start another and when and how they wrap it all up.

"I never forget a face . . . but names?"   How often have you heard that? Some people can remember names but can't match them with faces; others can remember faces but can't recall names. One way to impress people is to remember their name; to most people, nothing is more important.

Memory can be strengthened if you're willing to work at it. Below are some elements involved in developing your memory for names and faces.

Attention.   Whenever you meet someone for the first time, prepare to pay strict attention to the person because you want to remember her name. Observe her facial features — eyes, hair, ears, dimple, nose — for something striking or peculiar that may make it easier for you to recall her later.

Association.   Is there any way you can associate the name with the person's features or occupation? Perhaps Miss Smiley has a beautiful smile. Perhaps Mr. Pearlman is in the jewelry business or perhaps his teeth resemble pearls. It's amazing how, with effort and imagination, you can associate a name with a physical feature or occupation or hobby.

Comparison. Perhaps a person has a name similar to that of a very good friend of yours. Visualize this person in comparison to your friend. Compare their features. Search for a resemblance or vast difference that might make it easier for you to remember your new acquaintance's name. Again, you may be amazed at what you can come up with.

Repetition. When you meet a person for the first time, repeat the person's name as often as possible so that it is firmly implanted in your mind.

Be sure that you hear the correct pronunciation of the name. If necessary, have it repeated and spelled, then you repeat it. Repetition is one of the keys to memorizing. But be sure to pay undivided attention to the person and the person's name. I (AJV) recall a rather embarrassing situation when I was introduced to a gentleman and due to inattentiveness, I didn't catch the name and replied, "That's an unusual name, how do you spell it?" He obliged with "S-M-I-T-H."

"Say, I've got a friend who . . ."   One of the more pragmatic aspects of life is making business and social contacts. Let's not kid ourselves, the more people we know, the more pleasant life may be for us. You may have friends who were promoted or got jobs because they knew people. Others may have received certain benefits or special treatment because they have contacts.

Getting to know people is very important, but first you have to meet them. An excellent place to do this is at school. Try to get along with as many people as possible by being friendly and helpful and by keeping in touch. You never know who may be able to assist you in the near future or after graduation. If you're in a position to do someone a favor, do it. The day may come when you'll need a favor in return.

If you have a goal to achieve, make it a point to associate with people who can help you. Associate with people you admire and respect; some of their talents may rub off on you. Whether in your business or social environment, there are always key people, leaders who get things done. If you can help them in any way, volunteer. Do more than is expected. That alone will set you apart from the masses. When people in authority can depend on you, you're building a future for yourself.

TALKING ON THE TELEPHONE

For most of you, talking on the phone is an important means of carrying on and developing one-to-one relationships. Since you're not likely to speak on radio or appear on television, discussions of radio and television speaking are not included in this book.

But talking on the phone is something that all of you do, probably many times daily, at home and on the job. Here are suggestions to help you become more proficient at it.

Always treat telephone callers courteously.

Courtesy.   Always treat telephone callers courteously, not only because it's the right thing to do but because your response colors their impression both of you and of your company or organization. Even if you've had a rough day and your nerves are rubbed raw, don't let your voice and words show it. That's easy to say but hard to do. If you're too pressured to talk at the moment, say so, get the caller's name and number and tell her you'll call back in fifteen minutes, a half-hour, or whenever you can. But do what you said — call back.

Too many people today answer the phone, "Just a moment, please," and then keep the caller hanging for three or four minutes. It's far more considerate and businesslike to get the caller's name and number and return the call a few minutes later. Courtesy and tact on the phone pay off in the long run.

Voice.   Your voice will come through more warmly if you remember that you're not talking to a piece of office equipment but to another human being. If you feel what you're saying and visualize the other person (see Oral Visualization in Chapter 5), you'll probably even use gestures like nodding your head, shrugging your shoulders, and smiling, and your voice will reflect all that. As a result, you won't sound mechanical; you'll sound human.

For most people, the transmitter, or mouthpiece, should be about two inches away from the mouth and at the same level. If you tend to talk softly, keep the mouthpiece one or one and one-half inches away; if you blast, three or four inches would be better.

Pronunciation.   When talking on the phone, don't chew gum, smoke, or clench a pencil between your teeth. Any of those actions will result in slurred words so that your listener may have to keep asking, "What did you say?"

Brevity of calls.   At work it's a sensible idea to keep most of your calls short, say, five minutes or less. Plan your statement beforehand, and once on the phone explain the reason for your call and its importance. Then close with a few words on the course of action you or the other person is going to take. Avoid rambling on endlessly; someone else, with an urgent message, may be trying to reach you at the same time.

Expressions of goodwill.   Certain expressions "stroke" most people soothingly. Some of these are:

"Thank you."
"I appreciate that."
"I'm glad to help you."
"If you have any questions, be sure to call me."

When said sincerely, these expressions can build goodwill for you and your company.

Identification.   At work, rather than answering with "Hello," you should immediately identify yourself and your department. Not only does this save time, but the caller will know that she has the right party and, in that case, will most likely identify herself. Whenever you make a call regarding a serious complaint or problem, be sure to note the date and other person's name and number for future reference.

Security.   Once you pick up the receiver, don't make side remarks to anybody nearby. Even if you cup your hand over the mouthpiece, the caller may hear information through the earpiece that she shouldn't know. In a social sense that could be embarrassing; in the business or professional world, it could be costly to your organization or to your career.

Memory aids.   Always have a pencil and notepad near the phone so you can take messages promptly. Keeping on hand a list of frequently used numbers and emergency numbers can save precious time.

Taking messages.   When you answer for someone who's not in the office, avoid statements like:

> "She's having coffee now."
> "She's late today."
> "She's in the ladies' room."

A more tactful approach would be to say, "She's out of the office. May I take your name and number so she can call you when she returns?"

THINGS TO THINK ABOUT AND DO

1. Before class, at the cafeteria, or at your next social function select a person you've seen before but never talked with. Introduce yourself and engage her in conversation. Tell the class of your experience.

2. List the different sections of a newspaper and tell the class some features you discovered in each section.

3. Listen to a radio talk program and take notes. Then tell the class about the talk master and her line of questioning. Was she fair? probing? interesting? a good listener?

4. Try one or more of the techniques of starting a conversation discussed in this chapter and tell the class about it.

5. Tell the class how you feel about discussing politics and religion.

6. What methods do you use to remember names and faces? Share your methods with the class.

WHAT DO YOU REMEMBER FROM THIS CHAPTER?

1. What are some ideas to developing your conversational ability?

2. How can you become a more interesting person?

3. List several good conversational habits.

4. When is it permissible to interrupt someone?

5. Comment on the statement: Never discuss politics or religion.

6. Explain several ways to start a conversation.

7. What are some elements involved in memory development?

8. What is the key to making business and social contacts?

VITALIZE YOUR VOCABULARY

Farming and Gardening

agribusiness (n.)   the business that includes production and distribution of farm products and equipment.

agronomy (n.)   the use of scientific knowledge and methods in farming.

compost (n.)   a mixture of decomposing vegetable refuse, manure, etc., for fertilizing and conditioning the soil.

conservation (n.)   the planned use and protection of natural resources.

depletion (n.)   the process of exhausting land of its fertility.

erosion (n.)   the process of wearing away or blowing away soil by natural means such as wind, water, and weather.

fallow (adj.)   applies to land that has been plowed and tilled but not seeded, so that it can regain its fertility during the growing season.

fodder (n.)   food, such as hay and corn, for horses and cattle.

horticulture (n.)   the science of growing fruits, vegetables, flowers, and plants.

humus (n.)   the dark organic substance consisting of decayed plant and animal material that is essential to soil fertility.

insecticide (n.)   a poison for killing insects.

irrigate (v.)   to supply farmland with water through streams, ditches, and pipes.

legume (n.)   any of related pod-bearing plants, such as alfalfa, beans, peas, and clover.

livestock (n.)   animals raised on a farm, such as cows, pigs, sheep, and horses.

loam (n.)   a soil that contains silt, sand, clay, and decayed plant matter.

mulch (n.)   a covering of leaves, hay, etc., to protect plants against cold, to keep the soil moist, and to enrich it.

reclamation (n.)   the process of restoring soil for growing crops by watering and fertilizing it.

silo (n.)   a tall cylindrical building for storing fodder (see above).

16

Let's Go to Work

Too many job seekers expect other people to find a job for them. They don't do their homework. They don't evaluate what they have accomplished and figure out where their talent and experience might be most valuable.[1]

CHAPTER OBJECTIVES

After reading and understanding this chapter, you should know:

- The most effective ways to find a job.
- How to prepare a resumé that will sell.
- How to write an application letter.
- How to research a company before the interview.
- The importance of having a contact in a company.
- How to prepare for a job interview.
- How to handle yourself during an interview.
- Questions which may be discriminatory and illegal.
- What to do after the job interview.

---

[1]*Business Week* (March 23, 1974), p. 73.

CHAPTER DIGEST

This chapter is a culmination of the authors' combined fifty-two years of business experience, especially in regard to job search, resumés, and interviews. Supplementing this expertise are painstaking research into the latest techniques of job hunting and thirty-five combined years of teaching.

Your first step in finding a job is to determine your objective, without limiting your marketability to just one type of job.

Your second step is to prepare a resumé that summarizes in one or two pages (one page is preferred) your education, experience, and other capabilities. Resumés are vital in any job search because they can open doors for you; they get interviews or they don't. Along with exhibits of actual resumés that can serve as models for yours, numerous suggestions are offered for writing a convincing one of your own.

A resumé should include many or all of the following topics: personal data, job objective, education, experience, military service, community activities, interests. Whenever you mail a resumé to a company, you should include an application letter with it. Before your interview, you should try to learn as much as possible about the company. Ideas for doing that are given.

The three aspects of an interview — before, during, and after — are dealt with in depth. Numerous practical suggestions and cautions are presented, and they merit hard study. For example, there are many aspects of your life which an interviewer cannot legally ask about, and you need not answer such questions. Many of these questions are listed later in this chapter.

Applying the suggestions in this chapter should make your job hunt more efficient and more productive.

WAYS TO FIND A JOB

These are the most common ways to find a job:

1. Your friend tells you there's an opening where he works and, if you're interested, he could set up an interview.

2. Someone tells you that The Travelsmith is looking for management trainees. You telephone and are asked to come in for an interview.

3. You read an advertisement that representatives of a certain company will be in town, and if you're interested, call for an interview.

4. A close relative owns the company and offers you a position — no interview required!

5. You contact your college placement office.

6. You contact state and private employment agencies.

No matter how you learn of a job opening, before a final decision is made, you will be engaged in one or more interviews. Just as in preparing a speech, the more you prepare for an interview, the better your chances will be.

SET YOUR JOB OBJECTIVES

According to a national expert on career planning, employers say that the number-one problem with people coming in for their first job is that they don't know what kind of position they're looking for.[2] Because of your education and experience, you should know what type of work you wish to pursue. It may be to your advantage not to narrow down your choice to a specific job, but rather to think of allied areas. If, for example, you're interested in becoming a police officer, don't confine your search exclusively to police departments. If there are no openings there, you may consider private investigation work or positions in a penal institution or in industrial and commercial security. By accepting a job in an allied field, you'll shorten your job-hunting time and make yourself more versatile.

During your job interview you may be told that the position you're specifically applying for has been filled, and asked if you would consider a related position. Even though you might be disappointed, it may be wise to consider the second option because — one, you may have a job and two, after proving yourself, this may enhance your opportunity for upward mobility. Give it some thought.

PREPARE A RESUMÉ

A resumé is a one- or two-page (preferably one-page) summary of your qualifications. It is your "ad," your foot in the door. It can either get you an interview or it can land in the wastebasket.

A resumé serves a twofold purpose. (1) It is the only significant communication between you and your potential employer. (2) It can be helpful when you're filling out a job application, especially for dates, list of jobs held, and social security number.

High stakes hinge on how well you prepare your resumé. It is important that the resumé present all the necessary, pertinent information clearly and neatly.

The following elements usually comprise a resumé: personal data, job objective, educational background, work experience, community activities, military service, and perhaps references.

Personal data.   Give your name and address (include zip code), telephone number (include area code), date of birth (not required legally), and marital status (also not required).

---

[2]Peggy J. Schmidt, "That First Job: Finding It and Getting Ahead," *U.S. News & World Report*, 6 July 1981, pp. 67–68.

Job objectives.   Name the position you're seeking. If the position isn't specific, then be general.

Educational background.   Include the schools you've attended and years of graduation, your major and minor fields of study, degrees, certificates, awards received, and activities engaged in. Start with the most recent schooling first. If you ranked scholastically in the top quarter of your graduating class, state that fact; otherwise, don't.

Work experience.   List the more recent jobs you've held (full-time and part-time). Include dates and responsibilities, and any suggestions or improvements you contributed.

Community activities.   You may list organizations and clubs to which you belong and any offices held.

Military service.   This is especially important in an area related to your desired employment. Be sure to include the type of discharge or separation received.

References.   If you are asked for references, supply their names; otherwise, state that their names are available upon request. Be sure to get permission from your references in order to avoid embarrassment. Give your references copies of your resumé so that they'll know what to say about you.

Once you have compiled all your information, show it to someone who knows how a resumé should be set up and ask for constructive criticism. If you do not type well, have a competent typist type the resumé and then have clear photocopies made. A neat, well-typed resumé stands a chance of landing on the desk of the person who may hire you.

Production of your resumé can be a critical factor. For example, "having your resumé presented on pastel-colored paper instead of plain white can increase *its* chances of being noticed and *your* chances of landing a given job TENFOLD." So states Walter Lowen, one of the nation's leading personnel experts in his job hunting guide, *You and Your Job.*

You can get excellent copies of your resumé by having a printing shop reproduce it through the offset printing method. Your printer will have an ample supply of colored stock (paper) from which you can choose. Offset printing means you will probably get at least fifty professional-looking copies, whereas with a photocopy machine you can get only one or as many as you wish. Generally, it's more advantageous to have too many resumés than too few. In any event, be sure to keep the original resumé in case you need to recopy it.

As mentioned earlier, resumés may take many formats; Figures 16-1 and 16-2 show two acceptable formats.

WRITE AN APPLICATION LETTER

When you mail your resumé, be sure to paper-clip a short application letter to it. See Figure 16-3. Be sure to have the letter typed by a competent typist. Block format (no indentions) can also be used.

Walter A. Bryant   Fall 1983
88 North Central Avenue
San Diego, CA 92111
(714) 628-1936

Job
Objective   To work in the office of comptroller or treasurer of a
                         small manufacturing organization in order to qualify for
                         general management responsibilities.

Education

1979 to 1983   Stanford University, School of Management
               Received M.B.A. Degree in Business Administration,
               with honors, June 1983. Concentrated on finance with
               strong preparation in accounting and economics. Made
               Dean's List in first three quarters. Was member of
               business club and debating team. Financed expenses
               through outside work and fellowships.

1975 to 1977   Bunker Hill Community College, Charlestown, MA,
               Business Administration
               Received Associate's Degree, June 1979. Majored in
               Business Administration with several courses in
               economics, including industrial organization and public
               policy. Was president of Delta Kappa Epsilon and
               captain of soccer team. Financed expenses partially
               through scholarship, summer jobs, and part-time work
               as a sorter at the First National Bank Computer Center,
               Boston, MA.

Experience

1983 to   Kathleen Mullin Investments, Inc. Dorchester, MA 02124
Present   Security Analyst: Report to Director of Research. Duties

RESEARCH THE COMPANY AND POSITION

Finding out as much as possible about a company and the position you seek can pay off for you during the interview. How old is the company? What products or services does it provide? What is its geographical area of sales? If it has branch offices, where are they? Is the company growing or standing still?

If you're looking for a specific position, for example, sales, you may want to know the present size of its sales staff. How much traveling is involved? How large is the average territory? As a new member of the sales staff, will you be selling the whole line of products or will you be limited? What is the company's promotion policy? Is it usually from within the company, or does the com-

	involve analyzing current stock issues and industry trends, preparing weekly market letter for customers, and writing reports on specific stocks or situations as requested by partners. Am qualified as registered representative by the New York Stock Exchange.
Summer Work	Summer jobs during college years included camp counselor, construction laborer, and carpenter's helper.
Military Service	
1977 to 1979	U.S. Marine Corps Upon graduation from college, entered Marine Officer Candidate School, Camp Lejeune, North Carolina. After completing four-month program, was commissioned 2nd lieutenant and assigned to U.S. embassy in Rome as security officer. I was responsible for a 15-man 24-hour security force assigned to protect the embassy and its grounds. Received commendation and was released from active duty in June 1979.
Interests	Interests include swimming, soccer, tennis, and gourmet cooking.
References	Available upon request.

Figure 16-1
Sample resumé of a student with diversified experience.

Noreene Rowley   Spring 1983
45 Freedom Drive
Haddock, MA 02543
(617) 616-1936

Occupational goal

My immediate goal is to become a member of a corporate marketing division, with the eventual aim of a management position.

Education

Carnegie Mellon Institute, MBA, 1983
Wheelock College, BS, 1980
  Major: Marketing
  Minor: Psychology

Grades:
Graduated both institutions with high honors

Extracurricular Activities:
President of Speech Club
President of Senior Class
Member of Student Marketing Society
Public relations director of campus day-care center

Work experience

Summer 1980–Fall 1981   American Telephone and Telegraph, I started as an intern in the management training program and after four months was promoted to Assistant to the Director of the Northeast Marketing Division.

Summers, 1975–1979   Receptionist-secretary for the circulation department of *Redbook Magazine*, New York.

Figure 16-2
Sample resumé of a student with limited experience.

---

pany bring in outsiders? What are your chances for advancement?

The more you know about the company and the position, the better you'll be able to react during the interview. If you can't find all the answers you'd like to have, when the right opportunity presents itself during the interview, ask questions. This will demonstrate that you did your homework and are genuinely interested in the company.

Many sources of information are available about your prospective employer and the position you seek, for example, the public library, college placement office and library, company folders,

November 3, 1983

Mr. Albert W. Berger
Personnel Supervisor
Midwest Telephone Company
85 North Central Avenue
Chicago, IL 60603

Dear Mr. Berger:

In reference to your advertisement in the Quincy Sun on November 1 for a junior accountant, I am enclosing my résumé.

In college I majored in accounting and finance, and ranked in the top ten percent of my class. I also worked as an accountant for three summers and part-time during my last two years of college. I feel confident that my education and experience qualify me for the position.

I would appreciate an opportunity to discuss this position with you. I will phone you in a few days to arrange an interview at your convenience.

Sincerely,

Nancy Shea
37 Rangeley Street
Chicago, IL 60603

Figure 16-3
Sample application letter.

newsletters, magazines, and annual reports. If possible, talk to employees, visit a brokerage office, and look through business publications and the business section of your newspaper.

CONTACT THE COMPANY

Now that you know the direction in which you're heading, it's time to contact the company and arrange an interview. You have two courses of action: conventional and unconventional.

Conventional. You can mail your resumé and application letter to either the personnel office or to the appropriate individual respon-

Try to learn as much as possible about the company.

sible for the hiring. You can appear in person with your resumé to inquire of possible openings, or you can telephone the personnel office.

Unconventional.   Perhaps you have a friend already working for the company who may be able to deliver your resumé and say some good words in your behalf. Any action on your behalf by a contact within the company can expedite matters for you and give you an edge over the competition.

JOB INTERVIEWS

NOTIFICATION OF YOUR INTERVIEW

You'll be notified of your forthcoming interview either by telephone, by letter, or by your company contact. Be sure to write down the exact time, date, place (specific building, office), and the correct name (and its pronunciation) of the person you're to meet. You'll find it useful to take along a pen and a small notebook.

You should now put together some questions you may wish to ask at the appropriate time during the interview. Remember that it will be a conversation in which both of you will participate, even though the interviewer will probably take the initiative, at least in the beginning. Your questions may run something like this:

1. What exactly would my duties be?

2. Is there a probation period, and if so, how long is it?

3. When is the starting date?

4. What are the company's prospects?

5. What would be my chances for advancement?

6. Does the company have an educational program for self-development?

7. What is the company's policy on wages, vacation, sick leave, life and health insurance, and other fringe benefits?

Some or all of these questions may be answered during the interview, but if they aren't, don't hesitate to ask them. Keep question 7 until near the end of the meeting.

THE DAY OF YOUR INTERVIEW

The big day has finally arrived, and you're probably nervous — a normal reaction. Just remember that you've come a long way from your first talk in class. You've done your homework, you're confident, and you know what you want. You're ready.

Here are some helpful suggestions:

1. Plan to arrive five or ten minutes early. Sitting in the reception area and reading or talking with the receptionist or secretary may relax you and may provide additional information about the company.

2. Since your appearance is critical, dress neatly and be well groomed. An impeccably attired individual can blow the whole image with dirty fingernails, unshined shoes, or an overdose of perfume, jewelry, or aftershave lotion.

3. If you're requested to bring additional information (references, another copy of your resumé), put them in a brief case, large folder, or manila envelope. Don't fold them or stuff them in your purse or pocket.

4. Be sure to have a pen or two in case you're asked to fill out additional forms, and don't forget the notebook.

The moment of truth has arrived. The secretary or receptionist announces, "Mr. Nazzaro will see you now. Go right in." Or the interviewer may come out to greet and escort you into the office. Your job interview has begun.

You're probably nervous.

THE ACTUAL INTERVIEW

The purpose of the job interview is twofold. (1) The interviewer has a position to fill with the best qualified individual in terms of education, intelligence, ambition, imagination, appearance, dependability, and moral character. (2) You want to convince the interviewer that you are that individual.

The interviewer plans to find out as much about you as possible. Since his task will be simpler if you're relaxed, the interviewer will most likely try to put you at ease quickly.

After the initial introduction ritual (shaking hands firmly and offering you a seat), the interviewer may ask if you'd like a cup of coffee. When it arrives and there's no napkin with it, tear a sheet of paper from your notebook and put the cup on it. By not placing your cup of coffee on the interviewer's desk or other furniture, you automatically gain a few points. Your notebook will serve other purposes, as you'll see later.

YOUR NONVERBAL OFFICE CONDUCT

What you do during the interview may be just as important as what you say and how you say it. Here are some points to ponder:

1. Maintain the communication cycle. Focus your eyes and mind on the interviewer and when he speaks, you listen. If a reply is in order, respond. Total concentration will pay dividends.

2. Avoid distractions. The office may be laden with many interesting objects (on the interviewer's desk, on shelves, on walls, and so on). Although they may make for interesting conversation, remember that the primary purpose of your visit is to be interviewed, not to chat about curios. Obviously, if the situation presents itself to comment on an interesting piece, keep the comment brief. Don't digress from the main reason for your visit.

3. If you're sitting on a sofa or soft easy chair, don't relax into the contours or stretch out. While seated, don't fidget or change positions often because it can become distracting.

4. If you brought a briefcase or manila envelope, place it on your lap or beside your chair, not on a desk or table.

5. Keep your shoes away from furniture.

6. Don't smoke unless invited to do so, and before you light up, be sure that an ashtray is handy. (If the interviewer doesn't smoke, you should refrain from doing so during the

Don't be too relaxed.

interview. This gesture will very likely create a favorable impression.)

7. Don't play with your tie clip or tie, necklace, earrings, or other pieces of clothing or jewelry.

8. Keep hands away from hair and face. Constantly brushing hair aside from your eyes may annoy the interviewer.

9. Don't chew gum or anything else. If for some reason you must take cough drops or throat lozenges, be sure to tell the interviewer. Don't distract him by clucking and slurping them around.

10. If there's a confidential folder or papers on the interviewer's desk which looks interesting, mind your own business!

THE VERBAL SIDE OF THE INTERVIEW

At this point you should review Chapters 5, 11, and 15.

Although you may be sitting, "be on your toes" for a question or two that might catch you off guard. It's not unusual for an interviewer to toss at you something like:

1. "O.K., Andrew, what can we do for you?"
2. "Why do you want to work for us?"
3. "Tell me something about yourself."
4. "Why should we hire you?"
5. "Tell me exactly what you're looking for."

A practical way to prepare for these questions is to ask yourself, if you were in the interviewer's shoes, what answers would impress you? The reason why you may be confronted with such questions is that the interviewer wants to see how you handle yourself. Although most interviewers don't ask more than one or two of the questions listed above, you'd be wise to prepare answers to all of them since there is no way of knowing which one might be asked. A more popular approach today is for the interviewer to ask a question about current events. A person who's interested in what's happening in the world will probably be interested in the company he works for and in the job he is doing.

QUESTIONS YOU SHOULD BE PREPARED TO DISCUSS

1. Place of birth and where you grew up.
2. Schools attended, courses of study, favorite subjects.
3. Why you selected those schools and what extracurricular activities you engaged in.
4. Do you want to continue your education?
5. Did you work while going to school and to what extent?
6. Military service and present status.
7. What do you know about this company?
8. Your immediate and long-range goals.
9. Do you know anyone who works for this company?
10. Present occupation. Why you left other jobs.

11. Have you ever been fired? If so, why?

12. What specific job do you want?

13. A question or two about politics and current events.

14. Do you have any hobbies?

15. Do you like to travel?

16. Are you willing to relocate?

17. Are you involved in community activities and to what extent?

18. What can you do for us?

19. How much money do you need to start with?

Only the interviewer knows what line of questioning he may follow or how long a time he will spend with you. It all depends on his degree of interest in you. If the interviewer is impressed, he may keep you twice as long as planned.

QUESTIONS YOU SHOULD BE PREPARED *NOT* TO DISCUSS

Since passage of the Age Discrimination in Employment Act of 1967, Title VII of the Civil Rights Act of 1964, the Equal Pay Act of 1963, and any executive orders related to the above legislation, an interviewer must be very cautious about his questions.

Any questions pertaining to age, sex, color, race, religion, or national origin could be discriminatory and unlawful. If such questions are asked and the applicant is not hired, the applicant could file a complaint at the local office of the Commission Against Discrimination or the Equal Employment Opportunity Commission.

Although many interviewers may be familiar with this delicate issue and may refrain from asking any possibly illegal questions, you should become familiar with the following potentially dangerous categories and areas of inquiry.

Age

How old are you?
What is your date of birth?

"And do you know anyone else who works for this company, Sis?"

Sex

Any questions pertaining to your personal sex habits, convictions, and relationships.

Marital status

Are you married?
What is your spouse's full name?
What is your spouse's occupation?
Do you receive alimony or support?
Do you pay alimony or support?

Dependents

Do you have children?
How old are your children?
Do you plan to have children?

Citizenship

Are you an American citizen?

Religion

Do you attend church?
What denomination do you belong to?
Can you work on Saturdays and Sundays?

Credit

Do you have any money in the bank?
Do you have any debts?
How is your credit rating?
Have you ever been denied credit?
Do you own your own home?

Experiences with the law

Have you ever been arrested?

Military

What type of discharge or separation did you receive?
Were you ever court-martialed?
Were you ever arrested?
Did you ever serve any time in a military prison?

Salary

What's the lowest salary you'll accept?

Financial

Have you ever had money or property attached?

Bonding

Are you bondable?
Have you ever been refused bond?

Health problems or handicaps

Do you have any physical or emotional handicaps?
What is your present state of health?

Relatives employed

Do you have any relatives employed at this company?

Bear in mind that under certain restrictive conditions, some of the above questions may be legitimately asked. For example:

- An applicant's physical handicap would be of concern to the employer if the job involved loading or unloading heavy parcels.

- If a person is applying for a position which requires handling large sums of money or securities, then the question of bonding would be expected.

- For positions involving national security, the question of American citizenship would be legitimate.

- If the job requires a person to work on either Saturday or Sunday, or both, then the question on working weekends could be asked.

If the questions asked are directly related to the specific job classification and job description or to duties you will actually be performing, then, of course, they would be justified.

THE INTERVIEWER'S APPROACH

The interviewer may utilize one or all three of the following approaches:

1. He may do almost all of the talking and questioning to see how you respond. He will observe your poise, patience, immediate reaction to questions, and how well you handle difficult ones.

2. He may say very little so that the burden of sustaining the interview will be on you. This approach is the most difficult for the new job seeker, but the interviewer may be looking for someone who is determined and well-prepared and who can communicate intelligently.

3. He may employ the technique in which both of you will interact on somewhat of an equal level regarding conversational input. It will be a give-and-take interview.

TIPS TO FOLLOW DURING THE INTERVIEW

The moment of truth has arrived. How you behave, verbally and nonverbally, during the interview may or may not clinch the job for you.

1. Try not to respond to questions with one- and two-word answers. Occasionally, however, a *yes* or *no* answer is perfectly acceptable.

2. Your answers should reflect only the information sought by the question. One exception would be some valuable information that would benefit your cause and that you hadn't yet had the opportunity to mention. If the questioning allows you to slide in the information without being too obvious, do it. For example, if you were asked about part-time employment and you wanted to mention that you paid for 80 percent of your education, you could say something like:

   "Yes, I feel that working while going to school is worthwhile. For some of us it is a necessity. I've worked nights and weekends during the school session and full time during the summers. Not only did this work enable me to complete my education, but the experience was invaluable, especially for the position I'm now seeking."

3. Look for his nonverbal signs. If he takes his eyes away from you and looks around the office, or at some things on his desk, perhaps you've been rambling on without substance. If he looks at his watch or gathers papers together, he may be about to terminate the interview. If the interviewer tilts back in his chair while he's still looking at you, that could mean that he's interested in your response. Therefore, you should keep going.

4. Be honest in your answers and opinions because the interviewer is a pro who can spot phony talk. Although you shouldn't lie, don't hesitate to stretch the truth a point, but *only* if you can back it up. Remember, you may get the chance to prove yourself and if you can't cut it, you may be cut.

5. When answering tough questions, it's permissible to pause a second or two to gather your thoughts. Then look the interviewer straight in the eye and respond as confidently as possible.

Look for his nonverbal signs.

6. Never offer confidential information about a competitor for whom you worked. It could weaken your chances for employment because the interviewer may feel, and rightfully so, that you might do the same while in his employ. If you have any business or professional secrets, keep them locked up. If your prospective employer enters upon this delicate area, he could be testing your integrity.

7. Don't criticize former employers. If you've had an unpleasant experience on a job, admit that it may have been a personality conflict and share some of the blame. Don't convey the impression that "they were out to get me from the first day."

8. If you've ever been fired and are asked why, there's no better approach than to be honest. The practical reason for honesty is that personnel specialists in the same area usually know one another on a first-name basis. If the interviewer doubts the truth of some of your statements, he can easily phone the personnel director of your former employer and check you out. It's far better to tell the interviewer the reasons for the firing and then convince him to give you the job which you feel you deserve.

9. Don't beg for the position. Don't say, "I'll do anything just to get my foot in the door" or "I'll work for nothing to get a start." Your interviewer may feel that if you're willing to work for nothing, that's all you may be worth. No respectable employer expects anyone to work for nothing.

10. The last thing you need is an argument. If you find that you must disagree, be as tactful and as brief as possible. On the other hand, don't always agree just to be sociable.

11. If you're being considered by other companies, don't pressure your interviewer by comparing conditions and offers. Negotiate terms at your second meeting. If you play games during your initial interview, you could lose.

Don't beg for the position.

12. Keep your options open. There's always a possibility that the interviewer might feel that you may be better suited for another available position rather than the one you're applying for. Listen closely to all aspects of this other position because it may prove more challenging and rewarding than the original one.

13. If you should receive some information you consider very important (directions, a person's name, the title of an article to read), ask the interviewer's permission to jot down the information in your notebook. Your interest and conscientiousness will be appreciated.

14. If you're offered a position then and there and you have no doubts or questions, accept it and ask when you can start. If you have some doubts or would like to compare some of the other offers, then thank the interviewer for the offer but explain you'd like some time to think it over. Ask if you could call him in a few days, and regardless of your decision, be sure to call him at the appointed time. Requesting time to think over acceptance of a position is common. If the interviewer wants a definite answer immediately, you're faced with a major decision. Before the interview you might think about such a possibility, so that you'll be prepared if a decision is expected. An immediate answer, however, is rarely requested. Almost all companies will give you a few days to decide.

15. If you feel that the interview is not going well and that you're really blowing it, *don't give up*. Do your best and keep your cool. Many people tend to underrate themselves and be too self-critical. Have you ever taken an exam and felt that you did poorly, only to be pleasantly surprised later? It could happen again. Even if you did botch the interview, so what? You've gained valuable experience, and you'll have other opportunities.

16. No matter how much at ease your interviewer sets you, don't get overly chummy. Remember, putting you at ease and in a relaxed mood is one way the interviewer can see the real you. Always refer to the interviewer by Mr., Miss, Mrs., or Ms. Reply with a "yes sir" or "yes ma'am."

17. Be alert not to oversell yourself. If, either by facial expression or by words, the interviewer shows that he's impressed with

your qualifications, leave it at that. Don't ramble on and on about your abilities.

18. Many novice job seekers place too much emphasis on fringe benefits and starting pay, and thus jeopardize their start in the business world. Ask yourself, "Based on my education and actual experience, what am I worth to this company?" If you want a job, the important thing is to get one and do the best you can. Remember that you're much better off looking for another job when you're working than when you're not.

19. At the end of the interview you should be told when a decision will be made. If the interviewer doesn't tell you, ask. It's a reasonable request.

20. Before you leave, smile, shake hands (if the interviewer extends his hand first), and thank the interviewer for the chance to discuss the job.

TIPS TO FOLLOW AFTER THE INTERVIEW

Now that the interview is behind you, can you sit down and relax? No, not yet. There are still things to do. For example:

1. At the earliest opportunity after leaving the office, take out your trusty little notebook again and jot down notes and impressions you may wish to remember. Since you may be invited back for a follow-up interview, these notes can play an important role at future meetings. In fact, keeping notes on all interviews should help you in comparing other offers and in making a final decision.

2. Should you send a thank-you note to the interviewer? Why not? It'll give you favorable attention and another opportunity to make a subtle pitch — "after having the opportunity of speaking with you and learning more about the company and the position, I'm more convinced about wanting to work for your company and to make a contribution to it." Figure 16-4 shows an acceptable thank-you note.

3. Would a telephone follow-up be proper? Certainly. Showing your further interest by a short phone call will, more often

116 King Street
Avon, MA 02173
July 24, 1983

Mrs. Frances Adler, R.N.
Supervisor, Department of Nursing
Shalom Hospital
Boston, MA 02116

Dear Mrs. Adler:

Thank you for the opportunity of meeting with you today to discuss one of the openings on your staff.

The position appeals to me very much and sounds exactly like what I'm looking for. I am more eager than ever to join your staff.

I appreciate your kind comments regarding my qualifications and look forward to hearing from you soon.

Sincerely yours,

Evelyn Elisav

Figure 16-4
Sample thank-you letter.

than not, make a positive impression. Do one or the other — a note or a phone call — but not both.

4. If you didn't receive an offer, *don't get discouraged.* The more interviews you have, the more experience you'll acquire; and just by the law of averages, you're bound to find a job. Although the legendary Babe Ruth chalked up an enviable home run record, he also struck out often. It takes no talent to quit, but if you believe in yourself and your abilities and are determined to succeed, then come hell or high water, you eventually will.

Your college placement office is there to help you and your career. Get to know the Director of Placement and members of his staff. They have a great deal to offer you, but it is **you** who must take the initiative. It is **you** who must sell yourself. And it is **you** who must never get discouraged. Good luck.

THINGS TO THINK ABOUT AND DO

1. If you haven't already done so, visit the placement office at your school and become familiar with its function.

2. Either from your audiovisual library or from the placement office, get and study a videotape or film on interviewing procedures and demonstrations.

3. From your placement office get some job applications and interviewer evaluation forms. Team up with a classmate, with one filling out the application and the other the evaluation form to use when practice-interviewing each other. If possible, this class exercise should be videotaped for evaluation.

4. Select someone in your class to interview your professor in an effort to establish better mutual understanding.

5. Prepare your resumé, bring it to class, and be ready to discuss it.

WHAT DO YOU REMEMBER FROM THIS CHAPTER?

1. Why is it sometimes advantageous when seeking employment not to be too specific about a job?

2. What is a resumé and why is it important?

3. What is an application letter and what is its purpose?

4. When you research a company, what information should you look for?

5. Should you prepare some questions to ask the interviewer? Explain.

6. Why is it a good idea to carry a small notebook with you to the interview?

7. List some important elements to keep in mind relative to office conduct during the interview.

8. What are some questions you should be prepared to answer that could catch you off guard?

9. What areas of questioning during an interview could be discriminatory and illegal?

10. During an interview, could a job applicant be asked if he has any physical handicaps? Explain.

11. What's a good policy to follow regarding criticism of former employers?

12. At what point during the interview can you start calling the interviewer by his first name?

13. List several things to think about and do after the interview.

VITALIZE YOUR VOCABULARY

Words from American Indians

This last exercise in vocabulary building is dedicated to American Indians, or Native Americans as they are sometimes called. From dozens of Indian dialects many words have entered the English language. Here are some of the more common ones:

Barbecue	Papoose	Squaw
Canoe	Pecan	Tepee
Cougar	Potato	Tobacco
Hickory	Pow-wow	Toboggan
Hominy	Raccoon	Tomahawk
Moccasin	Skunk	Wampum
Moose	Squash	Wigwam

Some less well-known Indian words are:

calumet (n.)   a pipe smoked as a token of peace.

caribou (n.)   deer found in the arctic regions of North America.

caucus (n.)   a closed meeting of members of a political party to decide on policy and to select candidates for office.

chautauqua (n.)   an annual summer recreational and educational program.

mackinaw (n.)   a short double-breasted coat of heavy woolen material, often plaid.

maize (n.)   corn.

peyote (n.)   a drug derived from cactus.

sachem (n.)   the chief of a tribe or the head of an organization.

sequoia (n.)   giant redwood trees of California.

Communicate with confidence.

There are hundreds, possibly thousands, of Indian names of places in the United States, for example:

Allegheny	Milwaukee	Saratoga
Chicago	Mississippi	Seneca
Indiana	Niagara	Susquehanna
Kalamazoo	Oneida	Tallahassee
Kennebec	Penobscot	
Manhattan	Potomac	

Quohquinapassakessamanagnog (The name of a brook in New Hampshire; the name was changed in 1916 to Beaver.)

Appendix A
Evaluation
Guides

BASIC EVALUATION GUIDE

BEFORE TALK

	Yes	No
Did speaker walk to the front of class quietly and confidently?	____	____
Was posture acceptable?	____	____
When name was called, was there an oral reaction (groan or sigh)?	____	____
Was overall appearance appealing?	____	____
If she carried notes, were they inconspicuous?	____	____
Did she briefly pause, look around at audience, and then start to speak?	____	____

DURING TALK

If speech had a title, was it mind-teasing?   _____ _____

Did speaker greet class?   _____ _____

Did she constantly look at audience?   _____ _____

Were her notes hidden?   _____ _____

Could entire class hear her?   _____ _____

Did she pronounce words clearly?   _____ _____

Did she use gestures?   _____ _____

Did gestures seem natural?   _____ _____

Was introduction brief and to the point?   _____ _____

Did she remain frozen in one position?   _____ _____

Did talk follow a plan?   _____ _____

Was talk connected by transitions?   _____ _____

Did she make subject interesting?   _____ _____

Was she aware of audience reaction?   _____ _____

Was conclusion brief and to the point?   _____ _____

Did she seem to enjoy giving talk?   _____ _____

Was her voice expressive?   _____ _____

Was she animated?   _____ _____

Did she do anything distracting?   _____ _____

AFTER TALK

If audience asked questions, did speaker
handle them with confidence?   _____ _____

If some questions were difficult to hear, did
she repeat them before answering?   _____ _____

When answering, did she look at questioner
as well as other members of audience?   _____ _____

Did she return to seat confidently and sit
down quietly?   _____ _____

OVERALL EFFECT*

	Needs improvement	Passable	Good	Very good
Posture	⎯⎯	⎯⎯	⎯⎯	⎯⎯
Movement	⎯⎯	⎯⎯	⎯⎯	⎯⎯
Eye contact	⎯⎯	⎯⎯	⎯⎯	⎯⎯
Enthusiasm	⎯⎯	⎯⎯	⎯⎯	⎯⎯
Voice delivery	⎯⎯	⎯⎯	⎯⎯	⎯⎯
Language	⎯⎯	⎯⎯	⎯⎯	⎯⎯
Understandability	⎯⎯	⎯⎯	⎯⎯	⎯⎯
Overall presence	⎯⎯	⎯⎯	⎯⎯	⎯⎯

Additional comments: ⎯⎯⎯⎯⎯⎯⎯⎯⎯⎯⎯⎯⎯⎯⎯⎯⎯⎯

⎯⎯⎯⎯⎯⎯⎯⎯⎯⎯⎯⎯⎯⎯⎯⎯⎯⎯⎯⎯⎯⎯⎯⎯⎯⎯⎯⎯⎯⎯⎯⎯⎯⎯

⎯⎯⎯⎯⎯⎯⎯⎯⎯⎯⎯⎯⎯⎯⎯⎯⎯⎯⎯⎯⎯⎯⎯⎯⎯⎯⎯⎯⎯⎯⎯⎯⎯⎯

⎯⎯⎯⎯⎯⎯⎯⎯⎯⎯⎯⎯⎯⎯⎯⎯⎯⎯⎯⎯⎯⎯⎯⎯⎯⎯⎯⎯⎯⎯⎯⎯⎯⎯

*This guide may be used separately to evaluate any speech.

EVALUATION GUIDE FOR DEMONSTRATION TALK

	Yes	No
INTRODUCTION		
Did speaker greet audience?	____	____
Did he give reasons for selecting the topic?	____	____
Did he explain what was to be accomplished during talk?	____	____
BODY		
Was the talk presented in a logical sequence?	____	____
If technical terms were used, did speaker define them?	____	____
Did he know how to operate the audiovisual equipment?	____	____
Was equipment or audiovisual aids on hand ready to be used?	____	____
Were handouts used effectively?	____	____
Did too many audiovisual aids lead to confusion?	____	____
Were aids large and clear enough to be seen and understood by entire class?	____	____
Were aids in any way distracting to the presentation?	____	____
CONCLUSION		
Did speaker have an effective conclusion?	____	____
Did he gather visual aids *during* conclusion?	____	____
Did he wait until end of presentation for question-and-answer period?	____	____
Did he answer questions from audience during talk?	____	____

EVALUATION GUIDE FOR PERSUASIVE TALK

INTRODUCTION   Yes   No

Did speaker attempt to win audience goodwill
in first few sentences?   _____   _____

Did he identify with audience before starting
body of speech?   _____   _____

Did he reveal understanding and knowledge
of listeners' beliefs and attitudes in the first
minute or two?   _____   _____

BODY

Did speaker place most convincing arguments
at the beginning and end of main body?   _____   _____

Did he pay extra attention to leaders in
audience because they "carry" others with
them?   _____   _____

Did he use evidence and reasoning to
convince listeners?   _____   _____

Did he achieve high credibility with audience?   _____   _____

Did he get the most possible "mileage" out of
social, biological, and psychological needs and
desires?   _____   _____

Did he convince audience?   _____   _____

CONCLUSION

Did speaker close with the strongest possible
ending?   _____   _____

Did he answer questions with poise and
knowledge?   _____   _____

EVALUATION GUIDE FOR INFORMATIVE TALK

INTRODUCTION   Yes   No

Did speaker state purpose of talk?   ____   ____

Did she explain the importance of subject?   ____   ____

Did she ask a challenging question or two to
stimulate audience?   ____   ____

Did she use relevant quotations from an
authority on subject?   ____   ____

BODY

Did speaker exploit various principles of
learning to put message across?   ____   ____

Did she use enough facts, examples,
anecdotes, comparisons, and statistics to
support statements?   ____   ____

Did she use audiovisual aids (recordings,
movies, charts, maps, photographs)?   ____   ____

Did she occasionally ask audience pertinent
questions?   ____   ____

Did audience seem to gain understanding from
talk?   ____   ____

CONCLUSION

Did speaker signal, by pausing or by inserting
transitions or by doing both, that talk was
about to end?   ____   ____

Did she summarize key ideas?   ____   ____

Did she handle questions competently during
question-and-answer session?   ____   ____

Did she repeat questions some listeners might
not have heard?   ____   ____

EVALUATION GUIDE FOR INTRODUCING A SPEAKER

	Yes	No
INTRODUCTION		
Did master of ceremonies (MC) refer to the occasion?	____	____
Did MC refer to main speaker and main speaker's topic?	____	____
Did MC arouse interest of audience?	____	____
BODY		
Did MC refer to qualifications of main speaker?	____	____
Was main speaker overpraised?	____	____
Was main speaker embarrassed in any way during introduction?	____	____
Did MC explain why audience would benefit from listening to main speaker and main speaker's subject?	____	____
Did MC say too much about main speaker's subject?	____	____
CONCLUSION		
Was conclusion short?	____	____
Was main speaker's name saved until the end?	____	____
Did MC look at main speaker when mentioning her name?	____	____
Did MC start the applause?	____	____
Did MC wait for main speaker to arrive at lectern before sitting down?	____	____

EVALUATION GUIDE FOR PRESENTING AN AWARD

	Yes	No
INTRODUCTION		
Did MC refer to occasion?	———	———
Did he refer to award?	———	———
Did he refer to recipient?	———	———

BODY

	Yes	No
Did MC explain criteria for the award?	———	———
Did MC explain why recipient was chosen?	———	———
If a group or organization received the award, did MC mention the individual who would receive it on the group's behalf?	———	———
Did MC refer to past winners of the award?	———	———
Did MC mention sponsors of the award?	———	———

CONCLUSION

	Yes	No
Did MC make the award in behalf of the award's donors?	———	———
Was the award given with dignity and sincerity?	———	———
Did MC make a warm gesture to recipient (handshake or kiss)?	———	———

EVALUATION GUIDE FOR RECEIVING AN AWARD

INTRODUCTION   Yes   No

    Did recipient thank the person/group giving
the award?   _____   _____

    Did she acknowledge the award itself,
occasion, and audience?   _____   _____

    Was she sincere in her remarks?   _____   _____

BODY

    Did recipient share the honors with others
who may have been responsible for the
award?   _____   _____

    Did she express the meaning of the award?   _____   _____

    Did she state how this award or gift may
affect her future?   _____   _____

    Did she express surprise for the award?   _____   _____

CONCLUSION

    Did recipient again express thanks?   _____   _____

    Did she hold up the award for the audience
to see?   _____   _____

EVALUATION GUIDE FOR A NOMINATING SPEECH

INTRODUCTION   Yes   No

   Did speaker state qualifications for the office?   ____   ____

   Did she say that her nominee meets or
   surpasses those qualifications?   ____   ____

BODY

   Did speaker mention full name of nominee?   ____   ____

   Did she elaborate on the qualifications of the
   nominee?   ____   ____

   During the talk did she occasionally look
   directly at nominee?   ____   ____

   Did she explain why nominee should be
   elected to office?   ____   ____

CONCLUSION

   Did speaker present nominee's name in a loud
   and clear voice?   ____   ____

   Was nomination a formal declaration?   ____   ____

   Did speaker's enthusiasm intensify during the
   talk and climax at the formal nomination?   ____   ____

Appendix B
Speeches for You to Study and Evaluate

The following speeches were given by people who spoke with confidence and effectiveness. The first speech, delivered by President John F. Kennedy in Berlin in 1963, ranks among the best of this century. Our analysis, paragraph by paragraph, appears after the speech.

We suggest that you study and analyze the other speech in the same way.

One of the great speeches of the twentieth century was delivered by President Kennedy in Berlin in 1963. He had gone to Europe to support democracy and freedom and to strengthen our commitment to Western Europe. He spoke to the people and reached them most effectively. His entire speech—note how short it is—appears below, and our comments on each numbered paragraph appear following it.

The title won audience goodwill and interest because it is in German.

"ICH BIN EIN BERLINER"
President John F. Kennedy

1. I am proud to come to this city as the guest of your distinguished Mayor, who has symbolized throughout the world the fighting spirit of West Berlin. And I am proud to visit the Federal Republic with your distinguished Chancellor who for so many years has committed Germany to democracy and freedom and progress, and to come here in the company of my fellow American, General Clay, who has been in this city during its great moments of crisis and will come again if ever needed.

2. Two thousand years ago the proudest boast was *"civis Romanus sum."* Today, in the world of freedom, the proudest boast is *"Ich bin ein Berliner."*

3. I appreciate my interpreter translating my German!

4. There are many people in the world who really don't understand, or say they don't, what is the great issue between the free world and the Communist world. Let them come to Berlin. There are some who say that communism is the wave of the future. Let them come to Berlin. And there are some who say in Europe and elsewhere we can work with the Communists. Let them come to Berlin. And there are even a few who say that it is true that communism is an evil system, but it permits us to make economic progress. *Lass' sie nach Berlin kommen.* Let them come to Berlin.

5. Freedom has many difficulties and democracy is not perfect, but we have never had to put a wall up to keep our people in, to prevent them from leaving us. I want to say, on behalf of my countrymen, who live many miles away on the other side of the Atlantic, who are far distant from you, that they take the greatest pride that they have been able to share with you, even from a distance, the story of the last 18 years. I know of no town, no city, that has been besieged for 18 years that still lives with the vitality and the force, and the hope and the determination of the city of West Berlin. While the wall is the most obvious and vivid demonstration of the failures of the Communist system, for all the world to see, we take no satisfaction in it, for it is, as your Mayor has said, an offense not only against history but an offense against humanity, separating families, dividing husbands and wives and brothers and sisters, and dividing a people who wish to be joined together.

6. What is true of this city is true of Germany—real, lasting peace in Europe can never be assured as long as one German out

President John F. Kennedy, West Berlin, June 26, 1963.

of four is denied the elementary right of free men, and that is to make a free choice. In 18 years of peace and good faith, this generation of Germans has earned the right to be free, including the right to unite their families and their nation in lasting peace, with good will to all people. You live in a defended island of freedom, but your life is part of the main. So *let me ask you, as I close,* to lift your eyes beyond the dangers of today, to the hopes of tomorrow, beyond the freedom merely of this city of Berlin, or your country of Germany, to the advance of freedom everywhere, beyond the wall to the day of peace with justice, beyond yourselves and ourselves to all mankind.

7. Freedom is indivisible, and when one man is enslaved, all are not free. When all are free, then we can look forward to that day when this city will be joined as one and this country and this great

continent of Europe in a peaceful and hopeful globe. When that day finally comes, as it will, the people of West Berlin can take sober satisfaction in the fact that they were in the front lines for almost two decades.

8. All free men, wherever they may live, are citizens of Berlin, and, therefore, as a free man, I take pride in the words *"Ich bin ein Berliner."*

Here are our comments, numbered according to paragraph, on the speech President Kennedy made on that summer's day:

1. JFK's pride in visiting Berlin and his compliments to the Mayor and Chancellor further intensify his hold on audience goodwill and interest. His assurance of American military aid, if necessary, gives his listeners a feeling of security.

2. His knowledge of history enables him to compare Berlin with Rome. He identifies with his listeners by using their language.

3. Here is the President of the United States, the most powerful man in the world, poking fun at his German accent and at the same time complimenting the interpreter. Europeans are not used to this kind of humor from heads of state.

4. The President builds up powerful emotional impact through repeating "Let them come to Berlin." Again he relates to the audience by repeating that statement in German.

5. The President admits that democracy has its faults, but it does not have to erect walls to keep people as prisoners.

   Another compliment to West Berlin.

   Now JFK reaches out emotionally and touches people— husbands and wives, brothers and sisters, families.

6. Germans have earned the right to be free, to unite their families, and to live in peace. These ideas appeal to West Europeans. Note the transition to the conclusion. "So let me ask you, as I close, . . ." and the emotional buildup using parallel construction, "beyond . . . to. . . ." The President expresses hope for a better tomorrow.

7. He builds his conclusion on the idea of a better future.

8. Another compliment to Berlin. An extremely moving conclusion in German words, the title of the speech. Note the conciseness of the last paragraph.

The following speech was delivered by the vice president for administration, Macmillan Oil Company, to Speechcraft students at the Des Moines, Iowa, City Hall in February 1980 (reported in *Vital Speeches of the Day*, 30 November 1980).

PUBLIC SPEAKING AND OTHER CORONARY THREATS
Max D. Isaacson

In my job and at other functions, quite often I'm called on to speak and my wife says that I get up so often that I'm living proof of the old adage that hot air always rises. But I have something a little more substantial than hot air to talk about today.

I'm glad you are here because that tells me you've had the dedication and the interest in this important speechcraft course. I can tell you from personal experience that the ability to express oneself well in public is certainly valuable in my business and in every walk of life that I know of.

In addition to my interest in public speaking, I'm happy to be here for another reason. Since I'm on the staff of an oil company, I'm happy to be invited *anywhere* where there is a cordial reception . . . that's a pleasant accomplishment.

Speaking of accomplishments, your chairman asked me to speak on "Accomplishments Through Speechcraft." A more appropriate title might be: "PUBLIC SPEAKING AND OTHER CORONARY THREATS!" because in public speaking, many are called but few want to get up. You know and I know that it can be scary indeed to get up to address a group. But listen to these statements:

Daniel Webster said:

"If all my possessions were taken from me with one exception, I would choose to keep the power of speech, for by it I would soon regain all the rest [of my possessions]."

Sigmund Freud observed:

"Words call forth emotions and are universally the means by which we influence our fellow creatures . . . by words, one of us can give to another the greatest happiness or bring about utter despair."

The eminent Dale Carnegie said:

"Every activity of our lives is communication of a sort, but it is through speech that man asserts his distinctiveness . . . that he best expresses his own individuality, his essence."

Someone else has observed, and I certainly agree, that "self-confidence has *always* been the first secret of success." Of the known phobias—and there is a long list of them—the fear of public speaking consistently ranks at the top in public surveys. It's even more feared than death. But why should intelligent people fear public speaking?

Most of us have at least average intelligence and when we look around us—at co-workers, bosses, politicians—we know that our level of knowledge is as great or greater than theirs, but the thing that so often separates us is our *inability* to feel confident when expressing ourselves . . . we fear to speak up.

It's true that we make ourselves vulnerable when we speak up . . . vulnerable to criticism. It's usually easier and more comfortable to stay out of the spotlight and to languish in the comfort of the non-speaker's role, to avoid the risk of feeling inferior.

But I've always been fond of quoting Eleanor Roosevelt on the subject of self-confidence and it was she who said: "No one can make *you* feel inferior without *your* consent." Think about that for a moment. "No one can make you feel inferior without your consent." Isn't that a remarkable statement?

And here are some remarkable figures to prove that man is his own worst enemy. MORE PERSONS KILL THEMSELVES EACH YEAR THAN MURDER OTHERS. There are 25,000 suicides annually in the U.S. and 18,000 homicides. Suicide is the severest form of self-hatred. But a milder form of self-hatred is the inferiority complex many of us secretly harbor.

One of my kids recently told me a riddle. He said, "Dad, do you know what the largest room in the world is?" "The largest room . . .?" I replied that I did not. He answered, "THE ROOM FOR IMPROVEMENT!" That's why I believe in speechcraft, because it's a valuable means for improvement. It offers what most of us need to become better public speakers.

Isn't it incredible that there is so little emphasis throughout our educational and business training on this needed skill of oral communication? I've found that in high school, college, military service, graduate school and in business, any emphasis on oral communication HAS BEEN CONSPICUOUS BY ITS ABSENCE. And yet, you and I communicate orally more than in any other way when dealing with people.

Sometime ago I attended a conference whose main speaker was a nationally known management expert and he said that we are not in the oil business, the insurance business, the government service business, the manufacturing business . . . rather WE ARE IN THE *PEOPLE* BUSINESS! It behooves us to do whatever we can to improve our communications among people in all walks of life in order to improve human relations.

Where will you go from here? What will you do with the valuable experience you've gained at these speechcraft sessions? Unfortunately, most persons stop their training after the formal speechcraft course has ended. They apparently are satisfied with their progress or don't want to make the effort to continue. But can you imagine a pianist stopping after 10 lessons and saying, "I've arrived—and I'm now accomplished!"? Public speaking takes on-going practice so I would encourage you to stick with it through regular Toastmaster training.

I'm convinced you'll do better on the job, in your community organizations and in your house of worship. One of my biggest thrills was that of becoming a certified lay speaker in the United Methodist Church—just one of the many ways that experience in public speaking can be applied for personal fulfillment and self-realization.

Let me close with a thought that I've shared with graduating high school seniors and other groups concerning the value of self-improvement. It goes like this:

God said, "Build a better world,"

And I said, "How?

The world is such a cold, dark place and so complicated now;

And I so young and useless, there's nothing I can do."

But God in all his wisdom said, "Just build a better you."

Glossary

Because the following words and expressions appear throughout the book, they are defined briefly below.

assertiveness   the ability to express your true feelings and opinions honestly and comfortably, and to be able to say "no" without feeling guilty.

audiovisual aids   material that helps a speaker to clarify and reinforce his or her message: photographs, cartoons, diagrams, actual objects or models of them, sound or silent movies, film strips, slides, charts, maps, tape or phonograph recordings, chalkboard.

body language   see *nonverbal communication*.

body of speech   the central part of a speech that contains the key information, ideas, or emotions to be communicated by the speaker to the audience.

chairman   one who presides over a meeting, panel, forum, round-table discussion, or symposium; a moderator or discussion leader. Also referred to as *chairperson*.

code   message or method of communication.

communication   in this book, the interpersonal exchange of ideas and feelings between speaker and listeners.

conclusion of speech   the ending of a speech that often sums up the main points or stresses the major idea. A conclusion should contain no new material.

delivery   the way a speech is given; it can be read or memorized or spoken extemporaneously (with or without notes after preparation beforehand). Delivery may also refer to the use of voice.

extemporaneous   refers to a talk/delivery, researched, thought about, outlined, and rehearsed, with or without notes.

eye contact   a communicative two-way relationship in which the speaker constantly looks at the listeners and reacts to their feedback (cheers, boos, facial expressions, gestures).

forum   an open discussion in which selected participants speak on an issue and answer questions from the audience.

gestures   movements by hands, arms, head, shoulders, or body to emphasize or clarify spoken thoughts and emotions.

identification with audience   associating oneself with the ideas, opinions, and feelings of listeners, usually in an attempt to persuade them.

impromptu talk   speaking on the spur of the moment, without prior notice or time for preparation.

informative speaking   communication in which the chief aim is to share knowledge and understanding with the audience.

interpersonal communication   a verbal or nonverbal exchange of ideas, knowledge, and feelings between two or more people.

introduction to speech   the part in which the speaker usually explains the purpose and scope of the speech and, at the same time, tries to win audience interest and goodwill.

lectern   a speaker's stand with a slanted top that supports the notes (if any) of a speaker; a lectern may rest on a table or floor. See *podium*.

listening   making an effort to hear and understand a speaker's statement.

MC   master of ceremonies.

modes   certain elements which communicate nonverbal messages such as facial expressions, eye contact, gestures, objects, space, time, touch, and paralanguage.

monotone   the tendency of a voice not to move far up and down the tone scale, thus resulting in very little expression.

nonverbal communication   the transmission and reception of messages, knowingly or unknowingly, other than spoken words: through facial expressions, eye contact, posture and gestures by hands, arms, head, shoulders, and body. Also known as body language.

oral visualization   the act of feeling, experiencing or living the ideas and emotions in one's message.

pacing   to create an interesting rate of delivery and variety which will hold your listener's interest. For example, while speaking you may slow down or speed up your delivery, or you may pause.

panel discussion   a discussion in which from four to six people, led by a moderator or chairman, explore different aspects of a subject. The purpose is to inquire, deliberate, and enlighten, not to argue and persuade. Audiences usually ask questions after all the panelists have spoken.

paralanguage   the "how we say it" as opposed to what we say. Some elements of paralanguage or vocalics are the quality of our voice, its pitch, rate of delivery, inflection, emphasis, and even pauses.

pause   a momentary silence in speaking. It can stress a point, separate ideas, and give a speaker time to breathe and organize his or her thoughts.

pause, vocalized   a distracting hesitation filled with vocal "static" such as "ah, er, like, right, you know," and so on. It is caused by habit or nervousness or both. It can be cured by conscious effort.

persuasive speaking   speaking that tries, by logical reasoning and emotional appeals, to convince listeners to change their opinions, to hold fast to them, or to perform an action recommended by the speaker.

pitch   the highness or lowness of a voice. Normal pitch should allow a speaker to comfortably raise or lower his or her voice for varied expression.

podium   an elevated platform, not to be confused with lectern or speaker's stand.

proxemics   the study of space as a communicative mode.

public address (P.A.) system   an electronic amplification system used in halls or auditoriums so that speakers can be heard by a large audience.

rate of speaking   the average number of words spoken in one minute. The average person speaks between 130 and 160 words a minute.

round-table discussion   a meeting at which several people sit around a table and, under a chairman or moderator, discuss a given topic. See *forum, panel discussion, and symposium.*

self-image   what and how we think of ourselves.

speaker's stand   see *lectern.*

special-occasion speeches   speeches given under special circumstances and for a particular reason: presenting or accepting an award, nominating a candidate for office, making an announcement, and so on.

symposium a meeting at which participants, usually from four to six, speak on specific phases of the same question. Then the participants may question one another or answer questions from the audience.

vocalics see *paralanguage*.

vocalized pause see *pause, vocalized*.

vocal volume the loudness or softness of a speaker's voice.

Index

Movement, 61

Nervousness, 53–55
Nonverbal communication, 11–30,
    55–58, 105, 270, 299–300, 306
  codes of, 22–26
  elements of, 13
Notes
  taking, 116–120
  using, 61–62

Oral style, improving, 167–169
Outline, 124
  advantages of, 125
  preparing, 124–125
  types of, 126–127

Pacing, 79–80
Panel discussions, 252
  responsibilities of audience,
    256–257
  responsibilities of moderator,
    252–254
  responsibilities of panelists, 255
Paralanguage, 13, 14, 21
Paraphrase, 117, 119
Pauses, 21, 79, 165
Persuasive speaking, 207–224
  catering to emotions, 217–222
  importance of, 208–209
  purposes of, 210
  strategy, 212–213
Pictures, 174
  as a means of persuasion,
    174–176
Pitch, 21, 70–72
  monotone, 72
Posture, 16, 61
Practice, 145–146
Presenting an award, 235–236
Pronunciation, 74–78, 281
  problems of 77–78
  regional accents, 74
Proposing a toast, 241–242
Proxemics. See *Space*

Question-and-answer sessions, 7,
    52, 62, 202
Quintilian, 103, 120
Quotation, direct, 117, 119

Rate of delivery, 21, 78–80
*Reader's Guide to Periodical Litera-
    ture,* 113–114
Reading a speech, 92–94
Reagan, President Ronald, 94, 167
Reasoning and evidence, 214–217
  causal, 216
  deductive, 214
  inductive, 215
Receiving an award, 236–237
Rehearsal. See *Practice*
Research, doing, 110–116
Resumé, 290–294
Roosevelt, President Franklin D.,
    111, 160, 272
Round-table discussion, 258–259

Self-conficence, 6, 8, 15, 50, 90,
    110
  aids to, 50, 52, 184
Self-image, 15
Sentences, 166–7
Shyness, 275
Space, 24–25
  "bubble," 24
Special-occasion talks, 227–246
Stage fright. See *Nervousness*
Stevenson, Adlai, 174–176
Summary, 116–118
Symposium, 257

Talks, informative, 191–205
  autobiographical, 48–50
  body, 199
  conclusion, 201–202
  kinds of, 195–196
  introduction to, 198
  purposes of, 193–194
Telephone, 280–282
Time, 22–23
Title, of talk, 141–144
  criteria for selecting, 142–143
Topics
  to demonstrate, 185–187
  to inform, 202–203
  to persuade, 222–223
  for group discussion, 262
  criteria for selecting, 104–108
  narrowing down, 109–110
Touching, 20–21